Reminiscences

of

John C. NIEDERMAIR

(Naval Architect - Bureau of Ships)

U. S. Naval Institute
Annapolis, Maryland

Preface

This volume contains the transcript of six taped interviews with John C. Niedermair at his home in Stone Harbor, New Jersey. The dates of the interviews range from June, 1975 through April, 1976. They were obtained by John T. Mason, Jr. for the Oral History collection of the U. S. Naval Institute. Mr. Niedermair corrected the original transcript. It was re-typed and indexed. A number of documents have been added to the appendix as supplement to the interviews themselves.

John C. Niedermair was a longtime Technical Director of Preliminary Ship Design for the Bureau of Ships, U. S. Navy Department. Throughout his career combatant ship design was his primary concern. He is credited with many critical design innovations. Especial contributions were made to the ESSEX Class carriers. Perhaps his most dramatic contribution came on the afternoon of November 4, 1941 when, in response to a British requirement received in the Bureau that same day, Niedermair made a small pencil sketch and calculated the basic characteristics of an entirely new and radical ship which became the workhorse of World War II - the LST.

In another area - Niedermair's work on watertight integrity and ship stability has left an imprint on practically every merchant ship constructed in the United States since 1929.

John T. Mason, Jr.
Director of Oral History

January, 1978

MR. JOHN CHARLES NIEDERMAIR

Mr. John Charles Niedermair was born November 2, 1893 in Union Hill, New Jersey. During his youth he lived in Staten Island, New York where he attended grade and high schools. He was selected for a scholarship to and entered Webb Institute of Naval Architecture and Marine Engineering in 1914. He graduated at the head of his class in 1918.

After a brief period of duty in the Navy during the first World War as an officer candidate, he commenced his active career in the shipbuilding industry in December 1918 by accepting a permanent appointment as a ship draftsman at the New York Navy Yard. He remained at New York until April 1928 when the Navy Department requested his services in Washington in the Preliminary Design Branch of the Bureau of Construction and Repair. Ten years later, he rose to the position of senior civilian in this Branch and still holds this distinction. His present title is "Technical Director of Preliminary Ship Design" and he is the highest ranking naval architect in the U. S. Navy, as well as the highest ranking civilian in the Bureau of Ships.

Mr. Niedermair has attained international stature and recognition among members of the naval architectural profession particularly in the fields of salvage, stability, and basic design. While employed at the New York Navy Yard, Mr. Niedermair was instrumental in the prosecution of a number of special projects, the scope and variety of which attest to his versatility as an engineer. One of these was the design, planning, and active supervision of the construction of the battleship building ways laid down in the early 1920's. However, his most significant work during this period was in connection with the salvage operations of the ill-fated submarines, S51 and S4. In each of these instances, he provided on the spot technical direction of salvage procedures which he himself had devised. In recognition of these services, which were so vital to the success of these operations, he was highly commended by the Secretary of the Navy and received a special promotion. Since that time, he has served in a consultant capacity on many other salvage jobs.

Mr. Niedermair's transfer to the Bureau of Construction and Repair in 1928 was occasioned by the fact that his talents were needed in connection with preparations for the forthcoming International Safety of Life on Sea Convention. Mr. Niedermair attended the convention, which was held in London in 1929, as the Navy's technical expert, and was one of the signers of the resulting agreement. He was personally instrumental in securing the adoption of the United States' proposal that every passenger ship be inclined upon its completion, and that operating personnel be supplied with information regarding the stability necessary to permit efficient and safe handling of the ship. For his services on this occasion, he received a letter of commendation from the Secretary of State. Again during the Senate Investigation of the "Mohawk" and "Morrow Castle" disasters, Mr. Niedermair served on the Subcommittee concerned with the Watertight Integrity and Stability of passenger ships. As a direct result thereof, in 1935, Mr. Niedermair's services were loaned by the Navy to the Department of Commerce where he established the Technical Division of the Bureau of Marine Inspection and Navigation, an activity designed to safeguard the public's interests against further such catastrophes. Mr. Niedermair's contributions in the field of ship stability are marked by many milestones not the least of which is his co-authorship (with Vice Admiral E.L. Cochrane, USN (Ret.)) of Construction and Repair Technical Bulletin No. 8, "Sub-division, Stability and Construction of Merchant Ships" (1935), a document still considered the basic primer on this subject.

In the field of basic design, Mr. Niedermair occupies a preeminent position and might well be termed the father of today's modern United States Navy. In addition, his contributions to the merchant shipbuilding field are also substantial. In the course of the design of the liner "America", Mr. Niedermair was appointed by Vice Admiral Emory S. Land, USN, to act as technical conciliatory between the design agent and the building yard. His contributions have left a lasting imprint on practically every merchant ship constructed since 1929.

It is in the field of naval ship design, however, that Mr. Neidermair has made his greatest contributions. As the civilian chief and Technical Directory of the Preliminary Design Branch of the Bureau of Ships for almost 20 years, Mr. Niedermair has been primarily responsible for the basic design of all types of naval ships during this most trying and critical period. This includes Battleships, Aircraft Carriers, Cruisers, Destroyers, Submarines, Patrol and Mine Craft; Auxiliaries such as Tenders, Cargo Ships, and Tankers; Landing Craft including LST, LSD, and other special craft types. The designs which he guided from conception through construction became the ships which contributed so greatly to the winning of World War II and which excited the world by their performance. Worthy of particular mention is the part he played in the design of the LST. This ship, which was in large measure the product of Mr. Niedermair's originality and fine engineering judgment, was known as the work horse of World War II. Over 1,000 of these versatile craft were constructed, a memorial of which few, if any, other Naval Architects can boast. To date, approximately 8,000 ships, a staggering number, have been built from designs originated under Mr. Niedermair's guidance. It is improbably that a record such as this will ever be equaled. For his outstanding services to the Navy both prior to, and during World War II, Mr. Niedermair was presented the Distinguished Civilian Service Award, the Navy's highest honorary award, in 1945.

It is of particular note that Mr. Niedermair's genius has spanned the coming of the atomic age. The past few years have witnessed the advent of the first nuclear propelled ships. The NAUTILUS needs no introduction; SEA-WOLF and other submarines to follow will in turn be followed by the nuclear carriers and cruisers now on the drafting boards. FORRESTAL, SARATOGA and their sisters are other mighty milestones of this newer Navy. The basic designs of all of these vessels were made under Mr. Niedermair's direction and exemplify the versatility and scope of his ability as a Naval Architect.

Mr. Niedermair has always been active in the work of the professional technical societies. In 1932, he presented a paper "Stability of Ships After Damage" before the Society of Naval Architects and Marine Engineers (SNAME). In 1936, he presented a companion paper, "Further Developments in the Stability and Rolling of Ships" before the same group. In 1951 he presented a paper on "Ship Motions" before the International Conference of Naval Architects and Marine Engineers in London under the auspices of the Institution of Naval Architects. Local Sections of the SNAME have also heard Mr. Niedermair on several occasions. He addressed the Chesapeake Section in 1950 on the subject of his own design experiences, and the same year presented a paper before the Philadelphia Section of the "Subdivision, Stability, and Damage Control of Merchant Ships." Mr. Niedermair has been a regular contributor to the discussions of technical papers presented before the Society. In addition to such technical activity, Mr. Niedermair has contributed his services on many occasions to the Society's work. He has served as a member of the Local Sections Committee since 1949. Currently he is a member of the committee engaged in revising the Society's book on "Naval Architecture." He has served as the Chairman of the Chesapeake Section (1946-1947), and has since served on the Executive Committee of that Section.

One of Mr. Niedermair's greatest and perhaps most lasting contributions to his profession lies in the interest he has always displayed in the younger engineers. Vitally interested in the future of the profession, he has fostered a high degree of technical excellence and professional pride among young Naval Architects and has done much by precept and example to inspire them and instill excellence into their work. He has constantly looked toward the future and his insight into it has led the way for many who follow. He has wisely counseled two generations of Naval Officers. Almost every high ranking officer of the Navy now actively engaged in ship design work has learned the fundamentals from "Johnny". A gentleman, a scholar, a man beloved by all with whom he is associated and finally as well as first and always, a Naval Architect, he has added a considerable lustre to an already honorable profession.

DECLARATION OF TRUST

The undersigned does hereby appoint and designate as his (her) Trustee herein, the Secretary-Treasurer and Publisher of the United States Naval Institute to perform and discharge the following duties, powers, and privileges in connection with the possession and use of a certain taped interview between the undersigned and the Oral History Department of the United States Naval Institute.

1. Classification of Transcript.

   (X)a. If classified OPEN, the transcript(s) may be read or the recording(s) audited by the qualified personnel upon presentation of proper credentials, as determined by the Secretary-Treasurer of the U.S. Naval Institute.

   ( )b. If classified PERMISSION REQUIRED TO CITE OR QUOTE, the user will be required to obtain permission in writing from the interviewee prior to quoting or citing from either the transcript(s) or the recording(s).

   ( )c. If classified PERMISSION REQUIRED, permission must be obtained in writing from the interviewee before the transcribed interview(s) can be examined or the tape recording(s) audited.

   ( )d. If classified CLOSED, the transcribed interview(s) and the tape recording(s) will be sealed until a time specified by the interviewee. This may be until the death of the interviewee or for any specified number of years.

2. It is expressly understood that in giving this authorization, I am in no way precluded from placing such restrictions as I may desire upon use of the interview at any time during my lifetime, nor does this authorization in any way affect my rights to the copyright of my literary expressions that may be contained in the interview.

Witness my hand and seal this 27th day of October 1977.

John Niederman

I hereby accept and consent to the foregoing Declaration of Trust and the powers therein conferred upon me as Trustee:

R E Bowker Jr

Interview No. 1 with Mr. John C. Niedermair

Place: His home in Stone Harbor, New Jersey

Date: Tuesday afternoon, 17 June 1975

Subject: Biography

By: John T. Mason, Jr.

Q: Well, Sir, at last it's great to have the opportunity to meet you and sit across the table from you. I've been looking forward to this story of your remarkable career, so would you begin now in the proper way with a biography by telling me the date and place of your birth and something about your background?

Mr. N.: I was born in Union Hill, New Jersey, on November 2, 1893, and talking to my sister about this thing several times I was amazed to find out that she said I was born over a blacksmith's shop. So I always thought that any good fortune I had in my work, I guess, was that I was born over a lot of good horseshoes.

Q: Lucky ones!

Mr. N.: In about 1899 my father moved us over to Staten Island, which was one of the great things that happened -

Q: What was his business?

Mr. N.: He was an engineer, an operating engineer. He worked for several brewery companies at times, on and off, so I grew up on an island, on the hillside with a beautiful name. I lived on Hillside Avenue, and the place where I lived, our lot, ran from Hillside Avenue to Pleasant Valley Avenue. Those two names in a way will describe the pleasant sort of life that I led on Staten Island.

Q: Describe Staten Island, not today but as it was then.

Mr. N.: At that time you had trolley cars running down the middle of the island, you had the railroad running along the edges down to Tottenville and to Port Richmond, Staten Island, and trolley cars running nearly everywhere on the island, particularly down to the beaches.

I remember the trip to Midland Beach. Midland Beach was always a beach that you had to pay to get onto. It's interesting because I came down here and just the last few years here at Stone Harbor and some other places they want to charge something for going on the beach to take care of it, to clean up and so on.

Q: People litter so.

Mr. N.: Yes, and there's a big protest, but I grew up on Staten Island and going to this beach on a trolley car with my father, who was a great swimmer, taking me down there. He'd put me on his back and swim out to the ocean. You could do that then because the water was really great.

As time went on, I got to be old enough to go to school, but for some reason or other my mother didn't want to part with me.

Q: That's not unusual with mothers!

Mr. N.: I was the firstborn and she delayed sending me off to school for two years, till my sister was old enough to go, my sister Elizabeth, and we went off to school together. I was two years late in going to school, but that didn't seem to make any difference.

Q: This was to grade school, on Staten Island?

Mr. N.: Yes, Emerson School. It was at the foot of the hill that was called Emerson Hill, where Ralph Waldo Emerson used to come for his vacations, and some of his sophisticated background rubbed off on Emerson. Emerson was really a very fine school to start in.

I finished there and even then I got out early, at fourteen, I believe. I delayed my education for a while. I got jobs in different places and so on.

Q: What kind of jobs?

Mr. N.: Oh, I worked for a plumber and a baker and in a machine shop on and off, and on and off, of course, while I was going to Westerleigh Collegiate Institute, where I went to school.

Q: What was that? A prep school?

Mr. N.: To prepare myself. I had plans for going to Cornell.

I did all my work in poetry and mathematics and everything. I was getting ready to be finished at Westerleigh Collegiate Institute and they told me about Webb Institute of Naval Architecture where they had scholarships available. So I went off to the Bronx. Webb was up in the Bronx then, and I took my exams. One of the interesting things that happened during those exams was that I was having a little trouble with a math problem when a Professor McLean came to me and said:

"What seems to be troubling you, young man?"

"Oh," I said, "I'm having trouble with this algebra problem here."

He said: "Oh, don't let that worry you. Why, I solve more difficult problems than that every day."

But the interesting thing about it was that he was one of the consultant naval architects on the <u>Titanic</u>. Unfortunately, McLean died before I got into Webb in the middle of September.

Q: Of what year was this?

Mr. N.: That was 1914.

Q: Tell me, by the time you applied for a scholarship at Webb, had you determined the direction of your career?

Mr. N.: I had been watching ships back and forth from the hills of Staten Island, all the liners and everything, and I'd been along West Street in New York. I started going into New York City, along the maritime fringes of it, the docks that were there when I was ten years old. In order to get there I used to get on a horse car going up West Street to go uptown.

Q: First, you said, you had plans to go to Cornell, but you weren't going to find ships in Ithaca.

Mr. N.: No, what I was after was an engineering education. Even though I went to Webb, I studied the course intensely and in a very broad way so that I had a very broad background in engineering after I got through with Webb. I've forgotten now exactly what my average was, but I know that my average for the four years at Webb was over 95.

Q: What kind of degree do you get from Webb?

Mr. N.: They didn't have a degree at that time. Later on they did. They tried to get it and the only reason they didn't have it was that our library was too small. For some reason, we didn't have enough books, and at one time to get a little higher priority I told the people at Webb:

"Gee, I'll go down to Hinds and Noble and I'll get a truckload of secondhand books and bring them up, then maybe we'll get this degree."

As I went through I met people there. The dean of Webb at the time was Chaffee, Professor Chaffee. He was a graduate of Brown University. Then there was George Crouch, who was a professor of naval architecture and a great designer of speed boats. I remember the time that George Crouch had four boats in the Gold Cup races, each one of them won its race, won its heat, and all the boats that were competing at the finish were his own boats and they came in one, two, three, four! The leading boat was what they called stepped - it really wasn't a displacement boat because he had put the planking on transversely so that it was full of little steps. So the Rainbow IV I don't think got it and the Baby Bootlegger I believe won the Gold Cup.

Q: What kind of students did you have at Webb? Where did they come from?

Mr. N.: They came from New York Stuyvesant High. The people I was competing with were from Stuyvesant High and Stuyvesant at that time had a record of being almost equal to two years of college. I don't believe they have that reputation now but they had it then.

Q: Did they come from other parts of the country?

Mr. N.: Yes, they came from scattered around. Most of them centered around New York State, not Staten Island. I was the only Staten Islander. I was the only hick in the crowd, but I soon caught on to the city ways and I was finally secretary of the student organization before I got through with my time at Webb.

The summer work was the interesting thing about Webb.

Q: Like the summer cruises at the Naval Academy!

Mr. N.: Webb instituted this system long ago and every summertime - now they do it in the wintertime - the first time I went up to Quincy, Massachusetts, and worked in the yard there on the Nevada, the battleship Nevada.

Q: At Fore River shipyard?

Mr. N.: Yes, and there I met Wakeman. The interesting thing about that was that in my background I had met a lot of people when I worked for the baker and so on because I ran the bakery and was a bookkeeper for the bakery while I was going to Westerleigh Collegiate Institute. There I met a lot of people and I found that the people with the most money were the hardest ones to get pay from. I had to go round every once in a while and some of the boys who worked for me had trouble, too.

I also learned that you can't trust everybody because one of my boy collectors that I had started falling by the wayside. He wasn't turning in the money, which was a good experience for me, how to handle that.

Q: Tell me more about this summer at the Fore River shipyard.

Mr. N.: At the Fore River shipyard I met Wakeman. I was the first one up there. Wakeman offered me $7 a week and I said:

"Gee, I can't work for $7 a week," because I actually had earned more than that before I ever got into Webb. So we talked about it a while and he had me sit on the bench outside, then he called me in and gave me $12 a week, which was pretty good pay then, in 1915, and he said, "Keep it secret."

Well, I told him I couldn't keep it secret because my friend George Smith, I'm rooming with him and he's coming up in a couple of days. I can't keep it secret from him, so he gave George $12, too. But one of the other fellows who came up from my class he only got $7 and he always wondered what we did with all the extra money and George told him: "I have a big inheritance, that's why we can make all these trips."

Q: These jobs were provided by the Webb Institute? Did they make all the arrangements?

Mr. N.: They negotiated. They simply would contact the yards and the yards would say they would take so many.

It was really a great thing for me to get on the Nevada, and Wakeman evidently took a shine to me because I had a kind of tussle with him, so my assignment on that ship was really free. I had to work for the best shipfitter on the job, Tommy Grant, and my assignment was to go and inspect every part in that ship, brackets, where the desk beam would meet the side frame, and any part that was missing I would then have to check it out and find out what belonged there, go out to the ship and have them punch holes into the brackets, go back and have them put in. I wound up crawling down through the inner bottom because Tommy Grant and his friend the shipfitter got so interested in me that they told me about the big secret in the Nevada and that was where one of the frames had missed the shell by several inches, so we crawled in through the inner bottom to show me this. They were really interested in showing me what goes on and, sure enough, there was the frame two inches away from the shell, filled in with wood, and they had put in a fake that looked like a rivet on the outside, but it was really a bolt on the inside, because they couldn't put a hot rivet through the wood.

Q: Sort of makeshift?

Mr. N.: So I had a great experience in that yard because I think of my first contact with Wakeman.

Q: Tell me something about his background.

Mr. N.: He was the manager of the yard. He had quite a lisp. I don't know very much about him because my contact after I left him was with the people in New York. I was there ten weeks and when I came back I knew what a ship looked like inside. I'd never been on a big ship before.

Q: What was Wakeman's first name?

Mr. N.: Oh, I have no idea. I couldn't tell you. I can't bring it back.

Then I went back to Webb and I went through the sophomore year and the next summer I spent at Cramp's shipyard. That was in 1916.

Q: That was in Philadelphia?

Mr. N.: In Philadelphia, in the mold loft, and I worked there for a George Dewey, who was the loftsman.

Q: What did you do in the mold loft?

Mr. N.: I helped to make patterns for the shell plating and for the rivet holes and everything that a regular wooden frame or paper that went with it to locate the rivet holes in all the plating, also molds to show where they went for the framing and so on. So I learned the mold-lofting business in the mold loft.

Q: How much did you get paid for that?

Mr. N.: I've forgotten how much. By that time I evidently was paid enough that I didn't run into any trouble. Now I was a sophomore, you see. Before I was a freshman, and Wakeman was really a very good person to meet the first time because he could tell, I think, the sheep from the goats, the way he did it, and the stand that I took with him evidently paid off.

Q: He reported back, I suppose, on your performance to the school?

Mr. N.: I never had any difficulty when I got back.

Q: How long a day did you have to work when you were working in shipyards?

Mr. N.: Probably 10 hours. At that time it was very busy there. The yard was working on submarines and all that sort of thing, besides, of course, the Nevada was there. I was particularly interested in the Nevada and what happened to her. She kind of stuck with me till she was decommissioned after World War II.

While I was at Cramps I went over to New York Ship. I arranged with New York Ship to go over there and see that yard because the _Idaho_ was building there on the ways and I had a chance to see her.

Q: Did you get a thorough picture of her innards, too?

Mr. N.: No, I didn't because she was on the ways and there was a big strike in the yard at the time and I was unable to go aboard because strike-breakers were doing the work. It was really difficult for me to get into the yard, in the first place. The yard manager, I can't remember his name (Howard Towle-'00Webb) met me at the gate and took me in. I had called up and talked to him and he said he'd meet me at the gate and he personally took me around.

Q: How did you students from Webb fit into the labor picture in the yards?

Mr. N.: I worked right with the people. I got along very well with yard workmen.

Q: I mean you didn't have to join a union?

Mr. N.: Oh, no, no union problems. None.

One of the last things I did at Cramps - we were running out of work and I talked to Dewey about this and I said:

"I notice you're not laying out the shaftstools." There's a support that goes under the shafting in the shaft alley. "Why don't they do it?"

"Oh, we never do that."

I said: "Well, you haven't got much for me to do, why don't you let me lay them out? I'll lay out the shaftstools my way and we'll see what happens."

So, he said all right. I went to work and I laid out the shaft stools, because I felt if you were going to put a shaft in you've got to always measure from the inner bottom up. If you've got it almost close to where the bearing is going, it would be much easier to get it done in a hurry and get the shafting lined up easier. So I did. I laid out the shaft stools on that job, which was the first time they had ever done it.

I later got a letter from Dewey telling me - they were doing the work for the Henderson, which was building in the Navy yard at the time.

Q: The Henderson was a destroyer?

Mr. N.: She was a troopship. They put the shaft stools in the way I laid them out in the loft and they said it was a great job. They said, "We'll do it that way all the time," so I at least contributed.

I tried to find out while I was there how to work out shell expansions, plating, the shape of the plating. The loftsman who worked out that expansion wouldn't tell me. "No," he said, that's a trade secret."

I said: "Well, it's really not a trade secret. I know the principle of it. I studied that sort of thing at Webb and I know how you tackle it and I'd like to see you do it here in the loft and work with you." But he wouldn't do it, so I never did lay out a shell plate in the loft.

Oddly enough, at that time they had a real problem in Philadelphia, a religious problem. The Protestants and the Catholics were really throwing rocks at each other.

Q: At Cramps?

Mr. N.: No, in Philadelphia.

Q: In the city itself?

Mr. N.: Yes, sure.

Q: In the city of brotherly love!

Mr. N.: Yes. And so they asked me what I was. Are you a Protestant or are you a Catholic? I said:

"Now, look, I never had to tell anybody what I was before and I'm not in the habit of telling you now." So I never did tell them.

Once in a while you had to drill holes into the wooden things and you had an electric drill that you had to use, and they cut the electric wire on me. I didn't bother too much about that. I just let them get away with it. But that was one of the oddities that I ran into.

Q: Let me ask you at this point how much application there was from what you were learning at Webb and what you were doing in these various yards?

Mr. N.: What they wanted us to know was how a ship was built in a yard. We were learning how to design a ship. We learned descriptive geometry and we studied strength of materials and we learned about engines, but you went into the yard to see what was done with it. When I was on the Nevada I'd go down through the boiler rooms, down in the engine rooms. The ship had been launched now and they were getting her ready for commissioning. I did some work up in the fighting tops. They had a cage mast that you had to climb up. I put in the fittings for the portable mast that would fly all the signals and everything. I was working on the fittings that went with that at one time. Another job I did was work on the gun ports and get them ready for testing. We'd finally get them the way we thought would be tight, and I decided that that was the last time these gun ports would be tight. When she went to sea they wouldn't be tight. That's one of the advantages of going out into the yard and working because you'd see that it passed the test all right with the hose and everything, but we had a little pump that we designed, Tommy Grant and I, that squirted a very powerful little stream right along the edge of the rubber gasket that went around the guns. If the least little leak showed up, we'd tighten it up a little bit more, and so on.

I came back to Webb then and worked. Now I was going back to my second year. At the end of my sophomore year I was at Cramps, at the end of my freshman year I was at Fore River, which was a Bethlehem yard, and at the end of my junior year I went to New York Navy yard.

Q: What did you do there?

Mr. N.: There I had some very interesting things. One of the first jobs I got was to go over to Hoboken. The German ships had been seized. We had gone into the war in I think April of 1917 and we seized these ships, so there's where I first met Commander Henry T. Wright, who was greatly interested in me for the rest of my years at New York Navy Yard and also showed a great deal of interest after I left there.

He asked me to go over on the Leviathan, examine the ship, and decide how many troops it could carry, also check out and find where I would put life preservers on the ship.

Q: You might say that she'd been renamed, however, hadn't she?

Mr. N.: She was the Vaterland and she was renamed the Leviathan.

I went over to the piers in Hoboken. They had a guard at the gate, and I had my note from the yard, and so I walked down and climbed aboard that ship. There wasn't a soul in it. Everything was scattered all over the deck. They had damaged the engines. Everything was helterskelter over the decks, but my job was mostly on the outside. I did wander through the ship a bit and then I went and checked up in order to find out about accommodations and so on, and I made an estimate of how many people it could carry. As I remember it, I came back and said that it would be able to carry over 10,000 troops. I also figured out where to put the life rafts.

The life rafts were jury-rigged life rafts. As I remember,

they looked to me to be made up of five-gallon oil cans boxed in with wooden frames, and they stacked those one on top of the other, with several of these cans in this wooden frame, and they would toss it overboard. I thought to myself while I was doing this and figuring it out that, yes, I've got enough of these things on there to take care of all the troops if they ever got into the water.

Q: That took up a lot of room, didn't it?

Mr. N.: Yes, it did, but what I worried about was that if any of them were in the water and they started throwing these hard-looking life rafts out, they'd kill a lot of people, just throwing the life rafts overboard. Fortunately, the ship was never hurt. She was faster than the German submarines.

Q: What was her speed?

Mr. N.: I think it was somewhere around 25 knots, 20, 25 knots..

I came away from there and went back into the yard and worked on many other things in the yard. The Tennessee was on the ways. In another year she would be ready to be launched. She was launched in the following April. The New Mexico had been launched and she was at the dock being outfitted. I did a lot of work on both of those.

Q: What kind of work did you do?

Mr. N.: I was connected with the scientific section in the yard.

I was assigned to that section.

Q: What did that entail?

Mr. N.: It included all the technical calculations and ran the various tests in the yard, inclining experiments, strength calculations, launching calculations, all kinds of things that concerned basic naval architecture, I would say.

Q: Your math had improved considerably, hadn't it?

Mr. N.: Yes. Not to get too far ahead of it, I did so well that I didn't get back to Webb - Webb was willing to let me stay a month extra, so I didn't get back to Webb until October.

Q: Did you have the same buddies every year from Webb working with you?

Mr. N.: No. I remember one of the things I did was to work on a 100-foot sub-chaser, wooden sub-chaser, which was a great success. Later on, oddly enough now that you ask the question about what we did, I went down on that sub-chaser and did some work on it. Forty years later I made the presentation of a model of that 110-foot sub-chaser. I never thought of it until this moment. That model was made out of burley maple, a beautiful thing, and I inherited it when Bates left, and I felt I should give it to some place where they could put it up so I turned it over to the Mariners' Museum at Newport News. But I did board several of them in the early days when I was first in the New York yard, and ran several tests at sea including stabilizer experiments.

Q: And you say they did very effective work?

Mr. N.: Yes, they did.

Q: You also worked on other German ships, did you?

Mr. N.: There were a lot of other German ships in there. There were several big dockings and we had to go down and take off-set measurements so that we could make docking plans. We'd make up docking plans for these German ships and we developed naval architectural technical data.

Q: Had they been seized in other U.S. ports?

Mr. N.: No, they'd been seized in Hoboken. There were quite a lot of them over there. There was a Martha Washington, I think, and then there was a George Washington. There was a President Lincoln and the Amerika and others.

Q: Those were ex-German boats?

Mr. N.: Yes, and we had to get them into a dry dock, but the Leviathan was too big to dock over in the Brooklyn Navy Yard and I don't remember where they docked her (probably Boston).

Q: She was the largest ship in the world, wasn't she?

Mr. N.: She was one of the largest, yes. She bugged me for quite a long time afterwards.

Then I went back to Webb in October and I worked from then until about the 1st of May. The yard had latched onto me and they put me on extended leave until December and for Christmas vacation I was required to go to the yard and work about a week. Then they put me on extended leave again, which lasted until I finished at Webb. In that way, they really wanted to hang onto me.

Q: They had a latch on you!

Mr. N.: George Rock was the chief constructor at the yard at that time, Admiral Rock later on.

Q: What were you studying at Webb that final year?

Mr. N.: In that final year I was working on engine designs. I remember working on the design of a reciprocating engine, steam engines were being faded out at the time. We had a Commander Cathcart there. He was a real great personality. He took a great interest in me and he hoped I would write a book about these things some day. I soon dropped that idea because when I got away I didn't do any more work in the way of designing an engine. I did design an internal-combustion engine, also, while I was at Webb.

Then I became aware of the theory of carburetion. George Crouch had invented, who was an expert on streamlining and flow, was my professor in naval architecture, and I think he invented the first carburetor that looked something like a Zenith carburetor. George Crouch worked with the inventor of vacuum tubes.

They were trying to work out an electric torpedo, and de Forrest had invented a vacuum tube.

I asked Crouch why de Forrest had sold that patent. I've forgotten now who he sold it to but RCA got it afterwards for about $10,000.

Q: Wasn't it Atwater Kent?

Mr. N.: No, I don't think so. It had to do with RCA, I'm sure. Anyway, I asked George Crouch about this, why he got so little money for it, and Crouch told me:

"I asked de Forrest that, too, and all he said was bread and butter. He needed the money."

Q: So he couldn't bargain around?

Mr. N.: No, he couldn't. So that's a human-interest story to get into this thing.

Now, I was leaving Webb -

Q: Let me ask you at this point a question on your years at Webb and your summers in these various shipyards. What appealed to you most?

Mr. N.: What appealed to me most? I apparently had learned to tackle any job, regardless of which way it went. I soon developed a reputation for being a trouble-shooter. I had developed a multiple interest, and not a special single interest. I had perfected myself in the theory of naval architecture very well. I knew mechanics and materials and engineering, and I had Professor Cathcart, who was very good at that. He'd tell me stories about how the different yards and the engine tests that they went on and how they'd try to cheat the government with their readings on their instruments. Cathcart was pretty sharp. When they finished any test that required springs in something, he would take the springs home with him, to test them out and see whether they had the right tension or compression. He'd let me in on all things like that, so I had a broad knowledge when I finished, not very much as a designer, you might say, to create a whole ship, but I knew what to do with it after I had it, inclining experiments and all these other things, and to build it, which is why I went in the yard, and the theory that I learned at Webb.

Q: That must have been pleasing to the school because that was certainly what they planned, was it not?

Mr. N.: Well, yes, I guess they looked at it that way because I got quite a reputation because of this. They remembered me and they remembered me all the time.

I used to worry about certain things, even though I was getting good marks, now that you ask about it. To give you some idea about how fussy I was about my understanding of things, we were studying descriptive geometry and I invariably got 100 on everything with Crouch. He taught math and his assistant math professor was Chaffee, and also naval architecture. In naval architecture, descriptive geometry plays a very big part. So one day I decided I'd better go in and talk to Professor Crouch about this because

I was getting these good marks in descriptive geometry, but I couldn't see the thing in space. I couldn't see this solid in which I put planes through it and projected it this way and that way on three planes. But I couldn't really see the image in my mind.

Well, George Crouch said to me:

"Niedermair, don't worry about it. Some night, all of a sudden, you'll see it."

Do you know, the next day after I had gotten that off my chest, almost the next day, I could see these things. So I believe it was that sort of a close look at things, thinking about them and wanting to know myself whether I really could do them, that made the difference.

Then I finally got back to the New York Navy Yard.

Q: They still had a lead on you, didn't they?

Mr. N.: Yes, they did. George Rock was there and Wright. Then there was the chief draftsman whom I haven't mentioned. H. C. Fletcher was the chief draftsman and Ambrose Merrill was the assistant chief draftsman. Ambrose Merrill was an MIT graduate and Fletcher was a self-trained person. He studied at night school and everything and he was really a beautiful person. Those four evidently, in one way or another, kept feeding things to me, George Rock, H. T. Wright, and Merrill, particularly.

I still write to Merrill. He's now over ninety years old. I got a beautiful letter from him just recently and I've got to get in touch with him and go and see him.

It wasn't long after I got back to the New York Yard before I ran into what I call my first spotlight job. You know, you get all kinds of jobs but something happens sometimes with one that you get and it brings management in on it. Well, that spotlight job was that the people in the scientific section had worked out an inclining experiment that was sent to the Bureau of C & R in Washington and had been turned down a couple of times. The inclining experiment was to determine the location accurately of the center of gravity of the ship and also its weight, accurate readings of the drafts and all that sort of thing, so you would find out what the metacentric height was by this inclining experiment. You put weights on the deck and the ship would heel over and from it you could determine where the center of gravity of the ship was. You can calculate the metacenter. The theoretical center is called the metacenter. That's determined by the form of the ship. It's a volumetric and a water-line inertial calculation.

That had been turned down by the people in the bureau.

Q: Did they give their reasons?

Mr. N.: I don't recall, but I do know that now they were on the spot. They ran the experiment, they worked it out, but it was turned down. Why, I don't remember. So I think they decided that I, being just out of Webb, they'd try it out on me, which they did.

I remembered all my work. I'd studied some of the work that Professor Hofgard had done over the years, I knew about his what they called the "lost buoyancy" method that concerned when water got into a ship and you could figure it two ways: either use the water getting into the ship as an added weight, or you could figure it by assuming that the buoyancy of the ship, the hull of the ship, wherever the water was it wasn't there any more, so you lost buoyancy. So I applied what I knew about theoretical naval architecture and I had to make up all the data sheets, redo the whole thing, and bring in a brand-new report.

Q: This was for what specific ship?

Mr. N.: I've forgotten. I think it was one of the early submarines. It was the inclining experiment of a submarine. That's a very important point. I'm glad you asked that.

So what happened? It went to Washington and it came back. Apparently Rock got the notice in his office that it was approved. I guess they said "three cheers." Rock had a very gruff voice and he came to the doorway of the scientific section and he yelled out in a loud voice:

"Who worked up the inclining experiment on the submarine?"

Of course, everybody was willing to point me out –

Q: Because they thought it was going to be a turn-down!

Mr. N.: And Rock came over. That was really my first real meeting with Rock. He put his hand on my back, he congratulated me and shook my hand, and said what a good job I'd done. Then he left.

At that instant, I became a submarine expert, never having been on a submarine. The closest I'd been to a submarine was the old Iron Whale that was standing in the yard. I used to peek into the peephole to see a place where there was kind of a bicycle in there that turned the propeller.

From that time on, I was the one for submarines.

Q: That was indeed a spotlight job. I understand.

Mr. N.: I did get going very soon on that, but I missed a point here a little bit because in working all these things out - I arrived in the yard in May -

Q: Of 1918?

Mr. N.: Yes - and by the time September came around I'd decided that I wanted to get a commission in the Navy, so I enlisted in the Navy as a chief machinist's mate. This was the procedure that they had to become an officer.

Q: You already had the inclining experiment behind you, had you?

Mr. N.: Yes, I had that behind me and I probably had a few other things behind me. My note here tells that I had the submarine behind me.

Now I joined the officers' training and I went through all that from September and was finished with all the military -

Q: Where were you stationed?

Mr. N.: I was stationed at Pelham Bay, and it was a very rigorous training program. I remember some of the people who were in my group protested so much, they said they must be a bunch of Prussians who are running the place. But I timed myself very carefully. I was accustomed to keeping data, you know, so it was no problem. They used to tell me that I kept a stopwatch on them because I knew exactly when I had to wash my clothes and when I had to do this and when I had to do that.

I knew what I wanted to do and so I went through all the military training, including the Manual of Arms, company parades, rowing the boats, semaphore signals - I've forgotten how fast I could do the signals, but I passed all those tests, everything connected with that, and we were on our last company formation, in which we were being examined, and now we're on a company front when I was called front and center and told to report at headquarters.

The Secretary of the Navy, Josephus Daniels, had decided - I always thought that Commander Wright and Rock had something to do with this - they let me go through all this military training, ready for commissioning, and, of course, if I got the commission they would have no control on me getting back to the yard. So they wrote a lot of letters to the Secretary of the Navy, and the Secretary of the Navy ordered me discharged from the Navy and returned to the Navy Yard.

Q: That must have been a disappointment after you'd done all that?

Mr. N.: It was. I was quite disappointed, so I didn't report right away. I was a couple of weeks late in coming over.

Q: AWOL!

Mr. N.: I really wasn't because I was on a resigned status now and I could have gone anywhere.

Q: Did they try to get in touch with you?

Mr. N.: No. I had kept it quite a secret where I was going but I had told Wright that I was going into the Navy. I wanted to get this training. But I wouldn't tell them where or what part of the Navy or anything else. He said, Well, fine, but he did find out where I was. They let me go through the whole shebang so I finished all that, and it was very good because I had a lot of lectures on command. And one of the things I remember is when in doubt to carry on what you think the orders might have been.

Q: A common sense thing.

Mr. N.: Yes. Now the first thing that Wright said to me was: "What took you so long?" In the meantime the gradings had changed. They used to have a ship draftsman so much and so much, and now they had three grades of draftsmen. The lowest one was C, then B, then A. And I remember Wright told me all this. He said: "While you were away" such and such happened and the Macy Board awards had come in. "These are the grades," he said, and he described each one to me. "And where do you think you belong?" he asked me.

I said, A, top grade, and Wright said, "Fine, you tell that to Mr. Fletcher." So I did. I went in and told Fletcher that I'd seen Wright and had told him that I should be an A and "Wright said to tell you that that's where I said I belonged," and Fletcher put me there.

Q: On your say-so!

Mr. N.: So I started off at A. But you see those people really were on my side already because this spotlight job particularly, the construction officer was getting into trouble in Washington with the chief because, what's the matter, New York didn't know what it was doing.

In any case, I started off getting into really good jobs like launching calculations.

Q: Before you talk about that, would you give me a picture of the New York Shipyard in that time? That was World War I.

Mr. N.: Well, we had a couple of big dry docks then. No. 2 dock was a great big one. We had a building ways that could take two ships, two battleships, and we had quite a few shops - all kinds of shops, very good shops, a machine shop, an electric shop, a forge shop, and so forth, pattern-making, a full shipyard organization.

Q: What sort of personnel, how many people were there?

Mr. N.: I have no idea how many people we had there, but we must have had thousands of people working there because we had the Tennessee there, we were taking in all these German ships that were being docked there, and some of the people who ran those dockings were really geniuses. I watched them dock one of those big German ships, and it would be a matter of inches at the head of the dock and the tail end of the German ship would come in between the ribs of the gate that would come in. You had to put the rudder over and they did it so well. It takes a lot of people to do things like that. So I would say that we probably had 8,000 or 10,000 people there.

I got going on the launching of the Tennessee, and now it was 1919. The launching of the Tennessee was heading up close and that was on April 30, the day set for launching. I had a habit of staying over. I'd get in early in the morning if I had a job to do and I'd stay over if I was in the middle of something to try to finish it up so that when I came in the morning I would have that thing finished, especially since, in this case, the launching was going to be tomorrow morning.

While I was busy working on this thing, Rock came in, George Rock, and said:

"I've been down in the yard looking at the Tennessee and looking down the ways. I think the armor shelf will hit the concrete sidewalls. What do you know about it?"

I said: "As far as I know, everything's in the clear."

"No," he said, "I don't think it is. I think we'll hit it." On the Tennessee the armor shelf was going to be an angle that was put on the side of the regular shelf, so they had the angle on there to take the armor, whereas on the New Mexico, I imagine, they had the ship shape there and a kind of a shelf put into the side of the ship and then continued the side of the ship up, and the armor would be flush with the side of the ship instead of sticking over.

So I said, "The only thing I could do, Captain, would be to get a transit somewhere and I'll go down and set it up. It's getting kind of dark, so we'll have to get the transit and it must be locked up somewhere." So he called a yard watchman - Rock, I guess, knew where the transits were - to bust the door down.

Q: In the scaffolding, are they?

Mr. N.: This was in a building. It's a surveyor's instrument, and you set it up like a theodolite. I knew a little bit about them.

I went down there all by myself. I didn't have any help, but I worked out a parallel line and I took a sight as near as I could. It was parallel to the ship's ways, and I decided that it wouldn't hit.

Q: There was clearance?

Mr. N.: It was clear. So I went back and Rock was waiting

patiently, and I told him that I thought we'd clear. I said that the way I figured it, we'd clear. He took my word for it, so we launched the ship the next day and it cleared.

Q: Were there a lot of notables there?

Mr. N.: Oh, yes, but I was in the launching pit. I hadn't been on any launchings before, but I made out all the different schedules on when to drive the wedges and get the ship onto the grease and all that sort of thing. Now I was in the launching pit under the ship and it was going down over my head. I could hear it humming as it went down. I was busy watching the schedule because we were the ones who from the pressure on the trigger would have to give the signals. Now we were sitting on the grease and the only thing that was holding it were these triggers. Finally, we spot the time to go and release the triggers and down went the ship. Of course, they hit it with champagne and the ship went into the water.

Rock remembered that I did that job.

Q: You put his mind at rest!

Mr. N.: Yes. Later on theodolites and so on came in even more importantly. However, shortly after we launched the Tennessee, I was elected to the shop committee.

Q: This, you said, was at the order of FDR, who had ordered that this be done in the shipyards?

Mr. N.: Yes.

Q: Tell me that background.

Mr. N.: You mean about the shop committee?

Q: Yes, about shop committees, the order to set up these committees.

Mr. N.: Well, if there was anything that the men complained about or anything happened between the supervisors or the officers and the men in a ship, they would come to the shop committeeman and the shop committeeman would then take it up with the command and talk about it.

Q: He became their spokesman?

Mr. N.: Yes, automatically. I did that.

Q: Was this an election? Did they elect you?

Mr. N.: Yes, I was elected. Evidently, people liked me. Anyway, it was very unusual because it was 1919 or 1920 and I'd only been out of Webb two years. Now when you get out of college we put you in training for a couple of years.

Q: You were a youngster, really.

Mr. N.: Yes. Anyway, I handled that shop committee job and quite a few cases, but a particular thing happened. The question of layoffs came up. Also something happened in the way officers were arranged over the design people. Up until this particular time, there was always a construction officer in a straight line between the design people and the constructor. There might be an assistant constructor who would be with the chief draftsman. Now, there was a struggle between the line and the staff officers. It started to show up that early.

By the time this happened Rock had gone. He was down in Washington, and Henry T. Wright was a captain and he was the chief constructor of the yard now. They put a line officer between him and his contact, between his assistant construction officer, who was with the chief draftsman and communicated orders through the chief draftsman, and that line officer was Fredericks.

I got along very well with Fredericks because he was a nut in - and it was well taken, too - the way that he felt a little fresh air twice a day would be good and a little exercise would be a good idea. So, twice a day we'd open the windows and everybody would go out and stretch themselves and breathe some fresh air.

Q: This was the early coffee break, was it?

Mr. N.: Well, we didn't have any coffee break, really, but this is what he wanted because the room was too stuffy for him. He was a ship officer, you see, and was used to being out at sea, and with all the windows shut I guess he didn't like it. He and I got along fine until he did something that I took exception to.

They stopped work on the battleship that was building in the yard. I think it was the 49 that was in the New York Yard. I've forgotten now. Maybe they had her and the 50.

Q: They hadn't got names yet?

Mr. N.: No, they stopped work on them and so they had to lay people off. The work slackened off when they stopped work on those ships. They were going to scrap them.

Fredericks helter-skelter started laying off people without checking to see what their background was. Some of them were the best people during the war, but he would lay them off. It didn't make any difference how much seniority they had or anything. Of course, we didn't have any retirement laws in those days. I went to him and told him he was doing this wrong. I've forgotten his first name. He said:

"Well, Niedermair, there's a lot of hankypanky goes on with these things, and I've made my decision that this is the way I'm going to do it."

So he had these people get their notice. I went to the construction officer, who was under Fredericks - I don't want to mention his name because he's still alive - oh, well, I can mention his name, it's Johnny Hale - Commander Hale. He retired as a captain. I went to Hale and he would always try to fluff me off on these things, which I guess was a way of telling me he really couldn't do anything about it, but he didn't say so. He'd say things like this to me:

"You know what a white rat is, don't you?" You see, he was really carrying Fredericks' tale to me about hankypanky. I said:

"Yes, I know about a white rat. I was down on the _Falcon_."
The _Falcon_ was a rescue ship that was down in the yard, and it

was true, I had been on the Falcon. She had a diving tank on her and all that sort of stuff. Little did I know how I was going to be connected with that later. I was on that ship and some of the members of the crew told me about the white rat they had as a pet, and they showed him to me. He was walking around, his ears would be bitten off and everything, but they told me that that white rat would chase all other rats off the ship. That's why its ear was nipped and so on. There weren't any rats on that ship but that white rat.

So I told Hale, "yes, I know what a white rat is. I just met one today on the Falcon and he chases all the other rats right off the ship."

Hale didn't say any more about white rats!

So I went off to Wright and told him about this thing and he said: "I agree with you." But you see, I didn't know about this line officer business. I hadn't signed that up as a problem because that wasn't any of my business. Navy was Navy, see. So I talked to Captain Wright and he said:

"Yes, I know all about it, Niedermair, and I was in talking to Captain Butler." He was the yard manager. "And he threw me out of his office."

"Oh," I said, "I guess there's no point in my going in to see him then. That's the end of the line, isn't it?" And Wright said:

"No, it isn't. I can't go to see the commandant. I suggest you see Butler, anyway. He probably will throw you out, but you'd better go and see him."

So I did. I went to see Butler and told him what was going on. Of course, he was a line officer now and his contact was with Fredericks, in a straight line, which I didn't know –

Q: You were innocent of all that!

Mr. N.: All right. I went to work and talked to Butler just a few minutes when he got up and walked out on me. He didn't order me out because he knew better than that, and I walked out. But I never thought of going to the commandant about it because I didn't want to make such a fuss about this thing because Captain Wright couldn't do anything about it and so on, but I had sense enough not to go back to Captain Wright's office after I'd been in Butler's office. I went back to my drafting board, and then when the opportune time came in a roundabout way I went and visited Captain Wright. I told Wright what had happened and he said: "I know all about it." He always worked at a stand-up desk and he had glass all around so he could see what was going on. And Willie Francis Gibbs loved to work at a stand-up desk, too. Anyway, I said:

"So, that's what happened to me." And Wright said:

"Now you can see the commandant. I can't go to the commandant, but there are no strings on you."

Q: What was the commandant's rank?

Mr. N.: He was Rear Admiral C. P. Plunkett, Commandant of the

Third Naval District. The big boss of the Third Naval District.

Imagine the training I was getting here! All right. I called up the commandant's secretary and made a date. She made a date for me right away. That is the next morning I saw the commandant. I told the commandant my story and he said:

"Niedermair, the thing we'll do is to call all the supervisors and all the officers in the yard to the sail loft and you tell them exactly what you've told me."

But before I took such a stand on these things, as a sort of extra thing I did for my own self, I'd gone over to the New York Telephone Company and several companies on Manhattan Island and talked to them about what they did about their senior employees.

Q: When they had to reduce their staff.

Mr. N.: So in telling the story that I told the commandant, I told them about what I had done and I came back and was more convinced than ever that this was the wrong move, that it's always a mistake to lay off your experience, and what Fredericks was doing was laying off experience, and really the only sales talk you've got is your experience.

Q: It's continuity, yes.

Mr. N.: Plunkett agreed with me. I had never made a real public speech before anybody and Plunkett said, "And you'll tell the story. I'll arrange a date. I'll let you know and then you come in my office and we'll go over there together."

Of course, I hadn't told Fletcher or Ambrose Merrill all

the things I did, and they had to be at this meeting. Fredericks had to be there, Hale had to be there, all the officers in the yard who had any activity in the shops had to be there, all shop committeemen. Plunkett introduced me. I had a pretty good introduction. He told them that I was going to tell them what I'd told him.

Q: Weren't you a little nervous at this point?

Mr. N.: I don't remember because I had been secretary of my student organization and when I worked for the baker I was accustomed to meeting people long before I got to Webb. As a matter of fact, I always decided about things my way, anyhow, even when I was a boy. This stayed with me all my life.

Anyway, I told my story and in about a week Fredericks came in to me and said:

"Niedermair, I've come to say good-bye."

I said, "What happened?"

"I'm transferred to sea."

I said: "I'm sorry to hear that. Where are you going?" And he said:

"I'm going to be captain of the Nitro, and I think a lot of people here hope it blows up."

And I said: "Oh, now look. This was not a question of personalities, really. There was a point. I felt you did the wrong thing and I carried it out the way my job as a shop committeeman required me to do the best I could for the people that I represented. I told you the story. I had to take it to the commandant and the commandant, I suppose, is responsible for you going to sea."

"Yes," he said, "and I came to say that, yes, I see. I never thought of it that way." He evidently believed other people, you see.

Of course, there's no other way of having everybody in the New York Navy Yard know me, but when the commandant of the yard introduces you.

Q: The whole system of laying-off was changed then, was it?

Mr. N.: Well, FDR did me a great favor there. I learned to get along with top people. I never in all my life really asked for a favor. I never had to. I did ask for favors for other people.

Q: But in that particular case, as a result of all this action, the whole system of laying-off men was changed, was it?

Mr. N.: Yes. They brought these other people back. Some of them were already out.

Q: And they brought them back?

Mr. N.: Yes. Gus Wenninger, one of my lifelong friends lives on Long Island and I'm still in correspondence with him.

Q: And then they let go the men who'd been there the shorter time?

Mr. N.: I don't know how they worked it out. They probably found they had plenty of work, anyway. I think some of this was just prejudice. This other thing was just to try to make a big showing. The orders were to lay off people and I guess he started at the wrong end.

Q: There was another example you wanted to relate of your usefulness in this job, about the sick leave.

Mr. N.: Yes, the sick leave thing. That was another thing that was minor in a way, but actually it was a very important thing. It might have been most important with George Rock, now that you mention that. I don't have it in my list of things here.

There was a question that came up about sick leave. A man named Sassensheid had been injured in the boat shop, and Rock turned down his sick leave because he didn't think there was an "and" in there. You either had to be seriously ill and worthy.

Q: Worthy? That's curious.

Mr. N.: Yes. I'm using that word now because I can't think of any other word.

I talked to Rock about this. I had to go to him after working hours, though, because the first time you brought a complaint in you had to do it after quitting time. You had to make an appointment to see these people right after quitting time.

Q: Why? Wasn't it a part of a working day?

Mr. N.: You had to do it on your own time. You couldn't use government time for this. But, as it worked out, when the commandant got in on the act, it turned it around. When it got to be a big thing, I had to carry it through with everybody in the regular way.

However, on this sick leave, I went to Rock and protested it, because the man had been injured in the yard and I knew that he had these spasms coming on and off, and he was really sick. Rock, I think, thought that his sickness wasn't really too bad, even though it was the same thing. Before I left him that night I said to him:

"Well, we'll have to take it up in Washington and have the word 'and' changed to 'or' in the sick leave regulations."

The next morning Rock called me into his office. He had a telegram and the "and" was changed to "or."

Q: Sick or worthy?

Mr. N.: So either one would do, and so Sassenshied got his sick leave. But Rock kind of wondered, I think. This was before the commandant thing happened because Rock wasn't there any more by the time I arrived at that sort of deal. That was a big deal.

Q: Yes, I understand.

Mr. N.: I think he always felt that I must have had an inside track. I was trying to remember the name of the man who did work with the Secretary of the Navy on that project, but I can't think of it.

Later on, before Rock got away, I did do something for him that was most interesting. It was very odd. Rock called me into his office and said:

"Niedermair, what do you know about civil engineering?" And I said: "Gee, I don't know a damned thing about civil engineering. When do I have to know about it?"

He said: "Oh, in a couple of weeks." I said: "I'll know all about it by then. What is the job?"

And he told me: "Yards and Docks somehow or other can't understand what's required in connection with the shape of the ways. They'll turn all the money over to us and we should do the job ourselves."

I had planned new ways in this way. I had put down the type of surface that I wanted. I had read up on it and decided that in building heavy ships, battleships, I wanted a small slope under the center of gravity at the beginning, but I wanted a big slope at the end. If you had a straight line, flat surface, you couldn't get an increase as it went down the ways, so I selected a circle that was part of a five-mile radius. Then Rock said:

"Well, Niedermair, they've turned the money back and now we'll build the ways. You'll do it."

I said: "I can't do it alone. I'll have to get help."

"You can get anybody you want, all the help you need. Go out in the yard and get the yard set up and order the materials, everything to build these ways." They were to be built out of wood. Blocks were to be built up off the concrete base.

And so I worked all summer, and who did I pick to help me?

I picked people - I interviewed a few civil engineers who were around there. I knew one civil engineer who was very close to me, Friedenreich, his name was, and I told him my problem. So we ganged together and we built a sawmill outside the yard and we ordered the building materials. I made one mistake in the whole thing. It was a mistake that I regretted because I ordered 14-by 14-dimensioned timbers. They were pretty big. I thought about it and thought about it, because I think they denuded all the yellow pine trees down south in order to get 14-by14 timber. I always thought, gee, 12-by-12s would have been good enough, as it turned out, because they never built a battleship on the ways. The first thing that was launched on the ways after we got done with it was a cruiser, and that's a long story in a way, it was the Pensacola. I had a half-inch slope now and a cruiser was going to be launched on there. This was sort of a surprise when some of the people like Ernie Rigg from New York Ship heard that we were launching this cruiser on a half-inch slope.

But in my research on the problem I said the grease doesn't know the difference of what's on top of it. The thing that launches it is the pressure per square foot on the grease. Now, if I have a weight on top that is wide enough to prevent the grease from sliding outside the ways at, say, 2-1/2 tons per square foot, we can put the cruiser Pensacola on that half-inch slope, be very careful how we do it, and the ship will be launched. So I figured that all out and by the time launching time came up I was no longer in the yard. I was in London. I knew the day it was to be launched but I couldn't find out whether it was in the water or not. I was worried sick!

Anyway, that is a good end for that story about the ways. But it was an odd job to give me. Actually, I had them build a sawmill for me, and, of course, the people from the woodworking shop ran it. The 14-by-14 timbers were delivered and we built the ways according to the way we surveyed the yard. We had established the centerlines and all that sort of thing.

I did one foolish thing in connection with that, though. While we were doing that surveying work, I tried to get some of the laborers to go - I wanted to strike a very careful centerline and I took a spot on a bridge, I think it was the Williamsburg Bridge, that was exactly down in the plane that I wanted. I apparently had the thing set up so that the people were on the bridge throwing the sight, and I wanted the laborers to go out on the 6-inch angle beam when the ways was up about 100 feet or more in the air and establish it. I think it was the top of the crane that was there, then we could take that line and drop it down. The crane would stand still. I had the crane operator get out of the carriage when we were going to do this, but I couldn't get any of the laborers to walk out on this angle. Because I wasn't married then and I didn't have any family at all I said, "OK, I'll go out and do it."

I walked out on this 6-inch angle, kneeled down, and spotted it for them. I was quite well coordinated and, having worked in shipyards, you had to be used to climbing on things but not quite that way.

However, we finished the job and they launched the ship. Rigg from New York Ship was there and I talked to Ernie Rigg later about it, and he said:

"Yes, I went up there expecting to see the <u>Pensacola</u> stick on the ways. Actually, the ship was very anxious to get in the water. She broke loose a little sooner than they expected and down she went." That's the end of that.

Q: Why did Yards and Dock renege on the design?

Mr. N.: They couldn't quite figure out how to get this surface, this half-mile radius. We have cambers that we put on the decks of ships and everything and using all kinds of odd-looking curves is a thing that a naval architect is working with all the time. A curve doesn't bother him. One of the things you really learn is all kinds of curves. You know the names of some of them. One that pops into my mind now is Lemniscate of Bernoulli. That's one I love to think about. It's one of these oddities that sticks in your head. I had selected the five-mile-radius curve and I knew how to get all the elevations — they were a little cagey about it, so I worked it out for No. 2 ways, which is what I was working on.

After we got the No. 2 ways built — Yards and Docks built the No. 1 ways —

Q: Oh, they did?

Mr. N.: Yes.

Q: Do you want to talk about cost overruns?

Mr. N.: Yes. I got interested in this cost overrun thing which I talked about. I may have talked about it previously here. But the point was that I did take quite an interest in these cost overruns and so Captain Wright thought it would be a good idea if I ran these jobs, made the cost estimates and then ran the jobs through the shops and supervised them completely, all the way through the accounting office until the job was finished. It would be good experience for me and I would also find out why these things run over, which I did. But in the jobs I ran I also indicated or found out why they ran over cost often. The accounting office used to report to me every day all the charges to every job that I was interested in, which apparently no one else ever did before. They just waited till the job was done, then they added it all up, but I checked it practically every day on any job that I ran. I did very well on that. It was just about the time that I was studying economics and business management, so I was interested in a thing that had nothing to do with the metacentric height.

Q: You were a little before your time. You would have been a good member for McNamara's team, wouldn't you?

Mr. N.: Well, I carried that idea on quite a bit. I have one other comment I want to make here.

Now we were approaching 1923 and on April 22, 1923, I married Ethel May Victoria Irwin, and she was a great lady, who for fifty years gave me the greatest freedom imaginable to carry on my chosen profession. Through it all, she was a perfect companion always, with a strong buoyant personality, with a song in her heart. She had a beautiful voice, she loved poetry. As a matter of fact, we met because of her love for poetry. And we met through an oddity. We would never have met, there was no way that Ethel and I would ever have met, even though we lived on Staten Island - I was away from Staten Island more than I was on it at that time, except for one thing.

One day, as I was coming to the ferry to go on a ferry boat, there was a friend of mine there, Charlie Post. He had been in the Naval Reserve on Staten Island and when the war came he was in the crew of the <u>President Lincoln</u>. The <u>President Lincoln</u> was torpedoed and Charlie Post, after several days in the water, was picked up on a life raft and his life was saved, and now I met him at the ferry house and Charlie said to me:

"Wait a minute, I'm waiting for a couple of girl friends," and one of the girl friends was Ethel.

That, I always thought, was an odd way to meet.

Q: No, indeed, but tell me how on earth did you have time for any courtship with all your activities? And your dedication to your job?

Mr. N.: I was a problem for Ethel because I would leave and go down. I remember one time I went away and I came back and my tie pin was missing. I didn't put any significance in it but later on I found out that the thing that worried her about that time was my tie pin - I bet he met a girl down there or something. You used to give your tie pins away, you see, and I had a beautiful tie pin.

Q: That was a sign of interest then?

Mr. N.: Yes, sure, and she thought maybe the other girl got it. But Charlie Post had warned her about me. He said that I had a girl in Brooklyn and he made up a lot of stories because I think he liked Ethel, too. Ethel and I had a slow courtship, I would say. It lasted from about 1920 to about 1923. But you see I was just getting started and I couldn't even think of getting married. I wasn't sure that I thought of getting married in April 1923, but by that time I was a supervisor and all that sort of thing.

Q: What were you making per week in those days, when you got married?

Mr. N.: I've forgotten what it was, but I was completely preoccupied with my job. When I was over at the yard there, I'd go down to the Philadelphia Yard. That's where I was when I supposedly lost my tie pin. Then I'd be up in Boston. There were different jobs that would come up, or there'd be a ship in the yard that New York worked on and I'd go up and see it. I would always be pegged for one thing or another.

Some of the things that happened were quite unusual. I got connected with diesel engines. I told you that I was working on a design of engines while I was at Webb, but that's not knowing.

very much about an engine. That's not knowing anything about how to build it. Even though an inventor can invent an engine, he may not know how to build it. There's a big difference.

Q: I can see that, the theory and the application.

Mr. N.: So by the time 1923 got around, I wasn't doing too badly. I could afford to get married. There were pay increases. They weren't very much, probably $8 a day. That seemed like pretty good pay.

Q: It went a great deal farther than it does today!

Mr. N.: Yes.

Q: Shall we break off there?

Mr. N.: Yes.

Interview No. 2 with Mr. John C. Niedermair

Place: His residence in Stone Harbor, New Jersey

Date: High noon, 29 July 1975

Subject: Biography

By: John T. Mason, Jr.

Q: It's great to see you again today, Sir, and to see that obviously you're in fine fettle. Last time we broke off with an account of your marriage in the year 1923 to a very charming young lady with whom you lived for the next fifty years.

Now, Sir, will you begin with a further discussion of your period with the shipyard.

Mr. N.: Yes. It wasn't very long after we were married - about a year and a half - when the question arose as to why the United States Lines was having a lot of trouble with the Leviathan as a passenger ship. This problem was caused by the fact that the first-class ventilation, as we found out when we went into it, was almost an absolute failure.

The reason for it was that they had not connected the amount of air supply from the fans into the rooms properly.

Q: This was from the beginning?

Mr. N.: This was the way Newport News did the work and they made the installations, and Gibbs Brothers were the naval architects.

Ellsburg and I went aboard and Jake Cohn - Jake Cohn was a man who had worked in ventilation, that was his specialty. I was not particularly known in the way of ventilation, but again Captain H. T. Wright had loads of confidence in me. I noticed just recently, in going through my papers, that in the meantime, before I even got started on the Leviathan, it was in the wind that I was supposed to go off to a stability committee. William Francis Gibbs was to be the chairman of it, and this was for the Department of Commerce. It was an official government stability committee to investigate the stability of merchant ships in connection, I suppose, with steamboat inspection and so on, but I didn't know this. I noticed in the memorandum there that Captain Wright was speculating that I would have to miss the first few trips on the Leviathan. It was his note to Ellsburg in this regard.

I was unaware of what was happening. I was busy in the yard, doing the things that I was there to do according to my job specification, but I very seldom had a chance to work on. All of a sudden one afternoon, on a Wednesday of a week in about October 1924, Ellsburg, whom I had never met, came to me where I was working in the scientific section and asked me if I would be ready to go to Europe on Saturday. That was only a couple of days away, and I told him I thought I would.

Well, now, an interesting thing happened. He told me then that we would be traveling on the Leviathan, they were having trouble, and we would investigate this while we were at sea. That was a very intriguing invitation.

Q: A vacation and work combined!

Mr. N.: It would seem like that and it did work out partly a vacation, but it had other benefits for me that were far beyond that because I got the great experience of being in the North Atlantic, some 25,000 miles at sea that winter.

Ellsburg left, and it occurred to me that I didn't ask him how we were traveling, so I called him on the phone and asked him: "How are we traveling?" He said, "Cabin class, I guess."

I said: "Well, we're the experts, aren't we?" He didn't debate that, so I said:

"If we're experts, we should go first class - "

Q: And suffer the ventilation!

Mr. N.: I didn't know at that time where the trouble was in ventilation, and Ellsburg said, no, he thought we'd go cabin. I said: "If we're experts, we should travel first class. I'm certainly not going as an expert in second class. If that's the case, if it's cabin class, I'm not going."

That was the end of that conversation and a few minutes after I hung up, maybe ten minutes or so, I got another call back from Ellsburg saying: "We're traveling first class." But he never allowed for the fact that I was an expert. Actually, I wasn't in ventilation, but I was an expert in engineering, I suppose. Otherwise, I wouldn't be going.

Now we were traveling first class, and you've heard all the trouble about passports and one thing and another, how long it takes to do it. Well, by Friday, two days later, I had my passport and everything, and Saturday morning I left on the Leviathan.

We traveled back and forth on there and we were to investigate the ventilation, the first-class ventilation, which we did. I started to hit the thing pretty hard, and the first thing you know I was running that part of the show, and my expert in ventilation, Jake Cohn, got seasick to beat the band and I had an awful time driving him around all the time.

However, other things developed. Not only did we have the ventilation to take care of, but we found that the amount of air that was going into the boilers was insufficient. They had converted coal-burning boilers to fuel oil burning. Of course, fuel oil was a lot easier to handle and everything but it required air, more air than was coming to the burners. Tremendous cones of carbon would be deposited all over the first-class sections of the open decks.

So I not only dug into the ventilation but I dug into the amount of air that we would have to take care of on the boilers. And it so happened that when I finally discovered what the trouble was in the ventilation - they had overhead light fixtures in all the staterooms and around the edges of the lights they had a little screen in there that appeared like the stuff that they put in chair seats, woven chair seats. It was a pretty design but they didn't connect it to the air ducts. The air would be let into the ceilings of the staterooms and the best-ventilated space was between the ceiling of the stateroom and the deck over it, not the staterooms.

That meant that after we checked it all out we made the estimate and decided we didn't have to add a single fan, but we did have to go through the thing and put stateroom vent ducts into the ship, which we did when we came back, say, in December. Then we took the ship up to Boston.

But in going back and forth we also had to look into the forced-draft system, and there we did have to add fans to get more air because they were very-slow-moving fans and the pressurized boiler rooms needed more air, and we worked out a method of doing this. In one case where we broke through in the uptakes there to see over the boiler rooms, there we found pieces of two-by-fours that had been left in there had turned to charcoal. That'll give you some idea how hot those spaces were getting.

Q: What a hazard!

Mr. N.: A hazard, too, but there they were. They'd turned to charcoal and that was it.

Q: Let me ask, what kind of ventilation system did the Germans have when they operated her as a passenger ship?

Mr. N.: The old fans that were on there were the ones they were using, and I guess the Germans had the same thing. They even had controls at the doorway so you could turn a damper to open and close - the damper would be off in one corner in the ceiling space overhead - but it was never led over to this little thing around the light.

We changed all that. Where they probably got a change of the air in the staterooms once every hour or two, we had an average of less than seven minutes' change of air in every single first-class stateroom when we got through, without adding a single fan.

Q: The passengers must have been complaining, weren't they?

Mr. N.: They sure did. There's an interesting little story about that because when Francis Gibbs would be called upon to come aboard and inspect the ship, they had cork on the decks so that the heat from the boilers on the deck wouldn't burn your feet! And they had a twofold problem, the way they took care of it. In any case, the result was that Gibbs had to inspect it there. He'd come aboard and go into staterooms, and I understand that one time they went into a stateroom where they had a real great problem and they claimed they could fry an egg on the deck. Willy Francis came in and looked at it. There were women in this room and they were practically naked. One of them said to the ship's officer who had William Francis Gibbs along, "We need air. We don't want a minister here." They looked at Willie and he looked so sober and solemn that they said they didn't need a minister, they needed more air!

So those are some of the humorous things, but that winter in the North Atlantic was the worst winter in the North Atlantic on record, almost. It was that way and I haven't heard of one since or up to that time that was worse. Lloyds insurance company said that practically every ship that crossed the Atlantic that winter in one way or another was damaged - every single ship that crossed the North Atlantic in the winter of 1924-25 was damaged in one way or another.

By December when we were coming back with all the celebrities in the ship, not only was the ventilation system bad but the heating system was bad, too. They had little radiators in the rooms and so on and there was trouble with those. That was solved in other ways, but the main trouble was the ventilation. However, without the ventilation there the heat would be so hot that some of the Englishmen who traveled in the ship now and then couldn't stand the heat in these staterooms, besides the fact that the system wasn't too easily controlled.

However, coming back in December, just before Christmas, and my last trip back for that part of our job and before we took the ship up to Boston for repairs, why, the ship started breaking in two, off Newfoundland. Actually, through the two-inch-strength deck of the ship cracks started to appear early one morning in one of these bad storms. It woke me up and Ellsburg and I went up and took a look at it. The cracks were working their way across the deck and we had the ship's carpenters drill some big holes through the deck to try to stop the cracks from going all the way across the deck. That worked, and we got the ship back in to New York.

Now we had three things to repair. We had the ventilation to take care of, we had the forced-draft system for the boilers to take care of, which we had to do with extra fans, and we had to take care of the ship breaking in two. So we went up to Boston and got a certain amount of money to fix the ship.

Q: Why wasn't it done in your own shipyard?

Mr. N.: Because we couldn't get her into a dry dock there. The dry dock up in Boston was bigger than the one in the yard. We couldn't get the Leviathan into the New York dry dock.

Q: Refresh my mind as to the tonnage of the Leviathan.

Mr. N.: I don't know what it was. I see there was some argument by somebody that wrote a history about ships. There was a little article in the Institute Proceedings about the tonnage. I never checked into that but Gibbs had worked it out so it was the biggest ship in the world, according to the tonnage. It was pretty close to being the biggest.

Q: Before the "Queens" came along?

Mr. N.: Yes. They had her sister ships, you know. There was the Leviathan and then the British had one that was a sister ship to the Leviathan and it started breaking in two. As a matter of fact, on one trip over we landed at Southampton and we could see the sister ship of the Leviathan that the British had. It was in a dry dock because it started breaking in two before the Leviathan was breaking in two. But they both started breaking in two during that same winter.

Q: How many round trips did you make on the Leviathan?

Mr. N.: Oh, I don't know how many. To get some rough estimate, assume 30,000 miles and a round trip about 4,000, or say, 5,000 miles, so there were at least six round trips. That works out about right.

Q: She was in constant operation and you just stayed a few days in port in England?

Mr. N.: Roughly we made at least six round trips. I met Rudy Valintino on there and the top movie stars. I got Rudi's autograph for my wife. I have it around here somewhere. And Jackie Coogan was there, Mary Pickford, and, oh, all kinds of movie stars were traveling first class. Unfortunately for everybody the weather was so rough that most of them were seasick. I got to be friendly with all the crew because I had to go through all the crew's spaces - I had to go through that ship from top to bottom, even down in the engine room and everything, and they thought I was a spy looking for liquor and smugglers aboard.

One day they caught me taking these lights down off the ceiling to find out what was wrong with the ventilation, when a second purser opened the door and yelled in - Jake Cohn was with me and I was up on the ladder, taking this thing apart, and looking inside to find out what was wrong with the ventilation:

"What are you doing? Looking for liquor?"

I said: "No, not exactly, but I would like to find some." So I got very friendly with him and they thought that we were searching for the places where they had their liquor hidden, because you could lift these little panels out that were supposed to let the air in.

The second purser took us down to his space. He said: "OK, come down and we'll have a drink when you're ready." So we went down to his stateroom and, sure enough, that's where he had his liquor hidden.

Q: And we recall the fact that this was in the days of prohibition.

Mr. N.: Yes, there was prohibition.

The purser was very suspicious of us. It turned out that one time - this is a little ahead of time but I might as well say it now. Sometime after the Christmas project, near springtime, we were coming back and Jake Cohn and I were going down the gangway and the purser was going down ahead of us with his briefcase. We knew the customs officers, too. We knew everybody and they knew us. This purser, whose name was de Carow –

Q: de Carow?

Mr. N.: Yes. That's pretty good comeback. I haven't mentioned that name for a long time.

What happened was that the customs inspector was at the foot of the gangway. Everybody else was off the ship. The officers were leaving and we were behind the head purser. The customs inspector had looked in the head purser's briefcase and he said to Jake and me:

"Now watch. Don't walk ahead. Let de Carow walk ahead, because we're going to pinch him when he gets down through the next door. We suspect that he's smuggling diamonds."

And, sure enough, here was a man who thought we were making believe we were on board to fix the ventilation while we were looking for things like that. He said that he found the diamonds in Governor Smith's wife's stateroom. She was on the trip.

Q: Al Smith?

Mr. N.: Right, Al Smith's wife.

That gives you some of the atmosphere of this venture. It was full of color. de Carow got nicked and I don't know what happened to him.

Later on I talked to the customs people and asked them how

they knew de Carow was doing this. They said:

"Well, he was very foolish. He would get in to Southampton and he would fly over to Belgium in a little plane. Then he'd fly back again. Besides, he came from a little island in the Mediterranean" - it wasn't Sicily, it was a British-owned island, I can't think of the name now.

Q: Malta?

Mr. N.: Malta, yes. He said:

"He's a Maltese and they always end up in the end becoming smugglers. So he not only exposed himself by flying over there but also by the fact that he came from Malta and these people, no matter how well positioned they were, could be tempted to go into this sort of business."

So, however, the December trip came along and our ship was in a hell of a shape, as I was telling you. Now we had to leave for Boston. We went in the dry dock up there and we started working to correct the troubles from the ventilation system.

Q: Was this the Boston Navy Yard?

Mr. N.: The Boston Navy Yard and in the dry dock. We got going on that and we started to cut out certain plating. We took a crew of Navy Yard workmen with us when we came back again to New York, so we could work on the ship after we got back into New York until she was ready to go and take the passengers back.

I think that was some time in January. We had a very short time to do all this work.

While we were in the Boston yard we had to put up some staging almost from the inner bottom all the way up to the main deck, probably 100 feet or more of staging, so that the workmen could get at some of these vent trunks that we wanted to put into the ship in order to get a better distribution of this air, which was really up on the weather deck and they weren't getting it.

Darn it, if we didn't run out of money. We had used all the money we had.

Q: This was federal money?

Mr. N.: I don't know where they got the money from but Boston had to have the money to keep the workmen going, you see. I never knew where they got it. New York, I guess, from the U.S. Lines, they owned the ship and they had to pay for everything. It was poor judgment on the commandant's part, the commandant of the First Naval District. They didn't like us, anyway, because we came from the Third Naval District.

His solution to this no-money problem was to take all this staging down, which we already had paid for, but he said he owned the wood. We only paid for the labor. We wouldn't let him do that. It was solved later. They got some money and we left Boston and got into New York and got ready for the next phases of our trips across the Atlantic. In a lot of cases, in order to get this ventilation over the ceiling into the staterooms, we had to take the ceilings down, and they were made out of stuff that was like wallboard made up of residue like straw and so on. I've forgotten what the name of that stuff is. And the ceilings were all special. They had been sized for the rooms so there'd be no joints in the rooms. So we had quite a job to get these ceilings down because they wouldn't let us cut holes in them.

Q: Was that an early version of an acoustical ceiling?

Mr. N.: It has a name. You've seen it around. It was just like a very soft board that they put up. It came from some place out West and they had a hell of a time shipping it for that ship.

Q: It absorbed the sound, I take it?

Mr. N.: Yes, I imagine it was for sound.
We started going back and forth -

Q: You had to stay with the ship now?

Mr. N.: Oh, yes, I stayed with it all the time. When it got to New York, between the round trip I could go home for maybe a day, then I'd be gone again. I probably was home maybe two days in a month.

Q: And the purpose of staying with it after the repairs had been made was to see that everything was operating?

Mr. N.: A lot of the repairs couldn't be made and some of the workmen had to stay with us because we couldn't keep the ship in the dry dock because there were scheduled dates to carry passengers.

Q: She was only partially repaired then?

Mr. N.: That's right. We would be working on the forced-air system for the boilers. I'd be crawling around through the whole ship while it was at sea. There weren't any rest periods in this thing.

After January we got going again. The main thing that we had to repair were the cracks in the deck.

Q: That came first, yes.

Mr. N.: That had to be done first. Next we started to take the ceilings down in some of the staterooms and get the vent trunks connected up. All that had to be done while we were at sea. Some of the staterooms had to be kept vacant. I don't know how they did that, but we always had a batch of staterooms in which our people would be working. That took me from October 1924 all the way around to about the 1st of April, through March. In fact, we were there all winter, and it was the greatest experience and the roughest sea. I really liked that myself. I almost lost Jake Cohn one day when it was very rough and we were going up onto the boat deck. We opened the door and Jake stepped out. He'd never experienced this before. He was no seagoing man. The wind caught him and started to yank him and almost blew him in between two boats that were up on the boat deck. I just managed to get hold of this guy and anchor him before he went overboard.

When he recovered, we got our wits together and we went into the bridge and stayed around there, watching them navigate the ship. The seas would be piling right over the bow of that ship and the windows that were around the bridge -

Q: Was there any danger from icebergs?

Mr. N.: No, the iceberg business was taken care of by the Coast Guard. They had the ice patrols going by that time. They were put into effect after the Titanic accident.

Q: In a lighter vein, you must have gained weight, eating first-class fare for all that time?

Mr. N.: Yes, I did, and that's a thing I wanted to mention. The head waiter told me later, "Gee, I'd rather keep you in clothes than feed you."

So that's the adventure as far as the Leviathan is concerned.

As soon as I came back - in fact, I didn't have more than one or two days in the yard, when I had to leave again and go with the Stability Committee over at 1 Broadway, New York, and spend my time from then until probably around October some time.

Q: Now you're going to tell me about your service on the

Stability Committee, which began in 1925?

Mr. N.: Yes, around the 1st of April 1925.

The question at one time was where would I be stationed. It was agreed by Admiral Beuret, who was the chief of the bureau, that I could either set up a working space over in the Navy Yard or at any place that Gibbs would select. Gibbs gave me office space in his office, and I had complete freedom to start the preliminary investigations in connection with stability. One of the first things I decided to do was to research the stability of merchant ships.

I went up to the Lenox Library at Fifth Avenue and 42nd Street and made arrangements with those people up there to haul out all the information. It took me quite a while to do this because I had from April, as it turned out, until September 1925 with the Stability Committee. I have a notebook in there that's practically full of the notes that I took in connection with the stability of merchant ships. I advised the committee and I attended the meetings during that time, and I would tell them what I was doing. I was the only one really doing anything, any kind of research on that.

I have always had a good streak of curiosity and that led me on to doing all kinds of things the minute I got my hands on something. And, as luck would have it, I hit on this and it was approved, and I went up to the Lenox. I spent most of my time, outside of the few committee meetings that we had, between

April and September up in the Lenox Library.

Q: What were the particular problems?

Mr. N.: They weren't problems, but we had no stability standards for our merchant ships in this country.

Q: They just built them!

Mr. N.: They had laws making the Steamboat Inspection Service responsible for the safety of ships up to a degree, but they had various ways of protecting themselves against anything happening. They always had some legal loophole, you might say. They would do odd things in their regulations. They would pay the most particular attention to what to carry in a lifeboat.

I remember one one of the things that was really written out in black and white was how many matches they were to carry in the lifeboats. The trouble is you have to get into a lifeboat first before you can use the matches, but they had that all specified.

Here is the final report that the committee made up. That will give you some idea what that committee reported on afterwards. They gave me credit for how closely I had worked with them, and I did hlep them quite a bit.

In September 1925 the S-51 was hit. It was September 25th 1925 that the S-51 was hit by the City of Rome, and it wasn't very long before I got a telephone call that alerted me to the problem I was going to be faced with on the S-51.

Niedermair #2 - 68

Q: You were called from the Stability Committee almost before the job was completed?

Mr. N.: The job was not completed. They called me up and said that I'd better get ready to leave for the salvage area. And so on October 19th, as I have a note here, we left the yard on the Vestal, which was a repair ship -

Q: Who was "we"?

Mr. N.: Ellsburg was there, and that's about all, Ellsburg and I.

When we got out there the Falcon was out there, and there was Captain Ernest King and Lieutenant Hartley, who was the captain of the Falcon. He later on became a rear admiral in the Navy and he was the captain of a cruiser during the war. And then Dick Hawse who was an expert on handling small boats in the rough seas. He was a seaman gunner, as a matter of fact, but Ernie King prevailed upon him - he first had a warrant officer's rating and then King prevailed upon him to take a commission in the Navy. Hawse reneged a bit on that. He didn't want that responsibility, but King finally got him to do it and he became a rear admiral. His ship was the only ship in the Navy, as I understand it - I don't know the name of it, but it happened around the Philippines, that got two presidential citations during the war. And he was the fellow who didn't want all that responsibility! But Ernie King knew how to pick 'em.

Q: Will you re-create for me the situation you found when you went to the S-51?

Mr. N.: We got out there on board the Vestal -

Q: She was approximately where?

Mr. N.: She was off Block Island in Long Island Sound. You couldn't see Block Island except at times when you might see a mirage of it. We really couldn't see any land from where we were trying to salvage -

Q: How deep was she down?

Mr. N.: Around 150 or 160 feet down.

When we got out there we found that the Merritt, Chapman, Scott people were out there with their big crane, and they had attempted to raise the submarine. One of the worst things they did in maneuvering their crane around was to drop an anchor overboard and it so happened that they dropped it on the bow of the S-51. This gave us quite a bit of trouble later on because when we tried to get the buoyancy of that compartment air was leaking out of the rivet holes and the seam cavity sort of spread the plating apart, so we had to fix that up with white-pine wedges that we drove in there. They'd swell up and we solved it in that way. It was a simple solution.

There was a salvage crew out there that had been down in Guantanamo Bay, practicing the raising of a submarine. It was a German submarine that they had, one from World War I. They never did really raise it. I found out later on that they had done a lot of wrong things. They could always get one end up but they never could get both ends up.

I had collected some plans of the S-51 and some particulars about her capacity plans, and arrangement plans.

Q: Where had she been built? In New London?

Mr. N.: I never did check on where she was built. She probably had been built in New London. Until you asked the question, it never occurred to me to find out where she was built. She could have been built up in Portsmouth, up in Maine, or New Hampshire.

Anyway, in getting going on this, we had to start mooring the Falcon, put 5-point moorings down, so that you could always position the ship any way you wanted to over the wreck. That's where Dick Hawse I told you about was a real expert. In the beginning we only had a Navy small boat to do this job and it wasn't very long before we found out that the Navy didn't have a single small boat that we could handle out there. We had to borrow one from the Coast Guard, a 26-foot motor whaleboat, and that worked perfectly. Hawse managed that thing, he was really clever, all right, and we'd get our five-point moorings, no matter which way we had to have the Falcon arranged, depending on the weather and the way the sea was running.

One thing led to another. There was no one alive in the S-51. They were all gone, except three who had been rescued from the water. They had been up on the bridge when she was hit and they were rescued from Long Island Sound. And they were the most forlorn three people that I have ever seen. I still think of them, how forlorn they were. You can imagine. They didn't live very long after the S-51 went down. Somehow or other, they died one after the other in a very short time.

I right away got interested in making an estimate of the situation and how we would raise this submarine. I began to make some calculations, how much buoyancy we had to have by pontoons, what to do with the pontoons. But it so happened that this salvage crew that was there had their own way of handling the pontoons. I described my system of doing it to Ellsburg, but we had to let the salvage crew do it because that was their specialty.

When the day arrived to drop the first pontoon down for a test at the depth of 150 feet or so, I didn't go out because they weren't doing it my way and I felt they might be nervous about the fact that I was standing around, nosy on what they were doing. They were always conscious of the fact that I was there, so I stayed away for two reasons. One was my own reason, that they weren't using my method and I felt sure their system wasn't going to work.

Ellsburg left and I was in the office there. I had plenty of calculations that I had to make. He came back that night about eleven o'clock and I was about to ask him - in fact, I did say to him: "Well, how did you make out?"

He said: "Niedermair, first tell me again how you would handle those pontoons, how you would lower them."

So I told him how I would lower them. "Well," he said, "from tomorrow on, you're going to be in charge. We lost our pontoon today."

Q: They lost it?

Mr. N.: We finally found it, but they couldn't find it. They hadn't found it be eleven o'clock that night.

These pontoons had a problem because, unless you stopped the water from running into them - you know, when you opened the valves and you flooded them to sink them - because the pontoon had 120 tons of buoyancy capacity, the pontoon itself weighed 40 tons, and if you blew all the water out, you had 80 tons left, net. The trouble was when you opened the valves and let the water run in you'd have 40 tons pulling on your little lines with which you were trying to lower it down, which was all right when you were working in 60 feet of water or 50 feet of water. Then you could let it run before it gave you any trouble. But now when they had to go down to 150 feet or 160 feet, that was too much. By that time it got so full of water that the lines started snapping, they broke off.

Q: It would go down on the submarine and squash it.

Mr. N.: What you had to do was allow so much water to get in -

you had to put enough water in to sink the pontoon. I did it with a stopwatch. I would time it after we let the water run into the pontoon, and now the weight was beginning to come onto the lines before we started lowering. I would give it about five minutes or five seconds or some interval of time with the water still running into it to give it weight so it would pull it down. Then you'd shut it off, and you'd shut it off with an air bubble left in the pontoon. It was as simple as that, but they didn't realize that.

So we started working on it. Various problems we had in drilling underneath the submarine to get the chains down. The buoyancy problem of which end would be raised first. It appeared to me that the best thing to do was to raise the stern first because your chains could go through just forward of the propeller. The struts came out where the propellers were so you ran your chains down in between them and they wouldn't slide off.

Q: What was the S-51's overall length?

Mr. N.: Oh, I don't know. I couldn't tell you that. I could look it up for you.

Q: No, approximately?

Mr. N.: Maybe 200 feet. I used to know those figures right down to the last notch. My notebook has them in.

We finally got all our pontoons down, but in the meantime

we'd learned how to handle the pontoons.

Q: How many pontoons did you have?

Mr. N.: We put six forward and two aft. The winter weather was coming on and we tried to come back home in November, around Thanksgiving Day, when Dr. Flothy and I made an estimate of the situation, using the Farmer's Almanac to judge the weather. We judged that we couldn't get more than one diving day a month from now on, or some such figure we came up with.

Q: Was that more reliable than the Weather Bureau?

Mr. N.: Dr. Flothy happened to have a Farmer's Almanac with him, the famous almanac that they print in Maryland.

Q: I know.

Mr. N.: He had one of those and so we got together and averaged out the weather!

I remember Thanksgiving Day when we were sitting there. The Navy wouldn't let us come back home because the public wouldn't stand for this, they said, so we couldn't come home, because the bodies were still in the submarine. We finally prevailed on them to let us come back because we had certain other things that we had to do to improve the compressor up on the Falcon and the manifolds on the Falcon. There were certain things that had to be done to get ready for the final salvage. So they finally allowed us to come back home, but I remember listening to this Cornell-Pennsylvania game that they play every Thanksgiving Day. The radio on that ship was terrible but I was listening there.

The officer who was in charge of the crew's mess had Thanksgiving dinner with the crew, and the reason was that they were having turkey for dinner. I was eating in the officers' mess and we had meat loaf for dinner on Thanksgiving Day! Everybody chipped in about a dollar a day. The government paid me for that later, but I did it exactly the way the officers had to do it. I felt that that was the way to do it, and I didn't care, and we were allowed to come back.

My period back in the yard, in December now, sometime, we did a lot of things and worked on the **pontoons**. We also found out what it felt like to be in a diver's suit. Ellsburg did this, too, only he went further than I did. I only went far enough to know just what a diver was up against. I wouldn't dive. I felt that it wasn't my job.

Q: How many professional divers did you have?

Mr. N.: We probably had a dozen. He's got a picture in his book somewhere around that shows the whole diving team.

Ellsburg learned how to dive and he actually went down.

Q: To the submarine?

Mr. N.: Sure. He was a real daredevil. One of the bravest people I've ever known. He didn't mind it at all, and I found that later on in his career he did a lot of things and

I was beginning to wonder whether he had his wits about him! But he knew what he was doing, all right. He knew just how far to go, but it looked pretty risky.

We got all ready and sometime in February we went back out to the salvage operation and got started again. We were having trouble with the divers' air hose freezing up, air being cut off because the water was getting colder and the air would expand into the diver's suit, because the air was coming down at a higher pressure than was down in the suit and now had to bubble out through the helmet. That would drop the pressure at the valve, and the combination would be such that the moisture that was deposited would freeze up the air valves. So we had to work out a method of drying the air before it got down there.

We solved it partly so that by the time the next salvage operation came around we had to rig to take care of that. But on the S-51 we didn't have any way to take care of it, so we didn't go out there until the weather started warming up a bit. It must have been the end of February. We got out there and we started placing the pontoons, digging tunnels, and all. For part of that operation Ellsburg went down because we had to haul out the main induction line, which was where the air came in for the diesel engines, to run the engines. The valves on that, the hatch covers, and everything else - the hatch covers were all right, but quite a few of the valves were closed - no, the hatch covers weren't all right and these valves weren't right because when you put pressure inside the hull, they would lift because they were designed to be closed by water pressure round the outside.

So now we had no way of getting at the valve that was on this induction line. All we could do was to tear the deck out and get a section out of that main induction line. The divers went down and took the bolts out of the flanges of the section that we wanted to get. Then Ellsburg went down just as the risky part was coming, when you had to have something hauling from the deck in order to yank this section out between the two flanges, which was pretty tricky stuff, so he decided to do it himself.

Now he got into trouble with the salvage crew and the officer in charge of it, the warrant officer who was in charge of the salvage crew's divers. Ellsburg talked to the telephone operator and asked him to ask this officer how the lines were tending. All this officer would say was that it was OK, and that's what the telephone man told Ellsburg. Ellsburg wanted to know which way it was tending, because down there he couldn't tell and OK didn't tell him anything.

One thing led to another and they couldn't get together. I had never been on the telephone before but Ellsburg, who was down there, asked me to get on the phone. So they hunted me up and I came down and picked up the phone and talked to Ellsburg. And, you know, listening to someone under pressure down there is not the same as me talking to you. I finally understood through the squeaks what he was talking about, and he asked me the question, "Which way are the lines tending?" He had it all hooked up, with a line coming down and that was on the hook of the crane on the Falcon.

I called over to the officer and asked him which way the lines were tending. Ellsburg told me which way it was down below - when he had talked to the telephone operator that was Greek to him, but he told me all about it.

I tried twice to get him to tell me which way the line tended and he wouldn't tell me. Then I said to Ellsburg, "Hold everything. I'll go over and look myself." So I went over to the side of the ship, examined the line and the way the crane was going, came back to the telephone and told Ellsburg everything looked all right to me. He told me where he was standing, out of the way of it. So then we gave the signals to haul the thing up.

As a result of that little incident, this officer went to King and told him that I was ruining the morale of the diving crew. King looked him in the eye and said, mentioning his name: "You know, you're sick. I recommend you take sick leave, and when the reporters' boat comes in you go back in it." So King was on my side.

Q: He was in overall command, was he?

Mr. N.: He was in charge of the diving crew.

Q: I see.

Mr. N.: It was his responsibility. He came up from Guantanamo Bay, but King said he was sick.

Q: No, but I mean King was in overall charge, or what?

Mr. N.: He was the head man. He represented the Navy. Later on, of course, I got into more trouble than that, but that's another story.

Q: Where did Merritt Chapman fit into this picture?

Mr. N.: They went off the job because we decided - the Navy decided - that we would do it. They didn't have any equipment. We had the divers, we had the salvage ship. Their big cranes couldn't stand the rough weather out there. They could never get it that way, anyway, so they were sent back home. They never liked it. I don't think they like it to this day.

I had never been inside a submarine. I never took a dive in a submarine, and the S-50, a sister ship of the S-51, was right there. We could go and walk around on it but I wanted to be in it when it was diving. So I went to King and said:

"Why can't I go down in the S-50 and walk around while she's running submerged, just like the S-51 had been running?" I wanted to visualize this, where the doors would be open and what was the condition of the ship. I understood it. Everybody had told me, but now I wanted to see it, and not having been in a submarine I thought here's a good chance. King said no.

Q: Why?

Mr. N.: "No," he said, "I don't think it's necessary. Your place is up here.

I said: "Well, but I really think I ought to make a run in it," and he finally gave in to me and I went down in the S-50 for a short haul. He gave orders to the captain about how long he could keep me down, so we made a little runaround out there in Long Island Sound, not very long, back and forth. Just enough time for me to walk back and forth, climb up in the gun access hatch and look out and see how that operated. I came back and that was it. Now I was an expert!

I was never expert. I'd never been on a submarine before, actually. Like I told you about the incline experiment. Everybody thought I was expert from that day on, when Rock put his hand on my shoulder.

We were back again in the spring and got our pontoons working and so on. I told you about how Ellsburg became a diver and got into trouble and almost got me into trouble, but King could see through that. That's the way King was. When you had the responsibility, all you had to do was to carry it out. You never had to go to him for instructions or anything else. You had to do it as you saw it or as you thought he would want it done, and when that was the case you had the authority to do it. I think that's why he only had about 100 people on his staff during the war. When I was there last

March somebody told me: "Do you know Admiral King only had so many people on his staff?" And I said, "No, I never knew how many he had, but I don't see why he had that many because he let the people he put in charge of this group, they could add people to their group, but he only needed enough people that he could put his hands on." And if you didn't do it right, you were done.

Q: That day!

Mr. N.: We got everything ready by June, and a terrific storm came up. We had the pontoons up. Some of them were leaking. We went out in June to get ready to raise it - we were getting ready to raise it the next morning, about the middle of June of 1926, and the storm came up that night. We had to go out in the storm and get divers down to see how everything was going down below.

We thought we could get divers down but as it turned out we couldn't. We could see that some pontoons were leaking very badly. It was very, very rough. I remember looking it over and trying to put a little air into a pontoon that was leaking. I knew which ones. They had told me the day before, so I tried to compensate for that.

We now had all our pontoons buoyant and the amount of air that was in them at that depth and the amount of air that was in them to hold them up with about five tons of extra pull, if they moved up the least little bit the air would start blowing out the water and it would lift them. Finally when they reached the top - once they started moving up, you didn't have to blow them out any more because they would blow out automatically. It was that ticklish at that depth.

So the bow went up and the result was that we got into all kinds of trouble that day. I sprained my ankle. The result was that we had to let the bow down again. Then we got everything ready again and within two weeks' time we raised the submarine and brought it into the New York Yard. We took it down Long Island Sound and just before we got into the yard we had all shaved, ready to go home when we got it into the yard. The sun was shining. Thousands and thousands of people lined the shores of Long Island Sound to watch us come down with this long tow through Hellgate which was 1,000 feet long.

Just outside the Navy yard there was a submerged rock. We were to the right of the rock on the course we were going. I think they call it the White Horse Rock. We had a pilot aboard and that pilot was afraid that our tow was going to hit a yacht that was in the fairway. It wasn't supposed to be in the fairway, but there it was. So the pilot veered to the left. As he veered to the left, we were closer to that rock than he had estimated and we hit the rock and knocked out our middle pair of pontoons forward, and down went the submarine.

Q: In what depth there?

Mr. N.: It wasn't very deep but the speed of the water was terrific in the East River. It wasn't at Hellgate. It was down by the Navy yard, where you had a rip tide.

After we got the submarine up out at the salvage area, I had noted all the drafts on the pontoons so I knew how much reserve buoyancy I had in each pontoon. That was a lucky break, because now we'd lost the forward middle pair of pontoons.

Q: You had only four left, then?

Mr. N.: We had only four left. We had to have six because when you were lifting at the angle we were at, the water was deep enough so that we had about a 30-degree angle, which is about the maximum angle you could swing a bow up like this because everything would slip away from you beyond 30 degrees. It required a maximum moment to lift it, more than on how much buoyancy you had. You had to have a moment to do it. The ship's moment about the stern pontoons as compared with the buoyancy that we had there, you had to have more moment to do it.

I had made this estimate and I was pulling my notebook out and Ellsburg said in his book that as I was looking over my notebook - everybody was ready to go ashore - I yelled out: "Well, if we're going to hit a rock, it's a good thing we have a salvage crew on board." And all the people who had been kind of glum awakened to this, that now we all had to go to work again. I imagine he thought my statement really got them going. He was looking over my shoulder and he could see that my next idea was that if we lowered the four pontoons that we had up forward and had provide lift, we'd get some cranes out and hold the chains up, and sink them down till they were under water. Then we could get this reserve buoyancy, the amount of buoyancy that was sticking above the waterline when we were coming down the sound. That was just enough, the way I figured it out, to pick it off that rock.

By midnight we were able to do it. It was so close, I remember, that we had the floodlights going down, and I think Ernie King wanted a boat to go out with a sailor on it to stick a flag up on the bow of the submarine. In order to do that, the sailor stepped out of the boat, stepped on the bow of the submarine, and it started going down. I didn't know how far it would go. Maybe we had a little reserve buoyancy.

Q: Enough to have him get washed off, though?

Mr. N.: He couldn't stay there, anyway, but he noticed this happening and got off the bow right away, but it gave me a clue as to how close my figures were.

Now we had to turn it around 180 degrees and swing it into the yard at night, and the tide was going out in the East River, so when we got it swung around the tide was against us, and there was a very heavy rip tide there.

I had a bead on some way of telling whether we were moving or not. I was giving a signal when we were going to move. Ellsburg was ahead of me and he would get my signal, then he would signal the tugboats. What we wanted was to just get the tow moving forward, but not any more than that. We didn't want to have much speed on it because what we were pulling on was a bow piece that I had worked up to put a hook onto the bow of the submarine. It was like a shackle up there that I had made to hook the towline on, and we didn't want to lose it again, so if we could creep into the yard that was sufficient.

We managed to creep into the yard and got it moored alongside of a dock there. Then I went home. Everybody went home. I probably only got home for a couple of hours and then I came back again the next day, and we put it in a dry dock.

That's the story of the S-51 as far as the boat itself is concerned.

Now appeared a thing that had to do with people, the vanity of people. You see, while the S-51 was out in the salvage area the Navy Department was anxious to have publicity. The newspaper people wanted information. Ernie wasn't a very great guy for publicity.

Q: No, I know he wasn't.

Mr. N.: He thought it was a hell of a waste of time. We were out there to work. But Ellsburg was a gifted writer so he wrote a few good articles about the salvage operations for the New York papers, and that seemed to be great so he kept it up. The Navy had asked for somebody to do it, and in addition to all the other things he could write and as fast as he'd fill a page he'd throw it on the deck and write another one, just like that.

So he got the publicity but what happened when we got into the yard was that the reporters all wanted to talk to Ellsburg. Now the commandant, C. P. Plunkett, was left out. I don't think Ernie King liked it, either, although he didn't want them to bother him. He'd put up with a certain amount of hardship, you know, but he could do without it now.

Now Plunkett felt that this spotlight - it turned out that I felt he thought that Ellsburg was a bit insubordinate in this thing. The first thing I knew we were all called together outside of Plunkett's office and he gave Ellsburg a bawling out, a sort of a semi-public reprimand, about paying so much attention to newspaper people when we had all this work to do. I've forgotten just how the thing went, but it probably was along that line.

On the other hand, the Brooklyn Eagle came along and talked to Plunkett, and Plunkett gave them quite an interview. In that interview he talked about me. As I remember it, he didn't talk about anybody else, and he said that I was an unknown engineer when I went on this salvage operation and I now came back and raised this submarine with a lead pencil. I always thought that was a fine public compliment that Plunkett gave me. He at last got the papers to come in to see him, but the Brooklyn Eagle went out of business a couple of years later. I had a clipping with that statement by him in there.

Do you know about Plunkett, his background, at all?

Q: Not very much, no.

Mr. N.: When World War I was on they got a big idea that if they put a big Navy 14-inch gun, I think it was, on a railroad car over in France and ran it up, it would counteract the German long-range guns. So Plunkett went over there with a whole train. He was in charge of this operation, to get this whole train with the big gun on it, up to the front lines. I understand that he didn't pay any attention to the Frenchmen at all, and he put a crane at the front end of his train, and any time one of these little French cars got in his way he'd pick it off and put it on the side of the railroad. He went over bridges and everything else, never checking into whether they were strong enough, and he got quite a way along to the front when the French stopped him and warned him that he couldn't go any farther, he had to go back because the bridges and the tracks couldn't stand this weight.

He'd come all this way over any bridges that he had to cross and the tracks already, so he just brushed them aside and kept right on going. He got up to the front, but I don't know whether he ever fired the gun or not.

Later on, his crew got into trouble because it was wintertime and they went around through the village there and stole stoves and one thing and another to heat up their shacks. And the French came and complained to him again. Plunkett told them he didn't know anything about it. All he knew was that one day it was raining and snowing or stormy or something of that sort - he explained it to them that way - and the next day they had all these stoves here. He didn't know how they got there. He confused the French no end.

That was one of the things he did there.

Now the S-51 was in the yard and in the dry dock and our job was done.

Q: What about your regular duties at the shipyard during these two intervals when you were away?

Mr. N.: Well, they always had other people around and, of course, they got along without me to a fashion before I got there. So they did the best they could except that when any special hard jobs came around or new jobs, as you can see, I always got them. I evidently brought quite a bit of publicity to the yard by accomplishing these things. I don't have it here, but I have a letter from Rock - oh, here it is, 1926 he wrote that letter to me in which he complimented me on my success and said:

"You came to the yard early, in 1917. You have been there ever since, thus serving with me for a little over four years during my tour as construction officer at the yard. Your name also has come to my attention in connection with one or two other projects since my detachment.

Then he goes on to say that Commander Ellsburg's letter is a fine recommendation, and so forth. He goes on further to say:

"As you would quickly appreciate, it appeals to me (the things that Ellsburg said about me) just as I am very sure, as you would also know it would especially appeal to Commander Ellsburg, the salvage officer, and to Captain Wright, your construction officer. I am delighted with your prospective promotion, which the bureau is particularly happy to recommend, and I hope you will receive also the department's letter of commendation for your services, as recommended." And so forth.

That's the way the S-51 ended.

Q: With a promotion!

Mr. N.: Yes.

Q: Very good.

Mr. N.: Now I became supervisor of the scientific section.

Q: At the Navy yard?

Mr. N.: Yes. I became the boss of the section, which I hadn't been in for all those months.

Q: You were Civil Service, weren't you?

Mr. N.: Yes.

Q: Now you were back on duty in the shipyard?

Mr. N.: Yes, and I was supervisor of the scientific section. By the time that happened, Henry Wright had gone. He went to Washington, D. C., and was with the Shipping Board in connection with duty there. Later on he was relieved by Admiral Tawresey.

Land had his commander, Garland Fulton, write a letter to me.

Q: First, Land was assistant chief of the Bureau of Aeronautics?

Mr. N.: Right. So Garland Fulton wrote a letter to me but Jerry Land handled it by delivering it to the new construction officer because my friend, H. T. Wright, wasn't there any more. I've forgotten his name now, but he had a funny name. He addressed the letter to the construction officer rather than by his name. The thing was that I couldn't take that job -

Q: What was the job?

Mr. N.: It had to do with lighter-than-air. They wanted me to go down there and get a desk job in connection with the development of the Akron and the Macon lighter-than-air ships.

Q: They had not yet been built?

Mr. N.: No. They were being designed then, and they thought it would be a great job for me. In some ways, it would have been, too.

Q: Probably would have brought your career to a sudden end,

though!

Mr. N.: Not necessarily. I don't think so because H. T. Wright had dreams. I got a letter from him in connection with that and he urged me to go because he said that heavier-than-air is coming in and, as he visualized it, heavier-than-air would be going great guns and that would be a great field for me. That's the way he said it, and he said he had warned them that "a person with your talents I'm not so sure would leave New York." He told me all that, but I had to turn it down for personal reasons. I recommended a man named Ray Brown from Michigan. He got the job and he handled it and became quite an expert in handling helium gases. I think this is what caused trouble for these aviators. They used helium as a method of jetting. They had it under pressure and they had it in the double hull, too. It helped to support the inner hull and the outer hull together.

Q: You're talking about the astronauts?

Mr. N.: Yes. Ray Brown got to be an expert in that area, but he never drifted into heavier-than-air.

Q: Which is what you would have done?

Mr. N.: That's what Wright told me in his letter, but he didn't think I would go. They had offered me all they could, according to Civil Service regulations.

Q: What did you think of the lighter-than-air ships of that time?

Mr. N.: I thought they were doing all right, but they made a mistake in the design of those when they cut a hole in the main hull to put a little tiny aircraft in for reconnaissance. I think that weakened the hull structure and I believe it contributed something to the loss of them in the storm, because there was a concentration of stresses where this hole was. There was discontinuity in the strength.

I talked to Ray Brown about this later on. Ray was a naval architect. I said:

"Ray, how do you like all that thin stuff that you've got to be working on on this lighter-than-air?"

He said: "I'm slowly getting used to it but I'm not used to walking on some of these gangways that swing up and down as you walk along and they give as you walk, because this structure is so light. But it's all right if they let her bend the right way. It's like walking on a rope all the time."

I got a nice card from Ray after I got the top ten award, and he died shortly after that. He complimented me on what I had accomplished by that time.

I had to turn this job down. In the meantime, I had to work and get the yard people prepared so that we could use the building ways for a cruiser instead of a battleship. I had to get some special information about launching. Ray had been with Gibbs and Cox and had quit them because they ran into a shortage of work, and he guessed it wrong that Gibbs would have stayed in there and Ray would have stayed in there, too. But he went with New York Ship and from them and through Ray I got all kinds of information on launching that they used for launching heavy ships and so forth. In connection with the data that I got from him and other people, I decided that I could launch the Pensacola on the small slope that was used for the battleships.

I was in London at the time they launched her, and I certainly lost a lot of sleep because I couldn't find anything that told me she was in the water. I had left instructions that they were to iron out the paraffin and everything had to be nice and slick. Ernie Rigg, who was the naval architect for New York Ship, told me later on that he was a guest at the launching of the Pensacola and he went up particularly to see her stick on the ways because he knew that it only had a half-inch slope. They'd launch at maybe eleven-sixteenths or maybe three-quarters. He didn't know that I narrowed the ways down so that they had the same pressure - the grease didn't know what was on it. It was only interested in the pressure per square foot. If you have a low pressure per square foot, then you have to have a bigger slope. If you have a high pressure per square foot, it has a bigger component on it and it goes down the ways.

They launched her and I didn't find out - I got cards

from everybody and they had a dinner on her, but nobody told me. I should have guessed from what they said.

Q: I would think so, yes.

Mr. N.: But they didn't say it. I didn't see any pictures in The New York Times or anything - that it was in the water and that they did it according to my way of doing it. Of course, I was anxious to know I was right, and I was. Rigg told me the ship was very anxious to get into the water.

When I came back from the S-51 I did one thing that was very important. I wrote up a report on getting ready for the next salvage operation. I'd just come back from one, so I decided I'd better make up bill of materials, of all the things that would be needed if another submarine went down on the high seas. I had it all worked out, and the chief draftsman wouldn't let me send it.

Q: Sending it to Washington?

Mr. N.: Yes. I wanted to send it to Washington. H. T. Wright wasn't there any more. Ellsburg wasn't there any more. I could have gone to Plunkett, maybe. But anyway I didn't do that.

Q: Why did he object to sending it?

Mr. N.: He said we couldn't tell the bureau what to do. So by the time the S-4 happened all of a sudden, I had the material in my desk drawer.

Q: But Washington didn't have anything?

Mr. N.: No, they didn't have it. But I had it.

The only free period I had for a long time in the yard was from July 5th until December 17th, when the S-4 was lost.

Q: That was in 1927.

Mr. N.: That's the only time that I was in the yard for any length of time. So my next talk will be about the S-4.

I was still at the New York Yard in the interim after the S-51. About a year and a half had gone by since July 5th, when we brought the S-51 in, and during that year and a half I had prepared a report on what we would have to do in connection with the salvage of another submarine on the high seas, if it ever happened. But I was unsuccessful in having that report sent to Washington. In a moment you'll see how handy that was. I put it away in my desk and there it was.

During this year and a half between July 5, 1926 and December 17th, a Saturday afternoon, when the S-4 was lost, I was working on miscellaneous things in the yard. I described before about the Pensacola launching and so forth.

The unfortunate thing that happened on this Saturday afternoon was that just about four o'clock - we worked all day Saturday in those days, the week before Christmas - Admiral Plunkett's aide came in and whispered in my ear that there was another submarine down and Admiral Plunkett would like to talk to me about it.

So we started walking down to see Admiral Plunkett. We were all on the same floor of this building in the Navy yard, the New York Navy Yard in Brooklyn. When we arrived at Admiral Plunkett's office he told me what had happened. His first words to me were:

"What can we do to help the S-4?"

Q: Tell me where she had been sunk?

Mr. N.: The S-4 was sunk up near Cape Cod, just below Provincetown, at the end of Cape Cod, just outside the harbor of Provincetown.

Q: There had been a collision?

Mr. N.: She had been run over by a Coast Guard destroyer. The S-4 was running submerged on a trial trip there, running at periscope depth, I understand, and this destroyer came along and ran over her, and part of the bow of the destroyer was sheered off. There was a hole ripped into the S-4 and down she went with everybody on board.

Quite a few people were able to get into the forward torpedo room and seal themselves off in there. The rest of the crew were lost in various parts of the ship.

All I knew this Saturday afternoon was that the S-4 was down up in New England, in the First Naval District, but just precisely what had happened I wasn't too sure about, and

Admiral Plunkett wasn't either.

The problem was that I was the only one left in the yard who knew anything about what to do about this salvage operation, because Ellsburg had gone, and Fletcher had gone - not Fletcher, but Captain Wright, he had gone to Washington. Plunkett knew that I had been connected with the S-51 salvage, as noted in the previous discussion, where he had made the remark to the Brooklyn Eagle that I had raised the S-51 with a lead pencil. So he was fully aware that I knew something about what to do.

Q: Did he know of your report, which didn't get anywhere?

Mr. N.: No, he didn't know about my report but I made him aware of it in a very short time. I said, yes, we could do a lot because I had this report and we had the equipment in the yard, standing by for an event like this, but I knew of no preparations that had been made any other way, except that it was on the record that we stored these things in the yard.

I explained to Admiral Plunkett what the situation was, and he immediately said that the thing to do - I should mention here that while I was on my way to Admiral Plunkett's office to talk to him, or report to him, rather, the whistle blew in the yard and everybody rushed out, because, as I said, it was the Saturday before Christmas and everybody was getting ready for the Christmas holidays.

Q: And no one had been informed?

Mr. N.: That's it. It was in late December and darkness came early so very soon it was dark all over the Navy yard, too.

I explained to Plunkett that I had a report in my desk, so he said, well, the thing to do was to go down into the drafting room, we'll get a few desks, we'll push them together in a space in a passageway, and he would get all the duty officers of the yard together and get things ready. In the meantime, he snapped orders off to his aide to do these things, including the fact that he wanted the captain of the Sagamore, at least to come. I'm not sure whether the captains of any other seagoing tugs were available, but at least he got him.

Q: The Sagamore was a tug?

Mr. N.: She was a seagoing tug and had been one of the leading tugs in the towing line for the S-51, so he was familiar with some of these things that we did. He knew what pontoons were and all that sort of thing.

Plunkett sent me down to this desk and he sat on the other side of me. Then he looked at me and said:

"Now, Niedermair, you take over. You give orders. Take over the yard."

So I was in charge of the yard from that minute on. My desk was only a couple of jumps away, so in the meantime I'd gotten my report out and now I started to put it to work, to get the inch-and-a-half hoses out of storage. These poor officers who had to go riding round the yard in the dark on their bicycles apparently did a very good job because all this was to be piled on the Sagamore and another of the big tugs that was in the yard. How they did all this, I don't know, but they did collect all the material necessary in connection with the pontoons and the hoses and the valves and the piping and so on that you needed to get ready to raise this submarine. Not only to raise it but also try to save the people in the submarine, if they were alive.

I got into Plunkett's office just a little after the whistle blew, which must have been five o'clock, and I think that by eight o'clock that night we had pontoons under way. I remember objecting to the way the towboat captain was going to tow the pontoons and Admiral Plunkett reminded me that he was the expert on towing. But I told Plunkett that I believed he would get into trouble towing the pontoons in tandem. He wanted to put three in line, or something. I said, "These things are not directionally stable," but that didn't mean a thing. So Plunkett said we'd stay out of that. The captain of the Sagamore said he could do it so we let him do it.

By about eight o'clock the duty officers had scouted the whole yard and all I could do was go back home to Staten Island. In the meantime, he had wired to the New England people, the Boston Navy Yard, and told them that I would be up the next day, and they wired back about as fast as they could that they didn't need me. When the time came for me to go home Plunkett said:

"Niedermair, you go to bed with your shoes on," which

meant that I was to stand by, of course.

I wasn't home very long and to this day I don't even remember asking my wife whether I had called her up on the telephone that this had happened. I just got home late. By that time she was used to my wanderings with the S-51 and the Leviathan.

Q: She'd had four years' indoctrination!

Mr. N.: Yes. I don't recall ever thinking about that when I was so preoccupied with this submarine.

I finally got home and by about eleven o'clock I got a telephone call. This was Plunkett, who said I was to get ready to go up to Grand Central Station and get the Night Owl for Boston. There was a telegram in asking me to report out at the salvage area and a destroyer would be waiting for me in the Boston yard. I told the officer who was on the phone talking to me that I needed certain information if I was going. I needed a booklet plan on the submarine, the S-4. We must have some booklet plans around for that class. And stability data, the displacement and other curves, the arrangement plans. The booklet plan, if he could find it, would do all right. Then I gave him some other instructions, but I failed to tell him to bring an adding machine with him. When he got there he didn't have one, so I went out on the salvage area without one. For most of the things that I did out there I used the one that was on the ship, which I wasn't too sure about, but it worked.

I left Staten Island and, as you know, you have to go on a ferryboat and on a subway to get up to Grand Central Station, and you're not going to get there at twelve o'clock. So when I got into the station, everybody on board knew that there was a submarine down and everybody knew that the train was waiting for me. People were waiting to grab my bags and rush me into my compartment on the train, which had been taken care of, and Plunkett's aide had given me my ticket and all. I think the train conductor carried my hand bag, and in I went, and off I went to Boston.

Boston has said they didn't want me but I had sense enough - I've always given myself credit for this - that when I got in the Boston yard the next morning I could have gone in the gate and walked right over to the destroyer and left for the salvage area. But I had sense enough to go up and call on Captain Simms and Commander Enright, and those people, and say good morning to them. They said:

"Niedermair, what the hell are you doing here? I thought we told Plunkett that we didn't need you."

I said: "Well, but I have a dispatch here from the salvage area, from Admiral Bromby, that asks for my services. The destroyer is up at the dockhead some place."

And they said, yes, they knew about that. I think it was the Mann they sent and they said she had steam up and was waiting for me to go.

So I started off at least by calling on them because I was goint to need those people to help me with all the sketches that we took a look at a few minutes ago. It helped a bit but it turned out later on that they weren't too satisfied and they were waiting for a chance to get rid of me, which they never really fulfilled.

Q: I suspect a certain amount of jealousy within the organization?

Mr. N.: It was in their area, there's no question about it. I always tell something that's a flashback that goes back from that point up to about 1939 or maybe later, when King, who now was an admiral, came in to see me and asked why I wasn't out on the Squalus, which was lost then. I told him that I was no longer in that sort of work, that we had trained people for ten years how to do this thing, they had been in and talked to me and they knew how to do it.

King couldn't quite get that idea when I explained it to him. This thing now was ten years from the S-4 and he said:

"Niedermair, that's the trouble with the goddam Navy. When you know it, they don't want you." I never convinced him. He always felt that they didn't want me, they wanted this glory for themselves. But that wasn't true. He was away and he wouldn't know all that, but as it turned out later in many ways he was right to a certain extent, which I'll bring out along the way in this story.

I got aboard the Mann and the weather out there was really terrible. There wasn't a single person in the wardroom to eat because it was too rough, but I ate. I got my breakfast there. I've never been seasick in my life, so I'm pretty lucky that way - almost, but never really sick, which they found out on the Leviathan, too!

I got to the salvage area quite late. I've forgotten now why that was, but it was late in the afternoon. Maybe it was because of how rough it was. Got out there and everything was covered with ice. I've always said it was a foot thick on everything, from the sea, and that the night before they tried to launch a boat over the side of the Falcon to get the mooring lines arranged. The first try they made the boat was tossed back on board and smashed against the side of the ship. But they managed to get divers down that night.

The first diver down got tangled up in the wreckage - he was from the Coast Guard destroyer. His air line got caught in all the wreckage and they had to send another diver down, Edie, and Edie got a Congressional Medal of Honor for this task. He went down there and he had one hacksaw. I talked to him later on about having one hacksaw for this job. I asked him quite often:

"Edie, what were you thinking when you tried to cut this trash away from the air hose?"

He said: "I was thinking and praying that the blade wouldn't break."

I said: "Gee whizz, you should have really had two with you."

"I know," he said, "but it was too late. It didn't break so we saved his life."

I was there that day and I immediately got busy and tried to work out a system to get some food to the people who were alive in the forward torpedo room.

Q: How deep was this?

Mr. N.: This was about 140 feet deep, right off the neck of the cape. About 140, I would say.

The storm came up again and drove us away. We had done all kinds of things. I had an air hose hooked on to the Fessenden oscillator. By doing this, I could get air into the forward compartment and get a change of air in there.

Q: How would you get the food in?

Mr. N.: I was going to work it out by having them open up the torpedo tubes, the outside opening, and then we'd shove it in, and they'd open the valve on the inside and haul it in. Not very much water would get into it that way. I also thought maybe that was the way we could get the men out.

I had worked out a system of using inner tubes - they looked like inner tubes to me - and filling them up with water and lowering them down so that they would have fresh water that way. Quite a few schemes of that kind. I had these schemes in mind.

In the meantime, we had worked out a system of communication with the people in that compartment. Two close hammer blows together would be a dash, and one quick blow would be a dot. So we communicated by Morse code. He could read the regular Morse code off our oscillator, he could hear it in the water, and it would be transmitted into the boat. People were sending all kinds of messages of hope and so on to them.

Q: How many were in there alive?

Mr. N.: I've forgotten now. They were lying down. They were not moving very much, and they had quite a few bottles of oxygen in there, so they released oxygen on and off.

We were driven away from the place by the storm. We couldn't stay there. It was just impossible. You couldn't hang on at all, so we left - or, rather, were driven away. That's worse than just leaving. I mean just leaving would have been worse, wouldn't it?

Q: Yes.

Mr. N.: When we got back to the wreck we found that all our marking buoys had gone. We had an awful job trying to find the submarine again. We had to pass grappling hooks over here and there and everywhere, but it was no use. We didn't find it for quite a while. The sea was still pretty bad. When we finally got to them, why, they were gone.

Now, when we salvaged the submarine we found there was still plenty of oxygen there. They died from carbon dioxide. They fell asleep. That was the way that I found the ship.

We tried to work through the whole wintertime because we had worked out a way with the S-51 of getting moisture out of the air, washing the air clean of moisture, passing it over cold water, reduce some of the water in it and have it deposited and it changed temperature-wise.

Q: Yes, you explained that.

Mr. N.: And then we'd heat the air up again so the divers were able to work all winter long. We never had any time off until we raised it on March 17th.

Q: So, with the amount of time required, they wouldn't have lived, anyway.

Mr. N.: In the meantime, though, I found that the Boston yard wasn't keeping up with me in doing my work.

Q: What do you mean by that?

Mr. N.: Well, I sent sketches in to the yard of some of the things that I wanted them to do, like the sketches that you saw. They had to make one or two or three or whatever was needed in connection with all the hose connections or any other kind of connections that we needed. Or in connection with the hatches that had to be put into place, and so on.

They had to make some modifications onto the pontoons for us, too, because we had found a way of putting a little pipe on the inside so that we'd know when we had sufficient buoyancy to hold the pontoon up alongside the boat. We'd draw the water out, then we'd let it feed back through the hose. You'd get it so that it would blow just below the standpipe, the upside down standpipe, and when the water came up to that point, it would go back in through the hose, you would see it. We had to keep testing it. We had a valve in there to test it out.

Things like that they were doing on the pontoons to get the pontoons more modernized. The result of that was that I wanted to go in to the Boston yard to find out what the trouble was. The yard decided then that I was ruining their morale. King had to go in later on to salvage one of his officers who wanted to get a special job and King let him do it, but he fell by the wayside. So King was trying to rescue him from being tried by the commandant of the Third Naval District. He wanted to bring him home, which he did. He went in from the salvage area my last day in the yard before going back. He was in the yard. They went to him and wanted to get rid of me.

Q: How were you ruining their morale?

Mr. N.: Because when I got into a yard I didn't bother going up to the office or kowtow to anybody. I'd go around and take a look see how the job was doing because I didn't have forever. I'd want to go back on the next boat. It was because they didn't want me there, that's why. I was from the Third Naval District and they were the First Naval District.

They told my story to King and King, I was told later, would say, "That's exactly what I want him to do." But King didn't know what I wanted to do.

Q: He had that confidence?

Mr. N.: Yes. I wasn't fired. I went out on the salvage job and we raised the boat. I remember the last day. I had written out all the instructions on how to do different things, and King wanted me with him, to leave the ship there - I've forgotten her name - this machineshop ship or repair ship. And so I was standing early in the morning at the gangway on March 17th and King came out, stood alongside of me, and said:

"Didn't we say all boats should be in the water?"

I said: "Yes, I did. That was in the orders."

"What do you call that?" The captain's gig was hanging there. So he called the captain over and bawled him out in front of me, and they had to put the captain's gig in the water because if any accident happened or anybody was hurt in the boating operations out there when the thing came up, there were hoses to be collected - anything could happen. So King wanted that boat in the water and he got it into the water. Then he said to me, as we were going down the gangway:

"Isn't this the goddamedest ragtime ship you ever saw?"

And so out we went to the salvage and I went up on the deck to all the gauges and everything. Then we raised the submarine. The last few minutes were rather trying, but we got it up anyway. We had used the air from a sister submarine there and the people in the submarine thought they had enough air to raise the submarine. They were wrong. It wasn't true. It was high-pressure air, but it wasn't enough to raise the submarine.

Then I took the watch in to Boston.

Q: That's where she was to go?

Mr. N.: Yes, and that's where Saunders found out that I had this mystic way of judging things.

Q: Tell me that on tape.

Mr. N.: During the process of working and getting ready for the salvage operation, Captain Saunders, who was the salvage officer, came to me one morning and said:

"The boss - who was Captain King or Ernie King - said to empty the oil tanks, the inner bottom tanks."

And I said to Captain Saunders: "No, I don't think we ought to do that because I'm not too sure that it would help us any, and I don't believe I need them, so I'd rather not have any buoyancy from the bottom tanks.

"But the boss wants it done," he said.

I said: "Well, I tell you, Captain" - I hadn't met Captain Saunders before at any time. I just met him on this salvage job for the first time, so I'd only known him a couple of weeks.

I said: "I think it would be a good idea if you went back to Captain King, the boss, and told him that Niedermair said that he doesn't want to have the things pumped, he'd rather not have the oil taken out of those tanks."

Captain Saunders came back and said we wouldn't take the oil out of those tanks, so you can see King agreed with me. Later on, when Saunders took the watch after we got in to the Navy Yard - he took over the watch at the air manifold on the Falcon - and he tested my theory out by trying to push the oil out down low, and suddenly the submarine started heeling over, leaning on the pontoons a bit, and he decided to refill the tanks.

From that time on, he thought that my intuition was something to brag about, which he did. Quite often he introduced me as the person who had this wonderful intuitive mind. If British naval officers came over from the other side or any of these people at conferences or at a symposium and if Savvy Saunders was there, that would be my introduction - the man with an intuitive brain.

So we got the S-4 back and we then recommended quite a few things to do to continue research in connection with the diving bell, to develop further the lung -

Q: The Momsen lung?

Mr. N.: Yes, the Momsen lung, which was an adaptation from a mining apparatus, that's used in coal-mining districts in Pennsylvania. It was originally used for something on that order. Momsen and a man named Dobson - or Hobson - in the Bureau of C & R worked on that.

Momsen stayed with the development of the salvage equipment for the future salvaging of submarines. But as the submarines got bigger and bigger and bigger, those things were outmoded. The diving bell is still worked, though. That could still be used at quite deep depths if the submarine stayed whole and they went down in water that was less than their collapsed depth, but it would be almost impossible to raise the submarine.

So I think that closes off my salvage history.

Q: Did you have any recommendations that pertained to divers?

Mr. N.: No, not necessarily. They continued to work on diving training. They had continual training of divers down at the Washington Navy Yard. Momsen probably was stationed in the Bureau of C & R and Hobson was there. The only outstanding thing I remember about Hobson was that he won the first triple race - you know, where you bet on a race horse and you get two or three horses that would win races that day. Well, he won the first big one.

Q: Oh, he did!

Mr. N.: He was a real clever person. I remember he couldn't get out of the race track. They had to put a hole under the fence somewhere for him. That's how he got famous!

But Momsen's gone now. All the people are gone. I'm about the only one that's left. No, Ellsburg is still around. Saunders has gone. King's gone.

Q: Was Merritt Chapman involved in any way with the S-4?

Mr. N.: No. They were out of that sort of business. The Navy was doing all this sort of thing for itself now.

After I got back to the yard I wasn't there very long before there was a letter from the bureau, from Rock, with the approval of Admiral Beuret, and the Bureau of C & R, asking me to go to Washington. They sent a copy of that letter to Plunkett at the New York Yard. I'd only been in the yard about a week after we came back from the S-4 salvage and Plunkett called me into his office and said:

"I know, Niedermair, that you got a letter from the Bureau of C & R. They want you down there, and you're delaying your reply. You haven't answered it yet, have you?"

"No, I haven't," I said, "I can't make up my mind." Plunkett said:

"Well, I think you ought to make up your mind to go and I'll give you a suggestion. When you leave me, you go out in the office there and you look at all those people in that office and that's what you'll look like if you stay here."

I let another week go by and I then wrote a letter to Washington and said I would report in Washington on the 1st of May 1928. We had raised the submarine on the 17th of March 1928. I got home about the 1st of April 1928, and here I was leaving again on the 1st of May for Washington, leaving my poor wife back on Staten Island.

Q: Was it for family reasons that you were reluctant to go?

Mr. N.: I'd lived in New York all my life and it was a maritime center, and I had the connection with the Stability Committee. But it turned out later when I went to Washington I finally met all the top people in the merchant marine and the design people and the government people, the steamboat inspection people, and the Navy people. Then I went abroad and so on, but I did go to Washington. I did report in on the 1st of May 1928.

Q: Then your wife had to make plans for moving to Washington?

Mr. N.: We didn't move right away. We didn't move until two years later.

Q: You wanted to find out if you really liked it!

Mr. N.: Because I had to go to Europe in the meantime. A year from that time I was going to be quite busy. I went back and forth to Staten Island once in a while.

One year from the day I got there I was going away.

On the 1st of May 1928 I was in Washington from New York. On about the 1st of May 1929 I was on my way to Europe. That year wasn't the kind of a year to do it. Now I took her with me though, took her over to Europe with me. She was the belle of the show over there. I have a letter here to show it. People wrote in. She met the present queen and met the present queen's father and mother. She had a grand time.

Q: Are you going to tell me about that now or later?

Mr. N.: No, I'm only telling you what's going to happen to Ethel. We're not going to get into that. We're just getting ready for this now. We've ended the venture and I'm getting ready to leave for Washington.

Interview No. 3 with Mr. John C. Niedermair

Place: His residence in Stone Harbor, New Jersey

Date: Monday morning, 29 September 1975

Subject: Biography

By: John T. Mason, Jr.

Q: It's nice to see you this morning, Sir.

I think you want to begin by giving me something of a summary of the personalities and people who were important in your life, in the development of your career, as you approached the threshold of your service, your long service, in Washington?

Mr. N.: Well, what I would really refer to here would be the people I met before I got to Washington. It comes to mind that, of course, Captain George H. Rock, who later on was a rear admiral in the bureau, and Commander, later Captain, Henry T. Wright, who I feel was probably one of my greatest sponsors - he noticed something in me that was one of the most important things about my contacts with all sorts of peculiar, odd jobs that I did with him or for him. Towards the end, he became the chief constructor in the yard. Admiral

C. P. Plunkett was the commandant of the Third Naval District and the commander of the New York Navy Yard. I met him quite a few times and I believe I referred to him in some of the previous discussions.

Q: You did, indeed.

Mr. N.: He was, of course, a great person in connection with my work at the yard. He received very little credit for it, but I felt the way he stepped in when the S-4 went down in the First Naval District and he had all the equipment in the Third Naval District, and I was the person who made up a list that came in handy when it happened. He took charge immediately when I told him about this list. He had gotten in touch with me almost immediately when he got the telegram. All the people that were left in the yard on this Saturday night when the S-4 went down were assembled. He was seldom mentioned even afterwards, but his motivation to get active on this job - he started almost immediately when he got this dispatch - and he got all the equipment started out to the salvage area. The pontoons were all in his charge and all the hose gear and the various other equipment that they had to have out there - it wasn't the Boston yard that had this equipment. Boston was in the First Naval District and Plunkett was in the Third Naval District.

Q: You're really underscoring his executive ability?

Mr. N.: Yes, I'm doing that, and also the fact that he stepped into it so fast that by ten o'clock that night - I believe it was about five o'clock when he called me in and the submarine had only been down maybe an hour or so - we had pontoons and everything else under way and I went home. Then, later on, I got a telephone call, as I mentioned in the previous conversation. But I believe that Plunkett taking hold of this thing and putting me in charge of the yard and letting me give the orders there was a very swift move to get things going.

That's the way Plunkett got into the picture and that's why I mention him particularly at this point, because he doesn't get into my career in any way later on.

Then there was another person at the yard whom I have mentioned probably only in a sort of a passing way, and that was the assistant chief draftsman, Ambrose M. Merrill. He was assistant chief but in those days politics entered into these jobs. The chief draftsman and the heads of all the departments like the machine shop and the blacksmith's shop, all those had political connections.

Q: You imply they don't now?

Mr. N.: No, I don't. I'm only pointing out that it also existed then.

Fletcher, who was a very pleasant man, was the chief draftsman. He always liked me very much and he also took great interest in me, but Merrill was the one who really gave me great interest. He was a graduate engineer from M.I.T., a naval architect, and Fletcher wasn't. Merrill appreciated my understanding of these things probably a little better than Fletcher. So I only mentioned Merrill. I only found out some of this information just recently. I didn't know that that type of situation existed between Merrill and Fletcher because they never said anything to me. Fletcher would come to Washington to call on me but he never talked about things like that.

So there is Merrill, Ambrose Merrill, who is over ninety years old and I am still in contact with him. He's badly crippled. He broke both hips and one thing and another. I talked to him as recently as March, maybe.

Then, of course, there's Edward Ellsburg, a naval constructor. At the time, he was a lieutenant commander, a junior officer, and he went off on the S-51 salvage job, but he was no longer at the yard when the S-4 went down. Ellsburg had an outstanding thing to his credit. He gave absolute complete credit to the people who were working with him, one of the few that I've come across in my whole career who would go all-out the way Ellsburg did. There were others that went along but I could count them on the fingers of one hand. I'm still in contact with Ellsburg and my last letter to him was in about February or so, and you have a copy of his reply to me. He's a year older than I am. He's eighty-three, and I'll be eighty-two.

Then there's Captain and later on Fleet Admiral Ernest J. King. I met Ernest J. King on the S-51 and again on the S-4, and then I continued to meet Ernest J. King in Washington, as he was "fleeting up." Rock used that when I would be promoted into something, he would call it "fleeting up."

Q: Somewhat of a pun in connection with Ernest King, isn't it!

Mr. N.: I'm just beginning to get an understanding of a part of Ernie King's character. I think that if he detected in people who were playing what I call the school tie syndrome because they were either classmates or some other thing and they would have them drifting along doing things with this, that was one thing that I believe Admiral King detested more than anybody that I ever knew.

A seaman gunner who did a good job for Ernie King, as far as he was concerned, was as good as the highest ranking admiral, because he was good at what he was doing. This was a very important thing, and the school tie wasn't the thing that was so important to him. I believe that's why he doesn't very often get much backing.

I mention Ernie King again because my insight is getting better as I'm working on this taped conversation with you.

That sums up in a way, except on the S-4 Captain Saunders,

Savvy Saunders.

Q: What was his first name?

Mr. N.: I believe it was Harold E. Saunders. He never made rear admiral. I was always grieved about that because I thought he was probably one of the best equipped people in hydrodynamics and the theory of naval architecture. He was the author of a book on hydrodynamics. I came to understand later on that the particular detail that he paid to things really hurt him in not making a higher rank, by being so particular he evidently hurt some other people that might be on the selection board. But he was a very brilliant fellow and in one of the last issues of the Naval Engineers, the last president of the Naval Engineers gives a great deal of credit to Saunders and his brilliance.

That about sums up my time at the New York Navy Yard and the people that I met, some highlights that I wanted to get in at this point, because now when I go to Washington there'll probably only be Admiral Rock and King and Savvy Saunders now and then.

Now I've accepted the offer to go to Washington, D. C., and there were certain things about going to Washington, D. C., that I didn't know. I found out when I got there that I had to accept lower pay than I got at the New York Yard. You couldn't go from a field job to a departmental job at the same pay. You could only go at less pay, you couldn't get more pay or even equal pay.

Q: There was a field work proviso, then, was there?

Mr. N.: Well, I was in charge of the scientific section in New York and had people working for me, and all these different jobs that I had when I was at the yard doing my job, but when I got to Washington I found out that I couldn't get that pay.

I think the real reason was that they tried to keep people away from the outside jobs in Washington. When I was in New York, even though you had a good engineering education and everything, there were no engineering jobs available, certainly not at the Navy Yard. I was graded as a draftsman. And that brings up another point.

When I was working on the S-51, Ellsburg thought I was working such long hours that I ought to get a couple of hours of extra pay because of extra expenses at home and so on. Captain Wright was agreeable to this, but I noticed in a letter that I just came across just a few days ago that Wright wrote to Ellsburg and told him that the admiral, who I suppose was Admiral Plunkett, said that draftsmen can't work more than eight hours a day. You're not supposed to work more than eight hours a day. So Wright said that he was putting that request for overtime for me in his safe and when I got back it would be up to me to fight the battle.

And besides that, he said that he had pointed out to the admiral that I really wasn't working as a draftsman, I was working as a constructor. I mentioned this to you before, that I was working just as though I were a constructor in the Navy.

But when I got to Washington I was switching from a draftsman to a naval architect. Now I was entering a professional branch. It made quite a difference. However, when I got there - of course, I'd known Rock at the yard, Beuret wasn't too pleased about the fact that I was coming from the yard. He was chief of the Bureau of C & R. The reason he was unhappy was, as I found out later on, that there were a lot of civilian engineers in the bureau. They thought they could handle this job of getting ready for the international convention on the safety of life at sea, that they were well qualified to do it. I became friends with everybody afterwards, even those who wouldn't talk to me when I first got there.

I got there and I got going, and while I was working on the project for a year, getting ready for the convention on the safety of life at sea, we had to write up the rules and it was all for merchant ships. It had nothing to do with Navy ships, except that these merchant ships would get subsidized and the Navy could tell them where to put the bulkheads and so on. Our proposed rules for the new convention on the safety of life at sea had started about 1914 over in London after the <u>Titanic</u> went down in 1912.

Q: There was a system of regulations in existence, I suppose?

Mr. N.: No, the 1914 war came on and the only rules that were followed there - there was no convention that had been approved when the 1929 convention came along. They had certain interim things that they had worked on - certain methods, certain ideas. I always felt that the British started this thing, anyway, in 1914 to really get a platform to prove that the Titanic was really a superb ship, and it was. Even with the rules today and if the Titanic was around there'd be very little change you'd have to make in that ship to make her a good ship and up-to-date.

We got going at all that work, and then again I put on the other hat. Beuret would come rushing in and call me out because Portsmouth Naval Ship Yard would be working on something connected with salvage operations, modifying pontoons and so on. I wasn't a bureaucrat so my behavior pattern didn't suit some of the ways in the bureaucracy.

I remember saying to Beuret one time when I looked at something they sent down and he asked my opinion - I started giving my opinion by saying "Offhand - " and he cut me short on that. We were sitting with all these people there. He didn't want an offhand opinion.

Q: He wanted a memo on it!

Mr. N.: So I said, "I will give you a considered opinion, which will be about the same as I just said, that this is not satisfactory."

I turned on my heels and I went out.

This was where I got in trouble when I was with Ernie

King. He wanted me to do a job and I did it the way I saw it.

Afterwards - to jump ahead a long, long time - Beuret learned a lot about me and had a different opinion of me. I think he was influenced because he was having personnel trouble, but he never said a word to me about it, and neither did his people, but I sensed it.

I met quite a few people in connection with this safety of life at sea. There was James Pennypacker, a young M.I.T. man, that the Shipbuilders Council loaned us. Then there was Carol Roundy, who was with the Shipping Board, and John MacMillan, who was the head naval architect for Ferris, Theodore Ferris, who was the leading naval architect in the country at the time. There were many other people connected with this thing that I met in the shipping industry. All the government people who had responsibility in this field. They hadn't done a damned thing about it, actually, which was very aggravating. The only rules that were worth anything at all were the British Board of Trade rules and when we got over to London, at one hearing there they faced us up because we were demanding a high standard.

Rock was the chairman of our group, and they faced him up and said:

"What does the United States use for regulating their ships?"

And Rock said, "We use the British Board of Trade rules." I remember that incident.

Anyway, we got going and in the meantime - Willie Francis

Gibbs, of course. I met him on the Stability Committee and now again he was coming in on this. And there was George Sharp. There was the chief of the American Bureau of Shipping, David Arnett, and Ernest Rigg, who was a naval architect for New York Ship. Then there were the people who represented Newport News. I've forgotten who they were. They weren't quite as active as the people I've told you about. Ernest Rigg was one of the outstanding people. He was an Englishman, a previous Englishman, and Arnett was a Scotsman. Sharp, I was never sure whether he was English or Scots. The three of them came over to this country and became very prominent in our business. So the story went.

Knowing all these people later on helped me quite a bit when I'd finished with the convention.

My wife was living on Staten Island. I was working in Washington, and in April of 1929 to go to the convention in London, I took my wife along.

Q: How long did this convention last?

Mr. N.: It lasted for a month or so.

We had a congressman who was the political representative - Congressman White. I've forgotten his first name now. I think he came from Massachusetts or somewhere, Maine, up in that area. I hadn't thought of him but now, as I recite the story to you, these names are coming to me.

I remember that prohibition was on at the time and, of

course, there were cocktail parties given to everybody by everybody and we attended all those. There would always be liquor over there, but now the Americans were giving a cocktail party and I remember Congressman White passing the word down that all the delegates from the U.S.A. shouldn't really imbibe at this occasion because we were paying for it but it wasn't legal. So we felt we shouldn't drink our own liquor! I remember that and that's about the only important thing that he did, I think, on that trip.

Q: He was obeyed, was he?

Mr. N.: I imagine so. They knew the situation and we'd take some ginger ale and you wouldn't know the difference.

Over there we sat down with the Russians, who were very brilliant in lots of ways, but the odd thing about them was that they were all commoners and we had to dress according to the style. If you went to any night formal affairs, tuxedos were out. You had to wear tails, and they only wore their regular shoestring ties. They hadn't been taught any of these social things. But from an engineering standpoint they were very helpful. I remember one of the most important things that they insisted on. Even back in those days, at the beginning of their problem as the new government of the Soviet Union, when a question came up about the ice patrol, the United States was carrying a big share of that -

Q: The North Atlantic ice patrol?

Mr. N.: Yes, to find the icebergs before you hit them! They insisted at that very time that they were paying almost the same amount of money that we were putting into it. I thought that that was a gesture by these people. Socially they were really very embarrassed in lots of ways, but this was the way the rules were for them, and I didn't see anybody put on monkey suits.

Q: How many countries had delegations there?

Mr. N.: There were delegations from Norway, Sweden, Denmark, Germany, France, Italy, Japan, the United States, Canada, New Zealand, Australia - because each one of the British outposts was rated as a separate unit -

Q: They were dominions in those days -

Mr. N.: Dominions, yes. As I remember it, there was world representation there.

Q: Of the maritime nations?

Mr. N.: Yes.

Q: This convention was to be drawn up under the aegis of what, the old League of Nations?

Mr. N.: No, it wasn't. It was drawn up by agreement between these maritime countries. It had nothing to do with the League of Nations.

I sat across the way from the Japanese delegation, like

I'm talking to you here, and they seemed to take a stand against too much safety because it was too expensive. We had certain loopholes in the convention, such as pilgrims making trips down to Mecca and so on, those ships could carry people on deck and they wouldn't be counted as passengers - these migrants. The Japanese were quite insistent that where they were located and so on, the competition - they felt that they didn't want to go as far as we did in this safety business, which was a great thing for me because, later on, I remembered this.

Q: Did it have its roots in the attitude of the easterner to human life not being as valuable, as we place value upon it?

Mr. N.: That might have had some influence. There were all these people around and all these people wanted to travel and they didn't have much money, really. The Japanese were building big ships at the time and they went along as far as the convention went, but we were arguing for more than the standard that had been imposed by the 1914 convention. We went beyond that in our rules and we did get quite a few things accepted, specially one in which I was instrumental. I was advocating searching out the stability of ships, and I was credited with seeing to it that all passenger ships would be inclined so they would know where the center of gravity was, definitely know where it was, and certain other things concerning wing tanks and so on. They were modest improvements that we managed to get into that convention.

I thought we did very well, considering that until 1920 the Europeans and all the other countries thought we were still Indians - until World War I came along. But then after about 1920 a new age got in there.

Q: What percentage of the U.S. proposals were incorporated into the convention?

Mr. N.: I can't recall. I would say quite a bit of it got in there in words, but when it came down to putting down numbers we didn't do too well. For instance, we got the thing in about the inclining test, which was a very good start because later on that led to more and more investigation about stability. Shortly after I got back, I wrote the first paper on damage stability in 1932. I was quite active in that sort of thing.

Q: What proviso was made in the convention as it was written for enforcement of these regulations?

Mr. N.: Each country would enforce them itself, in a way. But the convention here had to be approved by our Congress and it took us two or three years to get the 1929 convention approved.

Q: That was remarkably fast.

Mr. N.: It appeared awfully slow to me! But I learned later on that it really was rather quick. We got it done and I still advocated stability. I made up a formula for what I considered the minimum metacentric height, which until that was put in that shape and made the metacentric height a function of the beam, as a percentage of the beam, it was so simple and yet it had never been attempted statistically to rate it that way. I was referred to by the naval architect at Newport News as O6B, and Sid Vincent, who was a naval architect, argued that it was too high, that it should be O-5B. When we wrote to each other, we'd sign "O-6B" and "O-5B."

But, you see, we were getting recognition and discussion back and forth, and I got very good support in the discussions on my paper, which was considered a classic at the time. Sid Vincent never did agree with O6. I never said that they shouldn't have more than that, but I said they shouldn't have less than that. No, I didn't. I didn't say it that way. What I said was that the legal requirement of the metacentric height need never exceed O-6B plus some other part of the formula.

I did that because I wanted them to get interested in trying to make the ships safe within the limits of O-6B.

Q: Yes, I understand.

Mr. N.: I also wanted that in because I didn't want some bureaucrat coming along when you'd finished your design and saying that he wanted O-8B metacentric height. A naval architect should know how far he would be pushed, and if he was wise he would take the upper limit, which turned out later on to be a pretty good one.

What they were worried about was the critical angle of roll on a passenger ship, because all this talk was only for passenger ships.

Q: But you did make the exemption in the case of pilgrims?

Mr. N.: Yes, and dhows. There was a ship that was used in India that was a dhow. I never knew what that was. That was like a Chinese junk, probably.

Incidentally, Chinese junks had watertight compartments in them way back probably to the year 1000. Watertight bulkheads in them.

Q: I'm not surprised to learn that at all.

Mr. N.: They did because they lived on them.

We finished our convention and Ethel and I spent two or three weeks after the convention going over to Germany and France. We came back home at the end of 1929, and we didn't move to Washington until maybe another year and a half after that, maybe 1931 it was - somewhere in there, anyway. I've forgotten.

So now I'm back in the bureau. I was supposed to understudy James L. Bates, who was the top naval architect in the Bureau of C & R. He headed up preliminary design and this is what they were aiming me for. But I still had to wear this other hat connected with the work on the merchant marine.

Some of the things that I started with when I got back had to do mostly with the merchant marine and I really didn't get going on the work that Bates was doing until about 1931.

Q: Was he approaching retirement?

Mr. N.: No, he wasn't, really. I don't believe it sat very well with Bates, because he left with Land later on, in 1938. Jimmy Bates was a very brilliant person and he might have been putting on a sort of high hat or superior attitude. Some people judged him that way, the officers who were there. He was very active. He did a lot of work. He wrote some of the best articles I've seen in connection with our business. He was crackerjack at the hull form, the shape of the ship, and so on.

I had this mixed-up background which led people like Admiral Taylor - I'd be working at a regular drafting table, we didn't have any desks - I introduced the desk idea later on. I had a great big 12-foot drafting table, and I'd be working on a little plan on a great big 12-foot drafting table. Well, who would come down but Admiral Taylor. He was the chief of the bureau during World War I, and others would come in to see me - George Rock, who became the chief of the bureau shortly after, would come down and sit next to me and spend an hour or two discussing things, then walk back. Of course, I was supposed to be working for Bates. As it turned out, I really wasn't.

I was not up in basic ship design. I had no access to

that sort of data. I was working in the field, doing the things that the bureau wanted and checking it out and seeing how often it didn't come out that way. This is the reason why I think they wanted me down in the bureau later on, because I knew all the difficulties they had with the machinery and with the cruisers, the Cincinnati class. They had trouble with inner bottoms when they'd go in a dry dock and then they would notice that the supporting structure would deflect. When you go in a dry dock and you sit down on the blocks, the inner bottom floors, which are the vertical girders, would deflect. So I ran tests on it. I'd seen this happen out in the field. For instance, I'd get involved with the ordnance people because the guns couldn't come back to zero when they rotated them. I found that out and they'd have to put in new rack and pinions to reduce the play.

So, with that sort of background, the naval constructors were all interested in me quite a bit. Bates was more of an office man who hadn't been working closely in those things all the time from 1920 until 1930 when I got there. I'd spent ten years roaming all over the place. He never showed any hard feelings to me or did anything to indicate that he was mad at me, but I know he was unhappy about it, because his means of communication was blocked because these people were coming directly to me and communicating with me and he was the top man in preliminary design. It certainly wasn't a good organizational way to do it.

Q: No, that's an understandable reaction.

Mr. N.: On the other hand, I visited in his home and he visited in my home. He met my family, I met his family, and we got along, but I felt that he was really hurt about this thing. Later on I felt this way. I didn't know it at the time, I was so busy wearing these other hats.

It wasn't very long before the Leviathan was getting into trouble again. I remember one day when I was in the bureau and the Leviathan started breaking in two again. You remember I told the story before.

Q: Yes.

Mr. N.: Well, now the thing busted up again. Either Captain Howard or Admiral Howard came to me and said:

"John, I've got another job for you." I said, "What could it be?" and he said:

"I just got a telephone call from the United States Lines."

So I took leave. I had been to New York. It was on New Year's Eve I came to Washington because for some reason or other I wanted to be in Washington on the 1st of January. That would have been 1929, I guess, but I was back in the bureau on the 31st of December when Howard came to me and told me about this trouble.

"Gee whizz," I said, "I just came from New York. Too bad that they didn't find me up there. Well, I'll go on leave again and go up there."

So I went up on leave and I was their consultant. The reason that they got hold of me was that the holidays were coming and it was costing them some enormous amount of money to have this ship tied to the dock. It mounted into tens of thousands of dollars. It wound up that they were right. There wasn't anybody available. The American Bureau of Shipping, which was supposed to have inspectors who would come over and help them, they were all gone.

I left Washington on the night of the 31st, was back in New York on the 1st of January, and went right over to the Leviathan and went aboard.

Q: Why was it necessary for you to take leave? Was this not an official duty?

Mr. N.: No, this was not official. I was working for the U.S. Lines. It's like when I went back and forth on the Leviathan. I went on leave without pay then. This time I went on leave with pay because I had the leave and I could go off and take an outside job during my leave. That wasn't against the regulations. Howard told me to do it that way. I was reluctant to go and he said, well, they're in a fix. You know, the usual story.

I spent two or three days there and I invented a couple of things for them on how they could drive rivets hydraulically because they were very thick plates. Some of the plating amounted to two inches thickness up in the strength deck. This time she really started to break in two in several places, so I worked out the method and made a sketch of what the trouble was. I transmitted the information to the U.S. Lines and they got in touch with the American Bureau of Shipping. That's what they wanted so they could start talking business right away, and so they repaired the ship and she went to sea. I certainly saved them a lot of time and a lot of money, too. I wasn't too particular about it. It was a very modest price I charged them. I only charged them for my regular time. I wasn't interested in doing any more than that.

I came back again to Washington -

Q: How long did that take you?

Mr. N.: It only took me three days. Within three days I was back again.

This was why they wanted me. They knew me previously when I was on the ship, or they might have kept track of me, where I was to be found. They called up the bureau, of course, and there I was. If they'd called during the week before I wouldn't have been there.

I was constantly busy working on these safety of life at sea rules and trying to get backing to have the convention approved. Then there would be questions coming up that we had to answer, technicalities that were coming up in the language.

People in different countries were working on the phrasing of the paragraphs. I would be in on that and I would have to help phrase those things. So I really didn't get going in the preliminary design work until about 1931.

In 1931 I started right off with a few preliminary jobs that I did. They were of no consequence exactly, but I got familiar with the routine in the bureau, which was altogether different from the routine in the field, because here now in the bureau you were creating a ship, whereas out in the field there it is, and that makes a lot of difference.

I was still busy helping out on things they were doing in connection with the salvage of submarines, the equipment and work on the diving bell. Questions would come up about the hatches and the ventilation valves. There would be constant interference of this type, and the first thing I knew it was 1931, when I made my first start on anything of any consequence as far as the U.S. Navy went. In the meantime I was sort of learning how to do it, you might say, learning where the data were and finally getting familiar with the people who were in the bureau, because you weren't going to get very far if you weren't getting along with the people there.

Q: It wasn't a one-man operation at all!

Mr. N.: No. It wasn't far from that, though. It continued to be a one-man thing because Rock would get in there all the time. And Jerry Land when he got to be chief was the same way. Land was the one who, when I got back from the S-51, wanted me to go with BuAir. These people knew me. The head of the General Board would come down and talk to me. They should have talked to Bates but I guess I had a more public image, for some reason or other. Anyway, Bates and I got along fine.

I very soon tackled the structure of ships. Bates took care of the lines end of it, which I wasn't too familiar with, but I got into ship structure, the arrangements and scantlings, as we called them, and the weight factors. You see, the hull lines and all would just be the outside imaginary watertight shell. Now you had to put structure on all this thing because these ship lines couldn't go to sea by themselves. They had to be hooked onto something, so I got into studies of the ship as a whole, you might say, and be in on the hull form also, because I would always be checking up on the stability of the ship. It might be less resistance with less beam, but on the other hand, I had to have beam for stability.

Q: Did you simultaneously have to have some knowledge of the ordnance that was going to be installed?

Mr. N.: I would follow that up all the time. I would get familiar with everything that went on. In battleships you'll see that I ran into some things there.

In 1931 and 1932 one of the outstanding things that I

worked out the weights and centers, the thicknesses of the plating, which we called the scantlings, the strength, and the subdivision and the damage stability. All those things I tackled. I became very familiar with the carriers, which was rather unusual because we didn't build very many carriers as a result of all this.

Q: This was a time when they were beginning to think more seriously of aircraft carriers, weren't they?

Mr. N.: Yes, they had the Ranger and they had the two cruisers that were converted, the Lexington and Saratoga. The Ranger was the first aircraft carrier that was designed from the ground up, but it was a modest attempt.

Q: But the carrier was beginning to come into its own, wasn't it?

Mr. N.: Within that short time that I was there I was already grabbing hold of this thing, because as I looked up my information that I'm giving you now - I had some notes on this. I then finished with this 10,000-ton flight deck cruiser, which came in very handy, as I will mention when we get started on World War II. You'll see the importance of my having this information.

Q: May I ask you a question? Were you, in planning this 10,000-ton flight deck cruiser, limited in any way by the arms-limitation treaties?

Mr. N.: To a certain extent, yes. That's what the 10,000 tons was, you see. The cruisers were limited to 10,000 tons, but the carriers were not. Carriers could go to 20,000 tons, because the next thing I did was study the 20,000-ton aircraft carriers which later on became the Yorktown and Enterprise - a long time afterwards.

This 20,000-ton aircraft carrier study that I made resulted in the Yorktown, CV-5, the Enterprise, CV-6, and the Hornet, CV-8. However, during the same period I studied a 15,200-ton aircraft carrier for the General Board, which turned out later to be the Wasp, which was the CV-7. I don't have the dates when they got in there but it was quite a long time afterwards - after I got going on this thing. When I did these studies I had to look into their arrangement plans and all that sort of thing, too.

Q: Did you take into consideration anything that the Royal Navy had in being at that time?

Mr. N.: We did to a certain extent. I was not too interested in that because the General Board was making those comparisons. The General Board was working on and studying the need for - I put a note here that these studies were made for the General Board. The 20,000-ton carrier was for the General Board at that time. Later on it developed that they became the carriers that I named to you.

Q: Who on the General Board was particularly interested in carriers at that time?

Mr. N.: I don't remember. I was only a beginner, you know, and I wasn't too familiar with these people yet. I have very little recall because these officers would come and talk to me and leave and I wasn't working with them directly very much, so their names didn't stick with me. And the General Board was constantly changing because that's where all the officers who had been to sea and were ready to retire - they were senior officers.

During that same period we started studies of large destroyers already from 1931 through 1932.

Q: Large, what tonnage?

Mr. N.: At that time the Farragut class got in there. She was the first post-World War I destroyer, but according to these studies here, she was not so big. My note says that at that time I was studying large-destroyer schemes, about 365 to 372 feet long.

Q: And that would be a tonnage of what?

Mr. N.: Oh, probably in the neighborhood of 1,400 tons or 1,500 tons. I think we were limited to 1,500 tons.

Q: Under the treaty?

Mr. N.: Yes.

During that same time I started getting into all these things, then I'd come across my interest in safety at sea. That began to pop up every once in a while. One of the things I did during this period was to make a research memorandum on the number and location of airports in foreign and U.S. naval vessels. You know, you put a nice heavy shell plating on a ship and carry it all the way up to the deck and then you cut a lot of holes in it so that people could see daylight down below. I was opposed to this and I took issue about putting air ports into these ships.

Q: And that's the term that describes that, air port?

Mr. N.: Yes, because they would want to open them up and get some ventilation in there, too.

Q: And that lessens the strength?

Mr. N.: No. We could take care of the strength, but when the ship got into an accident the water would run in through these ports. It no longer had a watertight side.

I submitted this memorandum and the same thing happened to me there as happened in New York when I made up a memorandum on plans for a future submarine accident when I got back from the S-51. I was told to file it away, that they couldn't tell the bureau what to do. This time I ran into trouble in the bureau, where they told me to file it away and to bring it up when an emergency arose.

Q: You mean when something happened as a result of an air port?

Mr. N.: Well, yes, but I kept watching it all the time, every chance I got.

Q: How were you going to provide a facility without the air ports? How were you going to do this?

Mr. N.: Well, they had lights in there and they had ventilation systems and everything. They just had to have more ventilation. Now, I understand, they have air-conditioning in all these ships. Nearly every ship is air-conditioned. We struggled along in the days before air-conditioning. But I ran into trouble on air ports. I got worried about it because a warship really expects to get into trouble. At some time in its life it may be called upon to be standing there and helping Uncle Sam out.

I also prepared a paper for Admiral Rockat this time, a lecture it was, on the safety of life at sea, and then a paper on the education of naval architects. I wrote a paper for him on that because he was advocating certain principles that he thought we ought to do something about, telling them what they ought to do about the education of naval architects.

Q: You mean a new curriculum for them?

Mr. N.: Yes, what they should be doing and so forth.

Q: Did you do this in conjunction with M.I.T.?

Mr. N.: No. I don't remember whether Rock finally wrote the thing or edited it and had it put in as a paper for the naval architects. I don't know what he did with it, actually. He left the bureau shortly after this, I believe, to become head of Webb Institute of Naval Architecture, where I came from. He was interested in education.

Q: He was going to apply the principles there!

Mr. N.: Yes, he did, and he was a pretty tough egg, too.

Q: Incidentally, may I ask you another question? Were you aware of what the Japanese were or were not doing under the terms of the convention?

Mr. N.: Oh, yes, that's right, too. I'm glad you brought that up. I studied the Japs' attitude and I decided they were either trying to kid us into not being fussy about safety or they really meant it. So every time they published anything about their ships, they'd make plans as a sort of publicity stunt and their regular plans would be copied on a small scale, I would take those plans and work out a scale for them in the technical magazines. I'd manage to make special scale because they would always tell you about the length of the ship, so I could make a scale that would fit that diagram. I'd study these ships and decide that the Japs really meant it when they said they weren't interested in the safety of ships. They (our people) knew that I had done this thing. I had told somebody about it, and they'd come to me and ask how many torpedoes did I think it would take to sink a Japanese ship, and I would say one would do it, or two would do it.

Q: And they were very vulnerable, weren't they?

Mr. N.: Yes, they were. I was right. But you see going to that convention and me being there - there were lots of other people there, but I was the only one who was constantly - evidently, that's one of my traits, to keep digging at these things when I don't know. I'm a great curiosity seeker. I'll search a thing out - I used to, anyway - to the limit, and I always had more time than anybody else because I still only use four or five hours' sleep a day. So I would always have two days to work on.

Q: When you gave that answer to them, how many torpedoes would it take and you said one, you still were not aware of the fact that sometimes the torpedoes didn't work?

Mr. N.: I found out later on that it bounced off, but my having been over there made me aware of the fact that their merchant ships - they put bulkheads in for practical reasons but they weren't worried about safety. So that was a great help. And, of course, that led to other things, my contact with the people in the Pentagon and the military people. I got to be known in the Bureau of Yards and Docks. Cdr. J. T. Reside (USNR) was there and Captain Laycock. Then the people in the Bureau of Aeronautics would come over to see me. I would be in contact with the people who worked on arresting gear. I would individually know all these people who were working in Ordnance. I'd go over there and talk to people - the designer of the 5-inch gun, which was very successful, one of the most successful. Then they would come over to see me. They would want to know what would this do to the ship and I would try to tell them.

Captain Diehl - I don't know whether you ever -

Q: Yes, Walter Diehl.

Mr. N.: He used to come and sit down and talk to me because I got interested in some very complicated methods of stresses in plates and he passed the word around. He'd be fascinated with this thing, and I was always interested in math, which I wish I could get at now, but I haven't had the time again.

You asked the question did I do these things. Yes, I did. I made myself thoroughly familiar, and in the contract design I would know all the people, all the leading men in there. And later on when they came back from the war, I would go and meet the officers who were on submarines, for example, or the officers who were going away would come in to see me. It was really a very happy relationship.

Q: And a very complicated one, I would think?

Mr. N.: It was very complicated, yes.

I mentioned before that I met Ernest Rigg in connection with this thing on safety of life at sea. Now, in a very short time I was running into Ernest Rigg because he was - this was 1932 about - busy designing the Manhattan and Washington, passenger ships. I got involved on the stability and the inclining experiments on those ships.

Q: What was their tonnage?

Mr. N.: Oh, I've forgotten now. They were very big ships, but I couldn't tell you. I could look it up for you. They were really the top ships in the U.S. fleet when they got going.

Rigg was always on my side when it came to stability, but unfortunately for him the Manhattan and Washington didn't turn out too well. They were rather fast rollers. I don't know just why they were troublesome. As a matter of fact, for stability they had to put in "ersatz" ballast, as he called it. It sounded to me that they were running deficient in stability and they had to put ballast in them. A passenger ship isn't going to carry very much cargo down in the bottom ever, that I know of.

Rock got interested in this, too. He was now up at Webb and he'd be writing to me and I'd have to write letters back to him. He'd ask me about the stability of the Manhattan and the Washington. I would know about it and I'd write back and give an opinion. Somewhere I have a letter from Rock.

To give you some idea of how these things worked out, I'm referring to a letter that's dated 1938, when he's still after me about stability:

"Thank you for taking time for me. I knew you would do it, although very busy in the bureau, but as you know I consider you quite the outstanding authority on stability and I wanted your phrasing and your touch in this particular important description."

That had to do with some people who were writing a book, in which they were hesitating to say the right thing about stability, and so Rock got interested in the Manhattan and Washington, because he was up at Webb and he wanted to know how they were doing.

While I was looking for that Rock letter, I came across an interesting letter that Ernie King wrote on the S-51 salvage operation, so that you can see the kind of letter he wrote. Here we were in 1932-1933 and, as I mentioned before, here again I'm working with Lieutenant Commander Edward L. Cochrane, who was now up in the Portsmouth Naval Ship Yard. I was co-author with him in writing Bulletin No. 8 on subdivision, stability, and construction of naval vessels. This bulletin was sponsored by Admiral Rock. We started working on it and we never finished it until Rock was up at Webb. It got to be quite the thing. A lot of people in the merchant marine, like Arnett from the American Bureau of Shipping - I have a letter from Arnett requesting a copy, he'd heard about this book and he'd like to have a copy of it.

Q: How did Ned Cochrane get to be an authority on stability?

Mr. N.: Because he was with me on the safety of life at sea.

Q: Oh, he was at that. I see.

Mr. N.: He was there and he knew the work I did on there and he knew about the convention. He was very familiar with it, so the two of us wrote the thing. I would put in all the things that I could think of and he would get hold of it and work on it, add what he thought and so on, and we got to be quite well known on this Bulletin No. 8. If you want a copy of it, I may have an extra one around.

Q: Yes.

Mr. N.: The next thing that I tackled from 1932 to 1933 - Roosevelt was elected president in 1932 and he was inaugurated as president on March the 4th, as it used to be in those days, so he wasn't there very long before he made himself felt. I have a note here that President Roosevelt was anxious to get work started, so we started on 6-inch cruisers, the Brooklyn class they were.

Q: Still in conformity with the limitations treaty?

Mr. N.: Yes, but we were limited this time to 6-inch guns. They had made an agreement that we could build more of these cruisers. We were building 8-inch cruisers up till this time. Only one of this group, the CVA-45, as I remember, was an 8-inch cruiser and that would be the last 8-inch cruiser. All the rest of them would be 6 inches.

Q: CLs?

Mr. N.: Yes, and that was a good thing. I always felt that Admiral Stark was responsible for that. I always gave him great credit for that.

Q: What makes you say that?

Mr. N.: Because he was head of Ordnance at the time when they developed that fast-firing, 6-inch gun. That 6-inch gun could fire faster and probably couldn't sink any ships exactly, but it could knock the intelligence out, get on target, because it turned out later on, in World War II when we got radar, that when we fought the battles down in the Guadalcanal area, when the Japs almost got through, really the 6-inch cruisers, I thought, were the ones that licked them. Betty Stark got into difficulty at Pearl Harbor, as I remember, but anyway he went to the last arms-limitation conference in London and he was in favor of the 6-inch-gun cruiser, and I personally favored it because it was a fast-firing gun.

Q: That limited the tonnage to what?

Mr. N.: Still 10,000 tons.

Q: Oh, it could be a light cruiser and still 10,000 tons?

Mr. N.: Sure, that's what they all were, down to 10,000 tons.

We got going on the Brooklyn-class cruisers and he (F.D.R.) was anxious to get the work started. I worked on the preliminary design for them, and it was decided to have New York Ship make the contract plans. Here's where my other hat comes in again. We had contract plan people and you would think they would have said to the people over at the contract plan division, "We'll do this at New York Ship." But instead of that they asked me to go to New York Ship and have them figure all the weights and the strength and make the contract plans up there.

I went up there to push those plans and all the weight calculations and all the usual stuff that contract design would do.

Q: That must have caused difficulties within that division?

Mr. N.: I don't think it did because it meant a heck of a lot of work for me and nobody ever objected when I got bombed up with jobs like this because I had to go to New York Ship once or twice a week, and it started in August 1933 and ended in December 1933. And during that time an odd thing happened.

You remember that fellow Cord who was developing an automobile? And when New York Ship built the Manhattan and Washington they had saved some money in their treasury, and Cord brought up their stock at a low price because there was a lull in there because of the depression. He bought New York Ship stock and got control of it, and I was there the day that the Cord people came into New York Ship and said that they were taking over.

Metten, who was the chief engineer of New York Ship at the time, finally became president of New York Ship through that performance.

I made these trips each week to New York Ship to speed up the preparation of the contract plans, weight estimates, strength, stability calculations, and so on. And I imagine it was about the spring of 1934 that we built the yard force up to about 4,000 people.

Q: There was no change in policy as a result of Cord's taking over?

Mr. N.: No, he was only after the money that was in the treasury. Somehow or other, he bled that out of the place, which is a typical way of doing it.

This experience that I had on the Brooklyn class I was able to do, why, because I met Ernie Rigg. He was the chief naval architect who had to do a lot of this work, and I knew him from the work that I did on the safety of life at sea. It may be that this is the reason why they sent me, but they never explained it. They just asked me if I would do it, and I did it. When I got up there and I knew these people and I had no trouble - Tom Bossett, Rigg, Joe Thompson and Metten. We finished up the hull plans first and I also had to watch the machinery plans at the same time. I wanted to get the hull plans signed as soon as I got finished with them and Metten said:

"No, Niedermair, why don't you wait till we've finished the machinery plans?" So I said, OK, we'll do that. We waited till they'd finished the machinery plans.

When they'd finished the machinery plans, he sent out the word that they were ready for signing, which made it look like he was the guy who finished up first! That didn't bother me too much.

Then when I got back and had finished with the Brooklyn class, which came out very handy later on when we worked on the Cleveland class - that comes in up the line a bit, I got to working on the Farragut class of large destroyers.

Q: You had worked on those long-range plans previously?

Mr. N.: I'd been studying them, now I had the job to really work on them. So I started working on it and one of the interesting ideas I had, the metallurgists told me - I can't think of the metallurgist's name, but I went up and talked about the new materials that I could put into this new destroyer, aluminum and stainless steel, so I went to the metallurgist and talked to him about it and he said:

"Yes, John, that's great stuff. We've been waiting three thousand years for this."

I always wondered why he'd been waiting three thousand years, or two thousand years, for this. Anyway, I got going on this destroyer, and the first time I worked on it I decided that I'd make a study to see what it would look like if I made it out of stainless steel.

Q: These were the destroyers they called gold something or other?

Mr. N.: Yes, those early destroyers. I designed the thing on the basis of stainless steel because that meant that we didn't have to worry about painting it and everything. This is what they told me. They told me what it cost for a pound of stainless steel and it cost quite a lot of money, so I decided I couldn't build this thing out of stainless steel because it cost too much money and didn't save enough paint. The paint would never cost as much as this ship would cost if I made it out of stainless steel.

And it's a good thing they didn't build it out of stainless steel because it turned out that stainless steel was a prima donna. The people who ran the salt tests made little test samples and set them up in salt spray. However, before they put the stainless steel into the bath, they had to clean this up so they could detect whether any corrosion was starting. They'd clean it up with a nice piece of velvet and stand it up inside there. If you could do that to a ship it wouldn't corrode. Newport News and others fell for this and the people who were interested about gasoline tanks and the carriers that were building - I think the Yorktown and Enterprise were building at that time, they built those gasoline tanks out of stainless steel, and they had holes in them before they could even launch the ships. They had to put holes in the side to take the tanks out.

Why? Because they used ordinary steel tools on them, and these steel tools would leave a little mark on the side of the stainless steel. That would start pitting, start electrolisis. I didn't fall for that one, but I did go along with the idea - I went along with the idea in my preliminary design work putting portholes into the superstructure made out of stainless steel and they pitted.

I also went into a modest amount of aluminum on the superstructure.

Q: This made for less weight, didn't it?

Mr. N.: Yes. The superstructure, as I remember it, on the Farragut class was the first one. Alloy aluminum wasn't too good at the time, and I don't know just how well we did with that.

Q: Aluminum has an age span, doesn't it? I mean there's a limitation in terms of years?

Mr. N.: A little bit, but we built things out of aluminum later on, and airplanes are built out of aluminum. There was that stretching that you get because they don't really have an elastic limit. That's what it is. Steel has an elastic limit. Mild steel has an elastic limit where you pull on it up to 30,000 pounds per square inch and you let go and it will always go back to its original size. But aluminum, no matter what you do, always comes out a little longer all the time.

Q: Like rubber!

Mr. N.: So, I got in there and got the Farragut going and that's about where I finished at the end of 1933.

Rock left the bureau in 1932 and Land came in - Emory Scott Land became chief of the Bureau in 1932. He was there then as chief of the bureau until he left to go to MARAD, when he retired from the Navy. So that would be some six years, until 1937, he was chief of the bureau. It was a very active time and it wasn't very long before I got going in connection with battleships, with battleship studies, and the North Carolina and the Washington resulted from these studies.

When I started to make these studies of the weights and the arrangements - the size of the ship usually is determined by - the speed has an effect and all the things you put into it have an effect and create the length, in a way. Then from it all comes the displacement. So this business of casting up the weights, as I told you before, and making up the structure plans and arrangement plans inside of this invisible set of lines that they started experimenting with — I'm not sure whether they got a twin keel on the North Carolina and Washington or not, but I do know that later on they brought that into the picture because we felt that a twin-keel arrangement for the inboard propellers, each one of the inboard propellers would be on sort of a keel so the flow and the lines of the flow to the propellers would be better that way. The outboard ones, then, of course, would be on struts, just like they usually are.

Q: Do I take it that when you first began working on these designs and plans they were to be 14-inch?

Mr. N.: 14-inch, yes. Four 14s are what I used at the time. But in my contact with the Bureau of Ordnance, I finally talked to them about it, I had an idea that maybe I ought to allow on the diameter of the barbettes, the cylinder on which the gun mounts would rest, and down below where the powder-handling was going on and all, would be inside this barbette where you'd sent the shells and the powder up to the guns. I wanted the inside diameter of that barbette to be able to take a triple 16, which was very important, as it turned out later on, and I found out after a certain amount of maneuvering around that if we could put 14-inch guns on there so that we made these turrets four 14s it would come out almost the same as the barbette for the 16-inch mounts, and by some juggling in there they could work it out. That is, the designers of the 16-inch guns could get it into the same barbette that I was putting the four 14s on.

Q: What induced consideration of the 16-inch gun?

Mr. N.: I've forgotten now but for some reason or other it got to be a fetish with me and I chased it to the limit. I think there was some talk about the 16-inch shell being a much heavier shell and could penetrate the armor of some of the other ships.

Q: Was it too early to think that there were rumors about the Japanese and their 18-inch guns?

Mr. N.: I doubt it very much because they were limited by the treaty, too. They couldn't have as many as we had. We could have the same number that the British had.

Q: 5-5-3, wasn't it?

Mr. N.: Something like that. Anyhow, the guns also were limited. They were limited on the size of the guns they could carry.

Q: But we were beginning to suspect, were we not, that they weren't living up to it?

Mr. N.: No. This was one of my big complaints as far as security went. I don't know just what caused me to do these things. I also checked into other things concerning the side armor belt, why they stopped it five or six feet below the waterline. I complained about that to Ordnance. I asked them whether they had any trajectories, what was the path of a shell under water, and they said they only had it for a 5-inch gun, and things like that.

I would go down to Indian Head where Ordnance would be running their tests. You asked how I got to dig into these other people. I'd go down to Indian Head where they were firing a 5-inch gun through the ring and they were testing out the powder cartridges with plastic sealers on them. I was standing so close to this firing that when they shot the gun off smoking plastics were falling down on the ground and hitting my feet. That's how close I was to this.

After the firing was all over, we had a conference, and I mentioned this but nobody had noticed it. This would have happened on the ship, and the personnel around would have been hit by all these fragments. I was the one who found that out because it was hitting my shoes. I was that close. I was close to these rings to see how they were getting the velocities of these guns.

Q: And when you were dealing with the battleships –

Mr. N.: With the battleships, I would be going over to ordnance in the same way. I would go into it and I would discover or complain about something they would be doing. I would let them in on it. I wouldn't keep it secret. I would tell them right away.

Q: I would suspect that the General Board had a lot of feed-in on battleships, didn't it?

Mr. N.: Yes, they did, and that's an unfortunate thing because look at all the battleships we built and the few airplane carriers we built. The chairman of the General Board came down to me at one time, we were talking about things and he asked about protection around the bridge. I was an advocate of protection around the bridge, and he said:

"You know, Niedermair, the boys sitting around on their desks over there when I talk about protection around the bridge they say oh, no, we don't need any protection up there. Hell, they're not going to sea any more."

I said: "No, you're right. I think we should have some protection up there, weather protection, anyway."

So he went back and talked to the boys. These boys were all about sixty years old and I'm sure they weren't all sitting on their desks. I've forgotten his name.

One of the pleasures I got out of this business that I was in - I always assumed the naval architect was responsible for the whole ship, everything that went in it. That was my philosophy. Somebody had to be responsible for the whole ship, and I felt the naval architect was. When the machinery went into a ship, I always told the machinery people how much room they could use, how long the engine room was, and if anything would happen they'd blame me when they couldn't get at some of the stuff they put in the engine room, and I'd say:

"Hell, if you knew you couldn't get the stuff in, you should have come back and told me about it."

We would fix the engine room length before they had their studies finished.

Anyway, I was getting into these battleship studies, and the Secretary of the Navy created a board to check into our design finally. We worked on these things from 1933 to 1936, and made 77 preliminary studies. I remember the chart that we made up. I remember going in to Captain Chantry, who was a real clever fellow, a fine design officer, and I told him that I thought we ought to make up a table for this board, tabulating all the different schemes that we made up. Chantry said — I think his name was Alan —

Q: Alan Chantry, that's right.

Mr. N.: He said, "No, John, don't bother," so I came out. Jimmy Farron was a young officer with me and Bill Leahy was another young officer, and then Bill Howard. They all became rear admirals later.

Q: Except one became a fleet admiral!

Mr. N.: Yes, but that was Bill's father.

Q: Oh, it was his father.

Mr. N.: Yes, he was with Roosevelt. That was Leahy's father.

When I came out, I think I told Farron. I said:

"Farron, I was just in talking to Chantry. I want this table made but he doesn't want it, but I think I want it. So why not get busy and make up this tabulation?"

They made up a tabulation and it turned out to be a set and columns, all about an inch or so wide, so we came up with a thing that was over six feet long. When it was all done, I took it and showed Chantry what I had in mind. I said:

"I wanted to make this thing up because I want that board to see that we didn't design this ship overnight."

When he saw the thing, he was really amazed at it. He grabbed it and took it in to the chief and for the longest time I never saw that thing again. I almost thought that the board might grab it.

Q: I should think it would have been very useful, however, for this special board?

Mr. N.: Metten was on that board. He was president of New York Ship. And Admiral Strauss. I think he's the one who became head of the atomic energy thing at one time.

Q: Yes. Louis Strauss.

Mr. N.: Professor Hovgaard was on there and so was Willie Francis Gibbs on that committee. There might have been one other man but those are the only ones I remember.

Something happened here. Bates and several people had to

appear before the committee. I was with them, when they went. Then when Cochrane and some of the officers had to appear before the committee, I think I went with them, and so on. Towards the end, the committee wanted to see me by myself. That was an odd occurrence, to say the least, wasn't it?

Q: Yes, it was, indeed.

Mr. N.: Everybody had been in talking, now they wanted me to see them alone. So, what did I do? It was now in contract design. The plans were being made into contract plans, you see, and I decided that before I appeared before that board I'd better go to work and study the situation with regard to weights and the trim of that ship - or the ships, the two of them. I did all that work at home at night. I didn't do this work in the office, I'd work at night. My testimony before that board was all prepared at home. I studied it and I decided that the ship was trimming by the stern, and the thing that had to be done in those contract plans was to move all the internals forward at least two frame spaces, which would be eight feet. The center of gravity was too far aft, so you just take everything inside and move it forward, cut eight feet off the bow and stick it on the stern.

Now I had another scheme. My other scheme was that I was not going to appear before that board with my notes. I wouldn't go with any notes whatever, no books, no calculations, nothing.

Q: What was the reasoning back of that?

Mr. N.: Because I didn't want them to take these books and copy them. I was security-minded. I didn't care who this board was. Gibbs was on it and he was a naval architect and all that sort of thing, and Hovgaard. They would all have wanted to see how this thing was done, I'm sure - I was sure at the time.

So I appeared before them without a single piece of paper. I walked in, and I might have had just an empty pad. I wasn't head of the section yet, when I did all this. Bates didn't know that I was doing all this stuff at night, but I finally told him that the thing was kind of heavy by the stern and they'd better move all the things forward two frame spaces. I notified the contract plans people about that, too. Now they had to change all the frames and they blamed me for it.

I didn't mind being blamed for that because I'd much rather have the change on the paper than have a ship come out heavy by the stern.

And the other reason I wanted to do that was that I thought maybe the committee might have made this investigation and known it, because the contract design had been out of our hands for quite some time. So I investigated what the contract plans were up to before I went to see the board. It was 1936 now and I was working on it in 1933. In fact, I was working on it longer, because you notice before I mentioned that I was working on it, so I was getting to be quite expert on battleships.

I appeared before that board, and I'm pretty sure that Gibbs knew what I was up to because he'd dealt with me on the stability committee, but I answered all their questions. I wasn't stumped on any question whatever. I just guarded against the fact that if I had a notebook they would like to see how I did it. Naturally, they would want to take it and look at it, I felt. And, you know, it turned out later on that Gibbs did design a battleship for the Russians.

Q: Oh, he did?

Mr. N.: Yes. I didn't contribute to that, although we became great friends and I was his chief consultant from 1959 until about 1968, almost eight years.

Q: When did he design the battleship for the Russians?

Mr. N.: I don't know, about the same time.

Q: As this, in the thirties?

Mr. N.: Yes. However, I guarded against anything like that. And that brings up the point of the things that are appearing in your magazine.

Q: The *Proceedings*?

Mr. N.: In the *Proceedings*. I always took the stand that you give a research job out to a laboratory and you spend a lot of money to find out something, and the professors and all these people who are working in the laboratory as soon as the job is done they want to write a paper about it. I never would allow that, not with anything I had to do with. I stopped a paper that was written at Notre Dame by one of the engineering professors out there. He made up this paper. It had to do with ships' motions, submarines' motions, submerged motions. He made it all up from unclassified material that had been published in the United States. Now he put it all together in the paper, and I said now that he'd done this I was afraid that the Russians would get it because now that he'd put it all together they wouldn't have to do it.

The head professor at Notre Dame at that time, in engineering, was Schoenherr. Dr. Schoenherr was the dean of engineering at Notre Dame, and I'm sure - a professor always has to write a paper, you know - that he suggested that he write a paper like that. He did such a good job that I classified it. Now that's an odd thing, isn't it, but there is such a thing as putting all unclassified, isolated material together and it's getting too close to what we know about the motions of a submarine we were going to have maybe faster-running submerged bodies in these submarines, and I wasn't going to let it go.

Q: All the blocks begin to fit together!

Mr. N.: It was that sense that I had then when I came before the committee. I was fighting that battle of security.

It's just about this time, you'll find, that ships' data

books that they used to publish by public printers was stopped. I have a 1934 copy of it and I wish I had a later one. I think it was about this time that I managed to get people to do something about this, because they could pay fifty cents for this thing and find out all about our ships.

Q: What about Jane's Fighting Ships?

Mr. N.: Well, up to a certain point, you've got to be careful about that, too. But I think that it finally reaches a limit. I never was in too much favor about it. Once a ship is in existence, maybe it's all right because really we never found out anything. My objection was the Japanese potential enemy, or we were their potential enemy, whichever way you want to look at it, and I never could find out very much about what they were doing. They were very good at keeping their own stuff secret, very good, and so I felt that I didn't want them to know in the early days - in the later days, when this submarine thing that I just told you about happened, was after World War II.

About this time, the Morro Castle caught fire, going up the ocean coast, off Atlantic City somewhere, and I think about 130 people lost their lives on there.

Q: This was September 1934.

Mr. N.: Yes. Now I got involved again. You see, 1934 was only just about five years after I'd been over in this other thing, so I got involved in this thing.

One of my first involvements in this Morro Castle thing was that the steamboat inspection technical stuff was very bad, so I was designated as a person to go over there, put this other hat on, and reorganize the technical division of the steamboat inspection service.

Q: Before it became a part of the Coast Guard?

Mr. N.: That's right, yes.

I went over there, and I wrote to Webb and I wrote to M.I.T. and I wrote to Michigan, and I wanted to get to the top people among the young naval architects who were coming out. I got two from Michigan, two from Webb. I don't remember who I got from M.I.T., but the two particular people that I got from Webb were J. J. Henry and Charlie Murphy. Charlie Murphy became a rear admiral in the Coast Guard, and J. J. Henry is head of J. J. Henry, naval architects. I got them their first job. They didn't really know that because we sent a telegram up to Rock, and Rock, of course, called them in probably said; "I've got a job for you." I asked for the best he could get.

In the meantime, I had talked to the Civil Service about this thing and the trouble I was in. I had to get good people and have some inducement to get the good young people from the colleges. I prevailed upon the Civil Service to let me give anybody that I approved of one grade higher than the grade that was officially called for by the regulations. If they came in on the grade P 1, professional grades at that time, I could give them grade 2, so they would get more money, as though they had at least a year's experience. I was the only person who could do that in Washington. They left it up to me. If I put my initials on it, they'd get this extra higher grade.

That's where I got tied up with the Morro Castle. I did reorganize the technical duties over there and I brought in my friend Carol Roundy. The man who headed up the steamboat inspection was Hoover's brother, Hoover from the FBI. Now in my going around and checking on who all these people who were working there - I found one man sitting in a corner that no one would ever lead me up to. Finally, when I came back, I said:

"Tell me, who is that person in the corner that you never introduce me to."

"Well, he's a presidential appointee."

The next week when I came around he was transferred to another department. This stuff was going to wind up in the Senate of the United States, you see, where it wound up later on. But I never knew that man's name. They wouldn't tell me what his name was.

Q: And that was J. Edgar's brother?

Mr. N.: No, J. Edgar's brother was the head of steamboat inspection before the Morro Castle accident, but he was removed and now there was a new man who headed it. That's kind of a mix-up and a very interesting mix-up. And who was chief of the Bureao of Ships? Jerry Land. He was a good guy and he didn't mind anything I did about these things. He never even asked me what I was doing and I never had to report back to him. Very seldom did I have to report back to these people. They let me do what I wanted and then they wouldn't be responsible for it! All through their lives they finally learned that they never got in trouble.

Q: How did steamboat inspection get involved with the Morro Castle? As a result of that?

Mr. N.: Because this thing was supposed to be inspected by them and all that sort of thing, and the rules and regulations were so ridiculous. They did all kinds of things. They were really criminally liable in lots of things, according to the law, but they did everything by committee, so you'd have to look up the whole committee. But the committee would agree and there'd be a general approval, and you could never lock up a group like that. There'd be a difference of opinion.

For instance, one thing that they knew very accurately was the number of matches that a lifeboat should have - the exact number of matches. If it carried that many, it was legal.

Anyhow, I worked that out and then the next thing I knew I was on a committee and Rock was on it, and so on. I was on this committee to come up with Senate Report 184, which was approved by the Senate in 1936. Rock was the chairman, and I got my stability formula and other things into that report.

Q: Had the Senate conducted an investigation?

Mr. N.: Yes. Senator Copeland was the head of the committee –

Q: Royal Copeland.

Mr. N.: And we were doing our work for the Senate. I have a letterhead that says "U.S. Senate." Maybe you ought to stick that in my file.

Q: Did the Senate Committee conduct an investigation of the Morro Castle accident itself?

Mr. N.: Well, we in a way were doing it because we were coming out with new rules. We found out that the steamboat inspection was lax in its attention to these technical details. For instance, their fire drills, the training of the crew. One of the worst things that happened on that ship was the fact that the crew got a couple of boats over the side and they landed up here in Brigantine somewhere, on the beach, and they were mostly filled with crewmen. So there was the matter of seeing that their training was done properly, and the equipment wasn't in very good shape. Fires don't happen every day, so the valves don't work, other things don't work, or the pumps don't work.

As a matter of fact, the fire started in a writing room

or something like that and in a matter of a very little while they sent signals off to warn all the passengers. The crew went up forward and the passengers went aft, or something like that. Some of the signals didn't work, warning them, to wake them, you know, to come out. A lot of people lost their lives on that ship. There were a lot of things like that. There was a lot of talk that there was subversion involved in it. I don't know whether it was or not. Somebody could have left a cigarette.

I rode on the Queen Mary and you saw signs all over "No Smoking" below because it was full of wood. It had been waxed and polished and waxed and polished for many years. If it ever caught fire - well - the Queen Elizabeth caught fire and she was a goner.

Anyway, I got involved in that and that took up a lot of time, working on the regulations to govern the subdivision and stability, fire-resistance for merchant shipping. It had nothing to do with the Navy, in a way.

Q: Senate Report No. 184, was this enacted as a resolution of the Senate, or what?

Mr. N.: It became the law for steamboat inspection, and the Maritime Commission used it in building the merchant ships.

Q: I see.

Mr. N.: It became a regulation. It was more drastic than the 1929 convention. When we did this one we got things in it that later on were put into the later convention.

Q: As a result of that — I mean it was more drastic, you say, than the convention of 1929 — did other nations take similar action?

Mr. N.: No, they didn't have to. This was strictly for our own ships.

Q: Yes, but did they go and do likewise?

Mr. N.: No. Look what happened not so long after to the Andrea Doria, when she went down. Everybody's been trying to salvage her ever since. I told them the day she went down that they couldn't do that. It's obvious that you can't lift a ship like that.

Anyway, it wasn't very long after I got through with that 184, which in our own country was controversial all the time because they were fighting that battle about my stability formula. They still said that 05 should be the maximum that they could go to.

Q: You mean the shipping companies were concerned?

Mr. N.: No, naval architects. It was a judgment on my part. Professor Lewis from M.I.T. said that my reasoning was too obtuse!

Q: Not flexible enough!

Mr. N.: Well, I had formulas that I put in the paper — later on I wrote another paper in which I expanded on this sort of thing and I put this stuff in it again and assumed certain wave equations and put them all together. Frank M. Lewis was in the class ahead of me at Webb, so we knew each other. He said I was too obtuse. I didn't mind that, that's all right, as long as he read it. I was always thankful that he read it, otherwise he wouldn't have known it. Besides, it wasn't his specialty.

Oh, yes, I notice here "On further developments in stability and rolling of ships." I presented that before the Society of Naval Architects and Marine Engineers in November 1936.

Q: Was this something that you generated on your own, or were you requested to do it?

Mr. N.: I was asked to do the first paper and I think I got the idea that I wanted to make some changes in what I wrote two years before. I think I initiated this one. The first one, I think Rock was the president of the society and he asked me to do that, or the secretary would ask me.

Anyhow, now the time came, about 1936. As you notice, I still had to do all these things for the Navy ships, and yet here I keep talking about what I'm doing for the merchant marine, but that's the way it went.

I have a note here that says that on February 1st 1936 Jerry Land called me in and said he had another job for me. He wanted me to be a go-between between Gibbs and Cox and

Newport News. They were fighting a battle for the design of a new ship for the U.S. Lines, which finally became the *America*. Newport News thought that Gibbs and Cox' prismatic coefficient was too low. They wanted to design a ship full of body and so forth, and they never got together. Newport News wanted to design the *America*. They wanted to be able to say that they designed the ship and built it.

Q: So they were seizing on this issue?

Mr. N.: No. They could do it, they were pretty capable people. I knew Sid Vincent down there. He's the O5 fellow. And then Comstock, who was his assistant. I knew all these people.

Q: Yes, but was this at the root of the disagreement between Gibbs and Cox and Newport News?

Mr. N.: No. It seemed that they couldn't get together. They finally wrote a nice letter and they mentioned me in it. I've got a letter where they mentioned me about that Senate Report 184 - I was on that committee, and so forth.

They apparently got in touch with Jerry Land and he didn't tell me who asked him. He just wanted me to go up there and get these people together. He said:

"They're at loggerheads up there, Niedermair. You go up there and pull them together."

And so we talked about it and then, with that, he said: "I'm sitting here waiting for a telephone call." I said:

"What for?"

He said: "Well, I feel like a goldfish in a bowl with the water pumped out." I asked him why, and he said:

"I'm waiting for a telephone call to tell me that the Senate approved my appointment to the Maritime Commission," or whatever they called it at that time. That's what he was waiting for the day that he called me in.

I remember turning on my heels to start towards the door and before I stepped out I thought of something. I turned around and said to him:

"Is there any agenda to this?" Because, here, I was getting this and I thought that maybe he might have something he wanted me to do particularly, or not to do. He said:

"No, nothing, except don't have it built in a Navy yard."

Little did I know that he evidently knew then that these people up there, maybe it was Gibbs or U.S. Lines, had gotten the New York Navy Yard to make an estimate to build this ship in a Navy yard. I didn't know this. All Jerry said to me was, "Don't have it built in a Navy yard." He didn't tip me off that this had been done. I only found that out a couple of months ago when I was going through my notes. I hadn't even remembered it.

Q: How could it be built - it was a commercial liner, was it not?

Mr. N.: Yes.

Q: How then could it be built in a Navy yard?

Mr. N.: It could be.

Q: It could?

Mr. N.: Sure, because we subsidized those things.

Q: I see, and it was a potential troop carrier?

Mr. N.: Yes, it did. It did a great job. It became the West Point, I think. Yes, it was the West Point.

I got them together. I got up there and I stayed at the Waldorf Astoria. I'd come down every day. They paid my expenses up there. The first day, I got them in there and I put them both to work. I studied their material, and I decided either that day or the next day, that I was going to put them both to work, give them each a job to do. I had touched on something to find out and I put them to work. I've forgotten now just how he did this, but I did get Gibbs to work on something, and Newport News had to work on something, and they both had to report in the next day or so.

Q: You were the government arbiter?

Mr. N.: Yes, but it wasn't done by mail or anything. There's nothing on the official record that I know of. Jerry was the one who told me. The only restriction that I found out when I went through the data and the material was these weight estimates made by the New York Navy Yard. They didn't tell me when I was there, but the raw material they turned over to me had it in.

Q: If it had been built in the Navy yard this would have taken it out of the hands of Newport News?

Mr. N.: Yes, it would. New York state would have been tickled to death because it would have put people to work up there. This was in 1938, the depression years. You've got to remember that, too.

Anyhow, that's all Jerry said to me and off I went. The usual thing. They had no restrictions. I did my stuff and got them together, and I faced Newport News up with the fact that they were trying to fit that ship into their dry dock. Now, that's a hell of a way to design a big ocean liner. If you had a small dry dock and you would design a ship to fit a dry dock and the ship wants to be bigger or different, and it won't fit in, that's not the way to design a ship. You'd have to dock it somewhere else, wouldn't you?

Q: You mean they did not want to go to the expense of having a bigger dock?

Mr. N.: Well, I don't know what. But they actually designed the ship and increased their coefficient because the thing would fit better into their dry dock, where if they built it according to the Gibbs line, which was a lower prismatic coefficient because that would be less resistance and less fuel oil to drive it and so forth, it wouldn't go into the dry dock. I never checked up to see whether it would or not, but this is what they said. I did face them up with the fact. I said to Vincent:

"It looks to me like you were trying to fit this ship into your dry dock down there."

And he said yes, and I said:

"I think, really, what it's coming down to now is that you want to build this ship and Gibbs is designing it, I guess for U.S. Lines, that's another story. Now it's up to you two people to come to some kind of an agreement, and then have the ship built."

The next day I came in and they had agreed. Evidently, what I told Gibbs to do and what I told the Newport News people to do, they got together and decided not to fight each other any more.

Q: What was the solution?

Mr. N.: The solution was that they took the lines that Gibbs had.

Q: And what about the inadequate dry dock?

Mr. N.: They didn't build it in there. They built it on the ways. They didn't have to have a dry dock to build it. They launched it. They didn't have to build a dry dock.

Q: But they wanted to?

Mr. N.: They wanted to fit it into the dry dock. I guess they wanted it to come down and dock in there every once in a while, then they would definitely have the repair work. There are all kinds of reasons why people want to do things and they don't tell you all the reasons. But I sensed the fact that that was the difference and that wasn't a good way to make the lines. I caught them at it.

I put them together and I came back and I told Jerry that they were all happy and the ship would be built in Newport News. Fine, said Jerry. Gibbs designed it in the first place, anyway.

Q: How many millions were involved? Do you remember?

Mr. N.: I don't recall that. I guess maybe 40 million. That ship went in as a troop ship almost immediately, and it ran all during the war. Maybe it did fit into the dry dock, the way it turned out, but anyway it went back to Newport News when they went down there to convert it back to a passenger ship. They lifted the heads off the turbine engines and looked at the turbines, put the thing right back again and pulled them up. Not a thing had to be touched. They were perfect, and they'd run all through the war. Gas turbines cannot do that. They may run for maybe a year.

Q: Who had built the turbines?

Mr. N.: General Electric, I guess, but Newport News had to put them together down there.

That was a great thing in favor of our engine-builders, though.

So that's that story.

By April 1st 1937, Admiral Land retired shortly before his nomination to the Maritime Commission on February 1, 1938. You see, at the time I was in to see him and he was in the fish bowl, he wanted to be nominated to that post, I guess. But by 1938 he was out of it.

Q: The Maritime Commission was not created new at that point, was it?

Mr. N.: No. I don't know. All I know is that he thought he was going to be appointed back in 1936, you remember I told you, but apparently it didn't happen until one year later. It probably took that long to get through the Senate.

Now we're coming to a climactic point here because Bates resigned about March 1938 and he headed up the design division at the Maritime Commission. Jerry Land was there and Admiral Vickery was there, too.

Q: Vickery was the deputy, wasn't he?

Mr. N.: Yes, and he took Jimmy Bates with him. He wanted Jimmy over there. And now I was heading up the basic design, preliminary design.

Q: Who became chief of C & R after Land?

Mr. N.: I guess it was Dubose. Admiral Dubose became chief of C & R right during that period in '37 and '38 when Jerry was getting adjusted to go.

In the meantime, of course, we were doing a lot of work on airplane carriers, the 45,000-ton armored carriers. You remember those? The Midway and so on. The Midway design came in there. Chantry was the officer in charge of design, and I came up with the sloping armor there.

Q: Talk a little about that, sloping armor.

Mr. N.: That trajectory that I mentioned previously, we had determined that you can't arbitrarily with these high-angle guns - you see, before when you were fighting a battle like in the Civil War, you didn't have to worry about this trajectory under water because they were horizontal trajectories.

Q: The range was short, you mean?

Mr. N.: Yes, and now the battleship armor was only five or six feet below the waterline, but if you missed the ship short the shell would come down and have a trajectory under water, and it could go through the ship below the armor. To my surprise, when I took this matter up with Ordnance at the time, they didn't have any information about this, except for a 5-

inch shell. Because of the gradual change in the trajectory of these guns, they began to shoot at higher angles, so they'd get a longer range. And then you would get what they call plunging fire through the decks.

Anyhow, we were still working on this carrier during that period, and Chantry was very intrigued. He really sat down at the drafting board, working with our people in preliminary design working up this Midway carrier.

Q: What new ideas were being incorporated into the new designs?

Mr. N.: He was the one who wanted the boilers to be moved outboard, and we didn't have torpedo protection of any consequence in there. We had some. But he thought if you put the boilers outboard you were getting extra spaces in there, and another longitudinal bulkhead, in your regular engine room - you don't have this longitudinal bulkhead. So he put the boilers outboard, and the machinery then would be inside this other inboard bulkhead. This is the way those ships were designed.

Q: Was that greater protection?

Mr. N.: Yes, against an underwater hit, torpedoes and so on. It would furnish a certain amount of added protection. And the deck was also thicker. It had heavy armor on the deck. I've forgotten just how much armor we put on there. It had side armor and it had a very heavy flight deck.

Q: Was there a new concept on arresting gear?

Mr. N.: A certain amount of arresting gear was getting in there because the planes were getting heavier and they had to work on that quite hard. They started about that time. They really didn't have it yet. In fact, they were continually working on arresting gear all the way up to the Forrestal, because planes got heavier and heavier, and the angled deck got in there.

Q: That came from the British, didn't it?

Mr. N.: Yes, the British thought they did, but that's not altogether true. They really got it from us because when we designed the United States we had an angled deck on there, and our Bureau of Aeronautics missed the point. We had an angled deck on the offside of the island to let the fighters go off independent of the bombers. We had one angled deck where the fighter planes could go off, just fly off, and then had the catapults down the center.

I think the British saw that and they decided that you could land on an angle, too. They just flipped it over 180 degrees and now they had the angled deck, but we really had that on the United States. The United States had other things, too, that got in there, but I remember working on that angled deck, but we didn't sense the idea that you could land at an angle like that.

Q: So that was original with the British?

Mr. N.: Well, also we were in another box and that had to do with the control of the planes as they flew off at the bow. The Bureau of Aeronautics wouldn't allow us to fill in the ship forward. It didn't make sense to have that flight deck going all the way forward and then supporting it on columns. Later on, some of the Essex-class columns were knocked loose by the waves and the flight deck collapsed forward, and the bow was filled in. The reason why we had to leave the structure open below the flight deck forward was that the air flow forward was interfered with by filling in the bow. It would create a low pressure forward of the bow, where the air would be parting company around the hull. And so, afterwards when catapults became improved, and the British came up with the steam catapult. That was their idea, I remember that, and that changed all this to a certain extent, because then when you shot the planes off they had enough velocity to get passed the bow and you could close the bow in.

Diehl was in Aeronautics at that time and I think he went along with that idea, too, that they had to have the clean flow, especially when the little planes were taking off in the old days. But they started getting bigger and bigger on the Essex, which we'll talk about at some later time.

Q: In the Midway design, was there any change in elevator structure or location?

Mr. N.: Not particularly, no. We still had the inside elevators, cut big holes in the deck. The angled deck didn't come in until later on. The Essex class had the first angled decks.

That angled deck, really, was promoted by a friend of mine named Ferris. He was the one who kept pushing everybody into an angled deck. They don't have his name tied to it. I don't have his name here but I will find it for you.

Q: You mentioned him once before.

Mr. N.: Did I? He was really the fellow who kept coming in with this design part of it. He was a very good structural man.

Just about this time, Dubose got in. He was now chief of the bureau. Chantry got through and we got through with the Midway. The Midway was rather an unfortunate design because it was a very big carrier and we tried to make it protected and all that, but it wasn't the kind of a ship you could bring out in mass production, like you could the Essex. It was ahead of its time, really. After that, other things changed and that design didn't become very popular.

I had a lot to do with the Essex and I see in your last publication they give the Essex a big salute. I was glad to see that, although the design isn't mentioned. It simply says it's very good. And that brings one thing up about designs.

When you design it wrong, you never can correct it

afterwards. It has to be a good design and that lends itself to a long life, a useful life, because we didn't have to use ersatz ballast, as my friend Rigg called the ballast they had to put into the Manhattan and Washington, you know, in those merchant ships. You built it to the philosophy that you used for that design. I'll get to that later.

Q: Well, they might well praise the Essex because I think the Essex class had a lot to do with victory in the Pacific?

Mr. N.: Yes, but those nine cruiser conversions also did their bit. You go and read the history. They were about all you had. When you read the history of all these ships, you'd think I was on all of them. I have in that little bunch of stuff over there at the New York yard all the battleships I worked on, the West Virginia, and Idaho, and there were several others that came in, and all the cruisers. The Tennessee, the New Mexico. I thought at one time I was the only person alive that had entered every compartment on the ship in one day or two days, not quite that.

Now we're going to get ready here for the battle between two chiefs, the chief of the Bureau of C & R and Admiral Bowen, chief of the Bureau of Engineering.

Up to this time the Bureau of C & R always had strong chiefs, and so what happened, appropriations on the Hill and everything were handled by the chief of the Bureau of C & R. For years that happened. Taylor was a very well-known chief.

He was the chief of the Bureau of C & R during World War I and he was the sort of person who would have a team pulling a load. He'd keep the traces tight but the reins loose. From Taylor all the way down to and through Jerry Land, they were all people who could appear before Congress and all and really pound the table and so on, and people would like it.

Now Debose was unfortunate in having Bowen who wanted to do that in the Bureau of Engineering. He didn't want to be passive, he wanted to be top dog. And so it happened that at that point there was public debate about the stability of destroyers. Their center of gravity had gone up, and blame was being handed out right and left and argued about in newspapers, whose fault that was.

Q: Was there an incident that caused this to arise?

Mr. N.: Yes. This ship was built and the destroyer had its center of gravity go up. The truth of the matter was that the Bureau of C & R was not at fault at all. I took this matter up with Chantry. There came the day when now the chips were down. Debose was going to be taken out of the Bureau of Ships and Van Kueren was going to step in. I think that's the way it went. Yes.

Chantry and I one Saturday afternoon were left. We had to write a triple bureau letter, Bureau of Ordnance, Bureau of Engineering, and Bureau of C & R. It came time to draft the letter and say why the stability, the center of gravity, went up. So the two of us were there, working out the letter, dictating back and forth. He did most of the dictating.

Q: To whom was this to be addressed?

Mr. N.: It was being addressed to the Secretary of the Navy. Charlie Edison was the Secretary of the Navy.

We were writing along and explaining all this sort of thing when I said to Chantry:

Chantry was now being transferred to Philadelphia. Bowen was staying where he was and Ordnance Chief was staying where he was, and our people in the Bureau of C & R were being transferred or quit, like Dubose. And I said, "It's really not our fault at all. I know where the fault lies. I checked it up. The fault is that the ordnance weights went up and the early estimates for the machinery had their center of gravity too low, even though that center of gravity is below the waterline. When you move that center of gravity up, it moves the center of gravity of the whole ship up, and the ordnance went up, so the whole lost vertical center of gravity is caused by engineering and the Bureau of Ordnance."

Chantry said:

"Now, look, John, let's not get into this. I'm leaving. Really there's more to this than this little talk about where the center of gravity is."

Q: He meant politics?

Mr. N.: Yes. Alan Chantry said that to me. He's gone now.

He later on made rear admiral at the Philadelphia yard. That's what he told me, "Let's not bring it up."

I said: "But I don't feel good about it when I see you going and all these -" Chantry was such a brilliant person. I met him later on at the Philadelphia yard and he was very happy there, but I wasn't very happy at what had happened.

That was the story. They moved out. Van Kueren became the chief of the bureau, and the two bureaus were not being combined.

Q: Let me ask you one question to continue the center of gravity idea, the basis of the argument. You say the ordnance was moved up -

Mr. N.: Their weights were heavier. Their weights were high and they were heavy, so the center of gravity. The moment of those weights above a certain point moved the center of gravity.

Q: Why were they heavier?

Mr. N.: Because it just so happened that the things that they put up there were heavier than they originally said they would weigh. When they put them up there, they were heavier.

Q: They were adding something else, then?

Mr. N.: No, they just didn't estimate their weights right.

Q: Oh, I see.

Mr. N.: The weights were more than they had said they would be.

Q: That was the issue as publicized?

Mr. N.: Publicly they said the stability was bad. I was hoping I might be called up before Congress because I was going to go before them and tell them that they weren't qualified to judge that technical matter and that we were as pure as Ivory soap. That's the way I was going to put it, 98 per cent pure, or whatever Ivory soap said. But I never had the chance.

Q: And you did discover that politics were involved?

Mr. N.: Chantry said to me, and I did find later on, but Bowen became a good friend of mine later. I have somewhere a book he autographed for me. He and Kettering from General Motors wrote a book and I praised that book one time when I was at a meeting, and he was so happy that the next thing I knew I got a copy of the book in the mail and he thanked me and it had his autograph.

Q: Tell me what was involved as the idea went forward to amalgamate the two bureaus.

Mr. N.: Well, they thought it would work better that way, to combine the two bureaus, to have one head of the two and then have assistant chiefs. They alternated the chiefs of the bureau.

Q: It changed the status of the naval architect, didn't it?

Mr. N.: The engineering officers felt second best all the time with the situation before and the machinery almost cost as much as the ship sometimes. But I never had any trouble with any of those people from engineering. I always knew almost before they knew what the weight was going to be. I could tell them the horsepower, the number of propellers, the diameter of the propellers - I would give them all that information because I also had to figure out the resistance and I practically decided what the machinery was going to be. I knew it would be steam. I kept track of all that.

I remember one day when Captain Logan McKee was head of design and he called up and gave me the weight of some cruiser machinery and I said:

"Have you got a margin in these weights?" He said, "No, I'll go and see my people and find out. I'll call you back." So he comes back a little later and says: "No, no margin." I said, "I thought so." And Logan said:

"John, why do you want us to do all this figuring and then you ask me have we got a margin and you know we don't have a margin when we give you a figure?"

I said, "I ask you to do it so the next time I get a job I know what it is. Then I can guess the next step. Costs the same way."

I'd hear them talking about the designed cost. I

designed to the cost all the time. I could make the cost estimates and had the curves and everything else in my files, and I'd make them up based on the costs of previous ships. Cost estimators would work it up, but I knew what the cost was going to be, and I'd give them hell too, and often would tell them, "You can't build it for that much. It will cost you more money."

I was doing that when they built the Mohole project down in Houston. I knew damned well those fellows were low on their cost estimates.

There was quite a bit of controversy about the Bureau amalgamation. Some people were in favor of it and some were against it. I was swayed to a certain extent in favor of it because I felt a lot of our good construction officers were being held back by their promotion system that existed under the existing staff officer position. Probably some of the best people that I met in the Navy were oldtime construction people.

Q: Some of the smartest ones, weren't they?

Mr. N.: They were all the heads of their class and all that sort of thing. Van Kueren was a particularly close friend of mine. Now Cochrane and Mills were the working team, the two guys who had to put the thing together. They were the underdogs. They were both captains.

Q: Captain Earl Mills?

Mr. N.: Yes, and Captain Ned Cochrane. They had to work for

the Secretary of the Navy.

Admiral "Mike" Robinson was a former chief of the Bureau of Engineering. He'd been retired for quite some time and he was called back into the bureau when this happened. It looked like the war was coming and that had something to do with it. He was the head of the committee, really, and Captain Cochrane and Captain Earl Mills were his assistants. I had never met Robinson for a long time after this happened, so I didn't know what kind of a person he was, but I was told by Bates and other people what a fine design officer Robinson was. He was one of the few engineering officers that they talked about as being a good design officer.

Q: What was the task of this committee?

Mr. N.: This committee was organized to bring the two together. That meant there would be certain supervisory positions that might be competing with each other, and there would be consolidations all down the line. They had come to me quite a while before when they were getting ready to do all this thing. They came to me and tipped me off that I didn't have a thing to worry about. They said Charlie Edison gave the group clear go but he said, "Don't touch Niedermair." I don't know whether we should put this in, but this is what they said.

I had not much contact with Edison but apparently he knew about me. Of course, he would know my record of why I got there, too, I guess. Maybe that had some influence, but he did tell them. I guess he told them that because he didn't want them to go dilly-dallying around. They had to have good reasons why they'd do things like that.

Q: I take it that Edison was very much in favor of this whole process?

Mr. N.: Yes, he was, and he was a good friend of Bowen, actually, as it turned out. Bowen impressed him quite a bit, and he was quite an active guy in lots of ways.

Anyhow, there was a lot of back and forth. As I said before, a lot of good officers - I remember Heberle. At the end of World War I he was a commander and I think by the time World War II came around he was just a captain. That was as far as he ever got - as far as he could get. Or maybe he was a commander and didn't get to be a captain until this bureau was combined. I don't know, but I remember that the war was on and a lot of people got higher rank, but Heberle didn't get it. After all these years he was still in that one single rank.

Q: Did this mean that there was a great deal of attrition? I mean men went out into private -

Mr. N.: Yes. I think a lot of good young people left because there wasn't any progress for them. And, as a matter of fact, their pay was low. I remember when Ernie King became fleet admiral he had $8,000 a year, believe it or not. Somewhere I have a note on this, because I was surprised, because by this time I got more than that.

Now, I have a note here that Julius Furer told me that he didn't favor the consolidation. Furer was one of the old-time rear admirals who was a real great officer and he worked with the historian, Morison, and so on in working up the history. Furer used to come to me and discuss these things with me, and asked me what I thought about the thing. I told him just like I told you that there were some things in favor of it. I don't think they have to change their staff position to do better. They should rearrange this thing so that promotion can happen to staff officers. But they apparently decided they couldn't do that because they couldn't become commandants of the yards, commander of a shipyard, and so on, which they did. I don't know what they do now.

I talked to Van Kueren. We were very close on this matter and other matters because I knew Van a long time and he knew me very well. I think I met him in New York, I'm not sure. Before he came on this job here, back in the bureau, he was head of the naval research across the river up there, and they were working on radar. They noticed the phenomena of radar but they hadn't gotten along with the use of it like the British did.

So they went ahead and they got reorganized, and for a little while Mike Robinson was chief of the bureau.

Q: Just to get it going?

Mr. N.: For a little while, yes. After that Ned Cochrane became the chief of the bureau. We're getting closer to the war now.

Q: Did the amalgamation work smoothly at that point?

Mr. N.: Yes, it seemed to. It worked in the beginning all right because the same quality of people were still running the show, actually. There were people like Charlie Brand. Charlie Brand, to my mind, was one of the greats. He became a rear admiral in charge of the Boston shipyard. He came to the bureau, and I met him when I was getting ready with certain stuff on landing craft and so on. I will mention that later on.

About this time the Essex started to be born, about 1939 to 1940. We've talked about the Essex. The design of that carrier got into the picture. The Cleveland-class cruisers were getting into the picture. We first attempted to use all the plans for the Brooklyns in the Cleveland class, but we decided very quickly that that wouldn't work. We'd better develop new plans because in lots of cases you needed a little more room and so on. It was a good thing because it made them better ships for carrier use.

Q: I take it there was feed-in when the plans were being developed from the operational fleet?

Mr. N.: To a certain extent, but not too much. There really wasn't not yet, no. There was no war on. Nobody was dreaming about these things yet, but fortunately we got the Essex going before the war was on. I had to do quite a number of odd things in these ships.

In the first place, the flight deck was all designed and I remember talking to Captain Les Kniskern, who was our design officer, and a real great friend of mine. Some people had gotten together and sent somebody to relieve me if anything happened to me. And so Pat Ryan came down to be my backup from the New York yard. He was standing there at the drafting board, Kniskern was at the drafting board, we were looking at it. Kniskern had just come over to tell me that the weight of the planes had been increased. The plane that was going to be put on the ship was heavier than the one that we designed the flight deck for.

Q: A new type plane coming in, I suppose?

Mr. N.: Yes, something or other. I pondered that for quite a while. I looked down and then I walked away from them - or, they told me later I did. I walked down to the end of the room with my head down, and I came back to Pat Ryan and Kniskern and I said:

"We'll change the steel to high-tensile steel," which would change the strength of the steel by 20 per cent, or whatever it was. From 60,000 to 80,000. So we made the deck high-tensile steel, and that took care of that without adding any weight.

Then I ran into trouble because they couldn't weld - the strength deck which was the hangar deck. We still had expansion joints in the flight deck. Now the question was what to do, because it had to be about two inches thick for this big ship, just for the strength. So I decided that it was really pretty thick stuff to try to weld, and also pretty thick to rivet. But I wanted to weld it. I got the idea that the thing to do was to put two layers of one-inch plating on it. You'd alternate the butts (the transverse ends), you would weld them, then put the next. You'd finish the bottom layer and you'd put it all on, weld it all up, and then you come in and lay the top - another inch on the top. You put holes in the top layer, and you fill up the holes with welding material and weld the butts alternately. You wouldn't put the top butts over the bottom butts. You'd just keep skipping them.

Q: And that would be equally strong, would it?

Mr. N.: We did that, and that was it. We never had any trouble with that.

Some of the _Essex_ ships were built in the New York Yard, so was the _Franklin_, I think. We had designed the _Essex_ class from the bottom up.

Q: You had discarded the design for the _Midway_? I mean you didn't use them?

Mr. N.: No, no. They couldn't fit this thing at all. The displacement of this ship was about 27,900 tons, the standard displacement, I think. Her standard displacement was 27,100, not 45,000, and you can see the big difference. They were a great success out there during the war, and you could build them in quite a short time. Some of these Essex ships were built in twenty months or something like that. This was one of the big things. Also, all this armor and everything else indicated that. You can't build that sort of ship in a hurry.

The horsepower was a lot less, too. I think the horsepower of the Essex was way down. The Midway had a horsepower that was quite high. It was probably something like 200,000. Here it is. The Midway's horsepower around 200,000, standard displacement about 45,000. Essex had 27,100 standard and the horsepower was 150,000. And the length of these ships - I don't remember now how long the Coral Sea was, but she was about 900 feet long. Well, the overall length of the Essex was almost 900 feet, 890 feet. So you got almost as long a flight deck, and that's why everybody was so happy with this ship.

Q: Yes.

Mr. N.: These numbers that I throw together here at one time and another, the Midway. Yes, oddly enough, the Midway with all its weight was only 968 overall. It was just about 90 feet longer than the Essex. Now the beam of the ship was another thing that you had to worry about. The beam of the Essex was quite a bit less again. Her beam was 93 feet and the Midway was about 136 feet. With a monster like that you couldn't build her in a hurry.

I don't know how far you want to go with this but I think maybe we ought to hold it.

On the Essex they really did a great job, and one of the problems that they ran into was the kamikaze situation. I think they invented the kamikaze to get these Essex myself.

Q: The Japanese did!

Mr. N.: The Japs really knew that they were finished. They had a few carriers. They were ahead of us for a little while, but it's amazing how we got in there. If we hadn't had this design of the Essex timed the way it was, you would never have been able to get all these carriers out there. The whole Cleveland class would have been airplane carriers. They did a good job but they certainly couldn't have done it like the Essex class. The Essex had a real weakness where the ready rooms were, up under the flight deck.

Q: And that's where there were some casualties.

Mr. N.: Yes. I went to New York to look at the Franklin. She got hit by a kamikaze and they couldn't get out of the place, couldn't get out of the ready room.

Q: Ship designers in the U.S. could not have anticipated the kamikaze?

Mr. N.: No. I think there was an error in their arrangement. The one thing in preliminary design we can't do - do all these things and take care of little things like doorways, exit doors, and so on. You would depend on your field people to take care of things like that. Those are everyday things, but actually I came across a funny thing about this door business, because I think on the <u>Franklin</u>, as I went on it, I believe that I discovered there was only one exit from that ready room. I never went back. I had no time to go back and check on it, but I was quite upset about the fact that the ready room only had one way out. That was the only thing I could find. I never checked up to see whether that was so.

But you know, some people I know built a $100,000 place up near Leesburg, where they bought a house that was ready cut. It would be delivered and they'd just put it together by some big company. But there was no way to get in the bathroom! There was no door there. They forgot to put the door on. When they put the thing together, no door.

I understand that's what happened down in Brazil when the architects built one of the buildings down there some place. They had restrooms but you couldn't get in them.

Q: This was Brasilia?

Mr. N.: Was that it? You can't blame the naval architects all the time. It isn't funny, though, when people lose their lives like that.

Q: No.

Mr. N.: When it came to the next class that I got involved in, which was the Forrestal -

Q: Yes, but by that time there was feed-in from the operational boys?

Mr. N.: Right, but surprisingly it's not always fed in. To mention a point ahead of time that I'll mention later, when I got into the design I decided that I'd better start putting an escalator into the ship. The Forrestal had an escalator. I put that in there primarily so that the ready rooms could be below the hangar deck, and when the flight crews came up they would come out down below the hangar deck, or at the hangar deck, and they could walk over and ride up the escalator. I think they've come up with a faster way of doing it, but I put an up and a down escalator in there, as I remember it, on the starboard side. I just put it in. Nobody asked for it. But when I put it in nobody took it out. I went down and rode on it myself and I decided it was too slow. So you just have to plan a little ahead of time, but it's better than being directly under the flight deck with a kamikaze.

Here we are talking about the Essex but the Cleveland-class design got in here and just about 1940 or so we finished the Cleveland class. I remember trying to make them all out of the old plans, and, gee whizz, we had trouble with the machinery spaces. The machinery was the same as in the Brooklyns, but we did change the hull form. We fixed it up so the Cleveland class was thought of just in good time so that we were able to get the Princeton and those things out by 1942.

Q: One last question for today. With the development of the Essex class and the Cleveland class, was there any indication that FDR himself was interested in these new designs?

Mr. N.: No. What FDR would do was go on a cruiser and then make sketches about how to modify the cruiser. He would then say, gee, why don't we put a flight deck here, and he'd make sketches. I'd several times want to keep the sketches. Jerry would bring them down and let me look at them, but he held them close to his stomach.

Anyway, the Cleveland class came in and the Fletcher class came in just about that time. They were 2,100-ton destroyers.

Q: They were sort of destroyer leaders, weren't they?

Mr. N.: Yes, they were very, very good. We got into this class before the war. The 445 was the lead for all these things and the continuous flush deck and no portholes, by the way, were on the side. I told you a long time ago about my interest in portholes.

Q: Yes.

Mr. N.: You'd be surprised at all the people who claimed that they were the ones who didn't want them.

Q: They had foreseen the problem!

Interview No. 4 with Mr. John C. Niedermair
Place: His residence in Stone Harbor, New Jersey
Date: Tuesday afternoon, 9 December 1975
Subject: Biography
By: John T. Mason, Jr.

Q: Well, John, it's delightful to see you again on a winter day, this time, because it is that.

Last time, you talked about the Essex-class carriers in great detail and your contribution to the Essex class. Now you have various things to add before we launch into the war period itself.

Mr. N.: Yes, that is right. I want to take a flashback on a few of the important things that were worked on before the Essex class got into the picture.

There was a considerable interest in PT boats and submarine chasers as soon as Franklin Delano Roosevelt got into the White House. He brought Starling Burgess in to our group for a while in case he had any input because he was the designer of the yacht that competed with Sir Thomas Lipton's Shamrock and so on. FDR, being quite a sailor, felt that anyone that could design a boat to beat this British boat might be of some help to us.

Q: Was Burgess in uniform?

Mr. N.: No, he was not. He was a civilian. He was a difficult man in lots of ways because he didn't like to work in the office with other people. He liked to take things back home or to the hotel with him, and his wife would make all the calculations and so on there. He was particularly concerned with working on the submarine chaser boats - the 110-foot submarine chasers - for which we did make up some designs, and he tried to compete with us in designing a better submarine chaser than we did. But he was soon phased out of our section because he didn't stay with us and he didn't gather some of the important things that we would consider in connection with the design of a war vessel. However, he did get in with FDR's uncle later on.

Q: Delano?

Mr. N.: Delano - in designing and working on what they called the bridge across the Atlantic. This is what they tried, and they brought the design in for my criticism. This carried on for quite a long time because there were several years between the time that Starling Burgess had worked on the submarine chaser and this bridge across the Atlantic.

Q: Tell me about this proposed bridge across the Atlantic.

Mr. N.: Starling Burgess came up with quite a few radical ideas. He attempted to provide a power plant by using a sort of exaggerated motor based on an outboard motor that was placed into wells that he had put into this ship. He also worked on some odd ideas in connection with the steering of the ship, and the end result was that Starling Burgess had ignored all the evolution, as far as I was concerned, anyway, of where merchant ship design stood after all the years of its development up to that time.

Q: This was a merchant ship he was working on?

Mr. N.: Yes.

Q: High-speed, I take it?

Mr. N.: He tried to come up - and he did - with these ideas, and they built one or two of them down in Texas.

Q: What speed were they?

Mr. N.: Oh, I've forgotten now. They weren't very fast. Maybe in the neighborhood of 15 knots or something like that - maybe less. My recall isn't good on that.

Q: What was the principal virtue, then, of this?

Mr. N.: Well, this is what happened. Since he had not paid any attention to what had happened in the design of merchant ships up to this time, the result was that when they launched the ship and it went on its first trials, it turned out to be almost a complete failure. Franklin Delano Roosevelt's friend was in the bureau, Loring Swasey.

Q: Was he a civilian also?

Mr. N.: He was a captain in the reserve. He was a person who had a lot to do with the design of the original World War I submarine chaser. The 110-footers were very successful. But Loring Swasey's partner, who was in business with him, was the designer really of the submarine chaser as far as the hull form went, but they were yacht-builders and so they worked it out together as kind of a team. And now Swasey came back and handled small craft. He became a friend of FDR because he was at M.I.T. when FDR was at Harvard, and he designed a racing shell for Harvard that was so successful - Swasey did.

So now Swasey came to me and told me that now that this Delano bridge across the sea had turned out so badly - I had turned it down before they did anything with it - Swasey told me that FDR - these were Swasey's own words: "FDR asked me to come over and talk to you and find out whether you could do anything about this Delano vessel."

Delano was a banker in New York. I said no, I couldn't do anything about it.

Q: The Delano vessel was the merchant one they were building?

Mr. N.: The one that was to become the bridge across the sea.

Q: I don't understand the bridge across the sea. What was it?

Mr. N.: Well, they were going to build so many of them and build them so fast and it almost would be a bridge across the ocean. It was a fantasy, you might say.

So, Swasey brought in a lot of other friends of his and he tried every which way to get me interested in helping them out if I could, and I finally had to tell them that no matter how hard they tried I couldn't help them with this vessel. So it became a complete failure.

Q: What did you find wrong with this vessel?

Mr. N.: It couldn't steer properly. This idea of using outboard motors in these tubes lined up inside the vessel, you could raise and lower them and they were located in four places in the ship. There were so many things that were not in line with good ship design.

Q: What tonnage was this?

Mr. N.: It wasn't very big. I've forgotten now - probably several thousand tons. But the main point was that Swasey and FDR thought that I could help them out, but I couldn't do it, so that was the last I ever heard of Starling Burgess. I knew his brother very well, who was in the Bureau of Aeronautics and was a pretty sharp fellow. It was too bad that I couldn't help them, but I just couldn't do it, so that was the end of that story.

However, at the same time, we got into the design of PT

boats, motor torpedo boats, and in investigating them one thing led to another and it was finally decided that we would have a design competition to find out what the industry would have to offer, and so we made up a set of specifications for two types of motor torpedo boat. One a small size, maybe somewhere around 50-feet long, and then another one 60, 70, or 80 feet long.

As a result of that competition, Professor George Crouch, who was my professor in naval architecture at Webb, designed a small PT boat, and Higgins was the award-winner on the big PT boat.

Q: Higgins from New Orleans?

Mr. N.: Yes. Higgins won the prize, and the prize was quite sizeable. I think we awarded them a sizeable prize of some $25,000 or $50,000, or something of that sort.

Q: Was this from Navy funds?

Mr. N.: Yes.

Q: What year approximately was this?

Mr. N.: I would say somewhere around 1936 or 1938. It was before the war. We weren't in the war yet. By the time the war came along, we had the PT program pretty well settled.

Q: Let me ask you a question at that point. Was the program

ever modified or changed because of the performance of the German E-boat?

Mr. N.: No, it was not. Scott-Paine, a British designer, had developed a very successful PT boat, and Sutphen and his son, from Electric Boat Company, were in Bayone at that time and they got the American rights to build the Scott-Paine boat.

Q: The British called them MTBs. Motor torpedo boats.

Mr. N.: I imagine so.

The small design that Crouch developed didn't turn out that we could use this small vessel to do the things we wanted to do. We tried to keep it down and find out what the small one could do, but we soon settled down to make the PT boats about the size of the Scott-Paine boat.

Q: What were the intended usages?

Mr. N.: They carried torpedoes on them and they were to patrol the coastal waters. Kennedy was on PT-109. They would run along the coast for coastal protection.

Q: And what kind of speed did they have?

Mr. N.: They had a speed running up sometimes as much as probably 50 knots, pretty good speed. In the meantime, we had the model basin working on these different hull forms - the Taylor Model Basin, and we had the Stevens Institute of Technology, which had an experimental towing tank, working on the theoretical part in connection with the best forms for a PT boat.

This report that I have in my hand here was EMB, Experimental Model Basin, Series 50, which was for V-bottom motor boats, and there were twenty of them tested. They had resistance curves something along the line of Admiral Taylor's resistance and propulsion curves, contours of total resistance, and plotted them out on various speed/length ratios and displacement/length ratios, and so on. So we did enter into this PT boat program.

We had a small boat section in the bureau, but they didn't handle this because this was more sophisticated than a small motor boat. These were very-high-speed boats that had plenty of horsepower and so on.

Q: Was Swasey involved in these?

Mr. N.: Swasey was the type desk that handled these.

Q: How large a program was contemplated? How many did you intend to turn out?

Mr. N.: President Kennedy was on the 109 and I imagine that we got up to some pretty high numbers - say 500 or more of these boats.

We kept them even after the war and developed aluminum - we were building PT boats out of aluminum. The idea of having these small boats around that could get out there and protect your coast. But I believe that has fallen by the wayside with the modern things that have happened.

That I should say gives you some idea of how we entered the war in connection with PT boats, and, of course, Jack Kennedy made PT boats pretty famous because he rescued some people when the Japanese destroyer ran him down or somehow or other wrecked his PT boat. He did some very great work in helping to rescue his crew.

Then, the war had started over in England and in Europe and a demand came along for a wooden minesweeper, a minesweeper that could stand the shock of the mines. It had to be built of wood because they attempted to make them safe against magnetic mines, mines that would be influenced by metal, because the influence on these mines if you had a metal ship the magnetic field would be concentrated in the metal ship, and that concentration of the magnetic lines would set the mine off.

Q: Was this as a result of British experience?

Mr. N.: Somewhat, but we knew about this before the British. This is what I'll tell you here.

Captain Cochrane and Lieutenant Forrest were over in England during the blitz, going over the design organization of British construction and all the material and information about what their ships were like. Captain Cochrane came back with a wooden minesweeper that the British had developed.

In the meantime, while he was away, I had come up with this minesweeper that I developed.

Q: A wooden one, also?

Mr. N.: Yes. In order to make it sturdy, I had to come with a new idea of how to build the frames for that design, because you had to have bent oak frames. You couldn't bend a 4-by-4 oak satisfactorily because when you would bend it in a steam box the inside of the curve would be in compression and the wood would be weakened that way, and the outside was in tension. So between the two of them it would work against you in trying to bend this big thing.

Q: It bent, but it wasn't very practical when it was bent.

Mr. N.: So I came up with the idea of making the frames out of two 2-by-4s back to back - bend a 2-by-4, which you could do.

Q: Of what wood?

Mr. N.: Of oak - and lay them together, glue them or fasten them together. This was before the days of laminated wood and the gluing of wood.

Q: Why wouldn't you with 2-by-4s have the strain and the weakness, also?

Mr. N.: No, because the depth was less. The horizontal

dimension was four inches and the vertical dimension was only 2 inches, and the curve, of course, that we gave the boat favored the curves not being too small. They made a good Mae West shape on her.

About the time that Cochrane came back on the <u>King George V</u> into Annapolis and he brought in all the plans of the British design, including their details concerning their design organization, the make-up of their construction corps and how they did their work. That was all brought from Annapolis into preliminary design. It was stored in preliminary design because we were under lock and key. They had me in a cubbyhole there.

Q: Under lock and key!

Mr. N.: Yes, well, we were not a big group. We were a group of top engineers and when we would need extra help we'd borrow it from other parts of the bureau or bring in people from the Navy yard to work on it.

Then Cochrane came in with a roll of these plans of the British design under his arm and told me what he had, and I said:

"Well, Captain, we developed a wooden minesweeper while you were away. You know what's in this English wooden minesweeper, so to save time why don't you look at our minesweeper, and if you like our minesweeper, we don't have to look at the British minesweeper."

So Cochrane went over and examined our design, the one

where I had developed a special wood framing and structure and he was thoroughly pleased with it. He walked away with the British plans under his arm and I never did see them. So we'd saved time.

Q: Theirs were not in being yet, either? They were just planned?

Mr. N.: They were plans but they were designed according to the old-fashioned way of building a wooden ship. It was put together with partial frames and so on. You see when you had to double a 2-by-4 type of frame, when you crossed the keel amidships, part of that inside frame could ride over the keel blocks and you could widen the space between the frame, which would be close together as you went up the side, and it would widen out as you came down, and we'd fill it in with a spacer, so that you had a good, solid structure of good oak.

There's a booklet out on the wooden boats where they refer to this design that I got up at the time as being the most advanced type of wooden construction.

Q: What tonnage was this minesweeper intended to be?

Mr. N.: I've forgotten now what their tonnage was. I could add those numbers for you later on in this text. I can look it up if I have the data. But just a few hundred tons.

These minesweepers were used in Italy and in the early hitting of the underbelly of Europe those minesweepers were over there.

Q: They were easy to turn out, then?

Mr. N.: Yes, they were.

Q: Who built them?

Mr. N.: Different yards. They would be built up in all the little yacht-building yards. Luders, for instance, up on Long Island Sound, would do it. They could build them over in Annapolis.

Q: And then were they convoyed across the ocean?

Mr. N.: I suppose so. I don't know, but they got over there. They were fairly big boats. They were about 135 feet long.

Q: That was the intent of my question.

Mr. N.: Yes, they were rather big. When we got into gluing these things up, we could make these wooden boats longer, and the next class of minesweepers were bigger. That was the post-war type.

These minesweepers got over there, into the Anzio landings, and I saw a dispatch that was sent over by either Captain or Admiral Haeberle, who was over there at the time. He was a constructor and he sent a dispatch back saying that the only ships that were doing the job they were designed for were these minesweepers. But I disagree with him because I found out that the LSTs, which I'll get into in a little while, were there also.

So that's the story of these minesweepers. They were very successful.

In that same period, the Bureau of Yards and Docks was busy looking ahead, and Captain Laycock, who was the head of the design department, War Plans Section, in the Bureau of Yards and Docks, and Reside, who was a commander, and finally, a captain in the Naval Reserve - yes, he was a Naval Reserve captain when he left, when he retired. But in any case, he was the creator of these portable, sectional dry docks. He was responsible for putting them together, but I'm sure that he was in contact with the big floating dry dock people. I think the Moreell Company was pretty big in floating dry docks.

Q: Is that Ben Moreell's company?

Mr. N.: No, this was another Morell. Ben was head of the Bureau of Yards and Docks. He went into the steel works. He worked for United Steel or something like that.

I was aware of what Reside was up to and, at the same time, we were working on the design of battleships during that period, so I could tell Reside the size of the battleships, which were then the biggest things that he would be called upon to handle.

Q: Was it the <u>Iowa</u> class you were working on?

Mr. N.: Yes, the <u>Iowa</u> class was coming along, and there were a couple of others that preceded it. I can't think of the names now. I don't have a list of them here.

He knew that we were working on this thing and so I was in contact with him, just as I was in contact with the people in the Bureau of Aeronautics who had to do with catapults and everything else. I made it a point to reach off into all these places, including the Bureau of Ordnance. For instance, I talked about the minesweepers. I would go to the Bureau of Ordnance and talk about them.

Incidentally, I went there in connection with minelayers, which we were working on, also, around this time, and, to my amazement, they didn't bring up the matter of magnetic mines. I called them on that. I said, "What have you got?" I asked for a model. I wanted to see a model of the latest mine, and they dusted off a thing there and I looked at it and said:

"Is this a magnetic mine?" No, it isn't, so I said: "Well, what does a magnetic mine look like?" And I never did see what it looked like. I finally got some dimensions and we went ahead and designed the minelayer.

What I'm doing now is show the kind of field work that I often got into.

So then in connection with the work that Ordnance was doing on the 5-inch gun, which was a very successful gun, probably one of the best in the world - it could beat any of the guns that the Army was testing down in Texas, because the clearances and all were very carefully worked out, so there was very little play and they were very accurate in their gear-ing, which was very important.

I went down to Indian Head - I think that's what they called the place - where they were testing these 5-inch guns and I tried to get as close as possible to the gun so I could observe how things were operating. They fired the gun and all these hot pieces of material were falling down at my feet. I didn't think too much of it at the time. Then, when we got into conference after the test was finished and we talked about our experiences and what we thought of it, I mentioned the fact that these pieces of plastic that were still smoking from the shot were landing at my feet. Up to that time they didn't know that these pieces were falling around like that. If you were firing that on a ship, these things would fall all over the deck.

They then redesigned the plug they had on the end of their container.

Now, I have one more person I want to bring in here, and that's Captain Laycock, who was working on a little module, a little box, that measured 5-by-7-by-5 feet deep. Now, the 5-by-7 is a very good number because you multiply those two together and that's 35, 35. And 35 cubic feet or so of salt water is equal to one ton. So when these little modules would go down in the water one foot, you'd know that it was displacing a ton. It was almost an automatic calculation. If you had ten of these in a row in there and they'd go down a foot, it was 10 tons you put on there.

Q: Unless you used brackish water instead of salt.

Mr. N.: You could allow for the density. Anyway, he put these things together. The idea was that you could assemble them to make barges and storage tanks and use them when the Marines got captured down on an island in the Pacific, why, they used some of his barges to store gasoline or to bring it in. And, later on, in landing operations we used those boxes all assembled in the roadways, which would work out. We'd put the Seventh Fleet transversely and put two next to each other so you'd have a roadway 14 feet wide. We'd make them any length we needed.

The Seabees, the construction battalions of the Bureau of Yards and Docks, were the ones who would have to work on the landing operations and get ashore in order to do the shore work with bulldozers and all that sort of thing.

Laycock would come in and talk to me about this and come up with ideas of using them as gunmounts - assemble them and put a gun on them. The Germans ran into a lot of trouble with trying to put their guns in for their landing operations along the coast, but Laycock was thinking about it for these little barges that he was coming up with. It turned out there were thousands and thousands of these little things made. I'll bring this up again, about how we used them when we got into the landing craft program.

So, there's Reside and there's Laycock from the Bureau of Yards and Docks. I brought in Ordnance.

Time is going on and now it appeared - the war was on now, the end of 1941, we were getting closer to it. The British had been in it since 1939, I guess it was, and we had gotten into it around that time. The big thing about it was that FDR managed to get lend-lease passed, and that happened somewhere around January 1941. So when we got into these building programs, and that also meant that he removed any tonnage limitations that were in effect. He had removed that long before lend-lease, as a matter of fact, because we were working on the big, 45,000-ton battleships.

Q: You mean those limitation treaties were abrogated at that point?

Mr. N.: Yes.

In 1941, according to a table that Admiral James made up in his paper, we had very few aircraft carriers. We had seventeen battleships in 1941 but only seven airplane carriers. We had no escort carriers. We had 166 destroyers, about 200 auxiliaries, we had no escort ships in 1941. We had only 47 submarines, and mine craft we had only 14, and landing craft we didn't have any - zero. This is large landing craft. That was the situation in 1941.

Q: The concept for some of those types had never been developed, had it?

Mr. N.: No. We started working on the escort ships and the

British destroyer, which we called the BDE - we designed the BDE for the British. They were right there, working with us.

Q: Was that a small type?

Mr. N.: That was a small escort vessel. It finally became the DE, our DE -

Q: And corvette?

Mr. N.: Maybe it was called a corvette but we called it the British DE, BDE. There was a Commander Cole who spent a lot of time in our section. He was with us right from the beginning. We worked very closely with all the British people. Before we got into the war and during the war, and I was still in contact with them after the war.

In 1941 we got busy and by the time 1945 came around we had twenty-three battleships, twenty-six aircraft carriers, sixty-four escort carriers - those were the merchant ship conversions. I don't know whether Kaiser's were included in that sixty-four.

Q: They must have been.

Mr. N.: Yes, they must have been there. These were all in the Pacific. We had 323 destroyers, 52 cruisers, as compared with 37 that we had, and the auxiliaries, they represented a lot of merchant ships that we took over. We had over 1,000, or 1,066, according to Jimmy James. Submarines, in 1941, we only had forty-seven, and in 1943 we had 181. You can see our shipbuilding capacity was pretty well filled up. Minecraft we had 160. That included minesweepers, minelayers, and the 14 minecraft that we had here in 1941 - we probably had a couple of minesweepers - but they were mostly minelayers.

Then, zero landing craft grew up to 2,783 and about 1,000 landing craft, which are the ones I'm about to tell you about.

The reason I'm bringing this up is to show that when the war hit us - I've always referred to this situation when the war hit us as being as though we were in the middle of a volcano. That's the way it was.

Shortly before December 7th, a very special day arrived which was November 4th 1941, when Captain Cochrane came in with a dispatch from the British outlining in a very brief manner the need for landing craft - large landing craft that could be seagoing.

Q: They had nothing of that type?

Mr. N.: They had designed landing craft and they were here in this country. We were building some, and some of them were called Winnies, named after Churchill, and so on. But their drafts were too high. They certainly couldn't be used for anything so they weren't very good.

The total weight of the military load, as I remember it, called for was 500 tons and they would carry the biggest tanks.

Some of the tanks that were getting into the picture at that time weighed somewhere around 30 or more tons, so you couldn't carry them on these little landing craft any more. In our LST that we were going to get into now, the landing ship, tank, with 500 tons allowed for at least ten of these big tanks and other equipment that had to be put in ahead of then in order to get onto the beach and prepare the roadway, or any guns that might have to be there.

In any case, Captain Cochrane recited the story and the British specified a design to go on a beach whose slope was 1 in 100, 1 foot in 100. I listened to that and then I started thinking and apparently, according to what Captain Cochrane said and others said later - but he particularly because he was there, and I understand that Lieutenant Evans was there because he mentioned it in a recent letter he wrote to the Naval Institute Proceedings. I think it's in the November '75 issue. He said he was there, but I apparently was concentrating so heavily on what Cochrane was telling me that I don't remember anybody standing there.

I got busy and made a few passing sketches on an envelope - I don't recall that I did this, but they said I did it. That seemed to be the way to do it. It had to have two conditions: one, it had to be able to cross the ocean and have enough draft to be able to get there; and then, when you got to the landing area, you could pump the tanks dry and you could go on the beach. Instead of taking the 1 in 100 slope, I decided that to make this design successful you have to design it to 1 foot in 50 feet, and that's the way we designed it. It turned out that that slope probably could satisfy 70 per cent of the beaches in the world, except those around Europe.

Q: Did you have a particular knowledge of beaches in your background?

Mr. N.: No, I didn't. Because I could trim this ship, you see, with the tankage that I had in it, I could make it 1 in 100 by simply moving the ballast forward and increasing the draft. But that meant that the forward draft would be greater than 1 in 50.

Later on, it turned out that we started to use these modules that Captain Laycock developed to make the barges, the 5-by-7-by-5 modules. We put those together to make roadways 200 feet long, 14 feet wide. And later on, we carried them on the sides of the LST and just let them flip off, the supporting angle bars. But that's getting a little ahead of the story.

Cochrane was satisfied that I had a solution. It seemed odd that we were able to do it so quickly, or that I would be able to do it so quickly because the British hadn't been able to hit on this scheme. But I did it.

Then I went home that night - and worked on it in my study which had a drafting board in it - I drew the original sketch in the office that afternoon in a matter of a couple of hours on a scale of 50 feet to the inch, which I think you have seen - this sketch.

Q: Yes.

Mr. N.: That's the full size. That's roughly 6 inches long and 4 inches deep. That scheme that you see there was never changed except that the ship was lengthened to somewhere around 300 feet instead of 280 feet and the beam was increased a little also, because the weights went up, and we were a little afraid of using quarter-inch plating on the sides and on the deck. We increased that to three-eighths of an inch. and to take the weight, we added a little to the beam and something to the length, but the machinery would be located just as you see it here and the bow would be like this with a ramp on it, and the details had to be developed.

This sketch was finished on the same afternoon that Captain Cochrane came in with the dispatch. Then that same night I took it home and made a larger drawing, one-sixteenth inch to the foot, and brought that in. They made copies of that and flew it over to England, and a short time afterwards the courier officer flew off with the plan to England. That was their way of getting secret material over in a hurry because they didn't want to talk about it over the air.

Q: No, and the courier slept with his dispatch and all the

rest of it!

Mr. N.: Yes, so it got over there. Then Admiral Darling and a team came over and they worked with the bureau in the development of the detailed plans.

Now, what happened was that, as I remember it, we had a scheme here where the Dravo Corporation, Neville Island, Pittsburgh, Pennsylvania - that's where they were at that time, became the prime yard. They were the leading shipyard to build this type. Gibbs and Cox was their design agent.

Then we in preliminary design got busy and worked on and made a complete design study and more detailed plans. We finished our study by some time in January. Mind you, all of this was started on the 4th of November 1941. Sometime after January 1st we had a preliminary design finished, and instead of taking those preliminary plans and turning them over to our contract design section, we turned them over to Gibbs and Cox to be developed into contract plans. They developed the details and the ventilation system that had to be put in there because the tanks had to be running inside the ship, and the ramp that was on the forward end had to be worked out. They made contract plans parallel with the detailed plans. Part of the detail plans were a set of plans that worked right in with the contract plans, and so the shipyards that got the job to do would get the contract plans and the detail plans were already ready for them.

Q: This was all a kind of telescoping process?

Mr. N.: Right.

As a result of that, by October of 1942, that is a little less than a year, an LST was finished. Then it wasn't very long after that when there was an LST available down at Norfolk Naval Base. It was cold winter weather, so I suppose it was either in early January 1943 or in December of 1942.

I went down there and Commander Holdsworth, who was a construction officer in the bureau and worked in preliminary design. At that time Captain Cochrane was the officer head of preliminary design, and Commander Kniskern was his principal assistant. Holdsworth came down with me so it could have been the latter part of 1942.

The reason I'm bringing this in is because when I went down to Willoughby Spit, Virginia, there was an officer who had been sent up from Texas, Captain Royal, and I think it was Forrest Royal but I'm not sure. It appears to me that that Forrest was his first name because I found some records on him later on, the only one who would have been connected with this landing stuff by the name of Royal. He later on lost his life in the Pacific.

I met Royal there and we went out to the naval base. Holdsworth was already there and the LST was there. We started loading that LST. We put a big crane in it and it seemed almost like magic that we had picked the size of hatch that would allow that crane to be lowered down in it without taking it apart, which was a very good thing because it could go ashore without having to be assembled.

It was very cold weather. I remember seeing the ice and calling attention to a couple of people who probably would have frozen to death if I hadn't found them down there, a couple of youngsters in the Army. I reported them and they went down and brought them back. They were soaked. They were on guard duty on a bunch of little barges off the end of a pier.

Anyway, we finished that job in Norfolk -

Q: That was a loading experiment?

Mr. N.: Yes. We ran some tests down there with sandbags and so on and tried to work out a method to get ashore. We weren't really practicing a landing operation, but we were practicing using the ramp location at the naval base there and then trying to drop sandbags over the end so that you'd have half a chance of getting a bulldozer ashore or something of that order.

We came back to Washington and it wasn't very long before I started going up to Quonset, up in Rhode Island, and also up to the Boston Navy Yard. The first thing I did during those months, the early months, I guess, of 1943, was to run a test.

Schuyler Pyne was on this test. The first landing operation we were going to make there, and I was there -

Q: Where? At the Boston Navy Yard?

Mr. N.: We took the boat out and landed on some beach - I

don't know where they picked the beach - but it was very rough weather and an interesting thing happened at that time. I was down inside, going through the great big tank compartment, and all this ship motion was going on, the waves were hitting the bow. They were testing a 50-mm. gun up on the deck and I was in this great big football field trying to listen to whether the ship was working in the seaway, the structure. I wasn't very successful in hearing anything because of all the racket.

During that racket Schuyler Pyne came down to me and said:

"There's a gestapo aboard representing the Secretary of the Navy and he says this ship is unseaworthy. Come on up and talk to him."

I said: "No, Schuyler, I don't want to meet him. It's too late to argue. You tell him when you see him again that if he has any complaints to make about this ship to write a letter to the Secretary of the Navy and tell him what he thinks of this ship."

It was a very prominent naval architect of New York who was representing the Secretary of the Navy.

Q: And his name?

Mr. N.: I can't think of it at the moment (Eads Johnson). He's dead now. I might be able to fish it up. He died a long time ago. He, incidentally, is the naval architect Starling Burgess tried to get to help him work on the Delano project, and he condemned it after he was with it for a little while.

I didn't want to see him, that's right, and Schuyler was really worried because he was a junior officer then, going and telling off a representative of the Secretary of the Navy, but I said don't worry about him, or something of that order, "Just tell him the best thing to do is write a letter and put all your complaints into a letter because we can't argue about it here."

Now we were getting ready for the landing operation and ready to make the drive to the beach when everybody wanted to know how fast to go to hit the beach. They came to me and wanted to know how fast they should hit the beach, and I said full speed. So they hit that beach full speed.

Q: That being what?

Mr. N.: About 10 knots. That's a pretty high speed and most captains don't like to hit a beach like that. I wasn't worried about it. I was standing up on the deck, at the side, and they had wire rope between the stanchions as rails so you didn't fall overboard. And now I was approaching the beach and now that speed of 10 knots began to get faster and faster and I began to look around to see what I would hang onto when we hit the beach!

Well, we hit the beach and it was just a gradual stop. It wasn't any problem. So it was quite successful. We didn't do any operational landing at all, we were just testing it.

I had made the plating under the bow 1-inch thick. The rest of the plating on the ship was three-eighths, but right up at the landing area, at the keel and around on the bottom in that section I had specified one-inch plating. I was always very glad I did after I saw some pictures of what happened to some of these LSTs landing on the Normandy beach, on top of rock and all that sort of thing.

Then I came back to Washington and, of course, as soon as Ned Cochrane heard that I was there he came down to see me and ask me about it, and I told him what would happen. I said:

"The Secretary of the Navy had a naval architect on board," and I gave his name, "he'll be writing a letter telling us where we're wrong on this thing and that it's unseaworthy," which he did. Then Cochrane came again with a letter from the Secretary, from this naval architect, and we discussed what to give him. Ned wanted to give him certain things and I said:

"No, no, let's not do that. Let's just give them plans of the completed ship. We won't give them any of our calculations. We'll give them our structural plans. We'll tell him the stresses that we figured, but we won't tell them how we figured them. We won't give them our work books because they may find a couple of 'ts' we didn't cross in there. So let's not do that. He's a naval architect. We tell him the principles on which we designed the ship, here are all the plans, and he can work from there."

We never heard from him again.

It wasn't very long after that, March 1943 arrived, and we had to make our tests for a real landing operation in Narragansett Bay. The Combined Chiefs of Staff were there. We worked up a roadway something like 200 feet long, 14 feet wide, that we towed alongside of the LST that I was on because I was going to handle that part of it.

Q: Was this to bridge the beach?

Mr. N.: Yes, because the beach was very flat. We knew that, somewhat similar to the proposed landings in the Mediterranean. We already knew that there were going to be landings there, but they didn't tell us where, but they would be in the Mediterranean. I always thought it was Malta but it turned out to be Sicily.

We made this roadway and the Combined Chiefs got onto my boat. There was another LST there. The one that I was on was Number 348, I think. Yes, 348 was the one I was on, and the Army had 359. The Army was to build a pontoon bridge when the LST hit the beach. They were going to put up their regular pontoons, a bunch of boatlike things that they have. They had a tank in their LST. I had a tank in my LST, but I had designed this roadway with studs on the side to hold it so that the roadway couldn't slip away from us in a wind or something.

Now I found that in order to do this I had to modify the ramp, in order to put a fair lead in there so I could get a line from the winch down through a fair lead that would go to the roadway that we were towing alongside. That line would go to the after end of the roadway. When we hit the beach, the LST would stop and the roadway, of course, would keep on going, which it did and hit the beach right on the nose. And that's how I met Admiral Brand, who was head of the Boston Navy Yard, and he sent a limousine so that I could go to the Boston yard from Quonset to tell them how I wanted to modify this ramp and the fair lead and things of that kind, and the yard would get these all ready and their mechanics would come down to Quonset and install the fair lead that I wanted.

Q: This meant that the roadway had to be moved laterally -

Mr. N.: Pulled over.

Q: Yes - in order to mesh with the landing ship.

Mr. N.: You put your fair lead in the center of the ramp and then the line would go down and up to the winch that was on the deck overhead and back to the after end of the roadway. And this worked like a miracle.

Here were the Combined Chiefs of Staff on the one I was on. Now the point of that was that Royal was there, too, Captain Royal, and he said to me:

"John, I'll take the bridge and you take care of the landing operation. You take care of the tank and the ramp and all the rest of it. I'll be up there and I'll see that we get the LST in. The rest of it will be up to you because you know how to do it."

So I did. I hit the beach and the ramp kept on running and hit dead ahead on the beach, ahead of my LST. We had the ramp down a bit and we pulled the roadway over, dropped the ramp on it. The beach was so perfect that I didn't have to do any ballasting in the roadway to bring it down solid on the beach, because it was flat on the beach. They got my studs down into the sand. They were simply like pipes with a pointed end every so often.

When I got the report from the Seabee people - we had another ramp on the end of our roadway that had to be lowered -

Q: Why was that?

Mr. N.: Because it was up too high off the beach. The tank had to have a ramp so it could ride right off onto the beach.

I gave the signal to the tank man to bring the tank down; then I discovered that the ramp was about a foot thick, and behind the tank was a towing rig in the back there. I didn't understand how clever tanks had their own roadway and that, no matter what happened to that tail end, that tank would keep on going. I stopped the tank before it got off the ramp because I was afraid that this thing that stuck out the back end was going to hit the ramp and then the tank would get stuck.

It didn't take very long, it took about a minute, but in that few minutes when we hit the beach, as we hit the beach, I was standing down on the roadway when Royal's aide, I guess, came down and said that we'd lost the anchor. There was a stern anchor they had to drop off aft and they dropped it too soon and all they saw was the bitter end of this thing and the wind was blowing broadside to us. What to do?

Here I was trying to figure out what to do with the tank. I told them instantly, though, just to push full speed ahead. Not quite full speed I understand that was the standard procedure, they always kept the propellers in motion after this. I read somewhere about that.

Then I let the tank come down, so I got the tank ashore in seven minutes, with all this happening. From the time the LST hit the beach and we pulled the roadway over, lowered the ramp, checked the roadway to see whether it was resting properly on the bottom, got the studs down, or the spuds, as they called them, I called the tank down, the captain asked me what to do because the anchor was lost, I got the tank going and it hit the beach in seven minutes.

Ernie King was there and all the Combined Chiefs were tickled to death. They knew that this LST could make the landing all right. And so nothing was ever held up by anything that we did.

The LSTs were very successful in the Pacific, in the Atlantic, the Normandy landings. They not only brought the tanks ashore, they were used as temporary hospital ships. The wounded were brought back onto the LST before it was backed off the beach and went back home. And it brought all kinds of supplies. We used them on special occasions to carry a top secret scheme for laying pierced planks on Pacific islands for landing fields. That was all done in preliminary design in a separate little room that we called - they had a code name for this. I don't know whether it's still top secret or not. I wouldn't think so. It was "Gold Rush." We can always just wipe it off.

The LST certainly proved itself to be a great thing, and it was all done in that short time. It never was really changed. Evans tells in his report that it always looked the same as what he saw that day. I wrote a letter to him and told him that in addition to that I had made a bigger plan that night.

Q: That's quite a story.

Mr. N.: That put the LST on the map, but oddly enough it was so successful, like anything else that's successful, like a big movie that's successful, a lot of other people try to take the credit for it or make a copy of it. A lot of people claimed that they were the inventors of it. In fact, Jane's Fighting Ships called it the British design.

When I was in Washington last Christmas, I got a telephone call from someone who worked for the Maritime Administration and he said he was helping historians and he said that the Maritime Administration designed and built the LST. But they didn't. The Navy did the whole job.

Then it wasn't long before we got going on other projects.

The next big one on landing craft that was very important was the LCIL, landing craft, infantry. That was a very interesting thing to develop. I, incidentally, got the idea early in the game, including the LSTs, too, that we had to keep the number of pieces and the number of plate thicknesses and the number of shapes down in all these ships - not too many sizes of things. There would be a small inventory, see, because you didn't want to have to go hunting around for this angle bar or that angle bar. I used to tell them that you can't have any more than you have fingers on your hands in shapes, plate thicknesses, five of each.

Also, welding came in pretty good at that time, so the LSTs were practically all welded, and diesel engines were put in there.

I must give credit to the engineering department, the marine engineers in the Bureau of Ships, because they worked wholeheartedly in getting engines for these ships.

Then Mike Robinson, Admiral Robinson later on - he was admiral already when he retired - he was a former engineering officer and head of the Bureau of Engineering, and he came back into the Navy when the war came on. He managed to get into this business of organizing the production end of it. There was a Captain Irish involved in the production department. He worked in New York, up at Gibbs and Cox. Gibbs was a great organizer, too, and he worked at this thing.

Gibbs was not only working on this sort of thing, he was also handling a lot of things for Maritime in connection with the "ugly ducklings," as they called some of the first merchant ships and later on Victory ships - I don't know whether he got in on those or not.

In the meantime, we were still struggling with modifications to destroyers and so on. The Fletcher class got in there. All the following destroyers were patterned after the Fletcher class. It was a flush-deck design, no portholes in it, and all that sort of thing.

Q: 2,100-tonner?

Mr. N.: Yes.

The LCIL, however, got in there. There was a demand for this small infantry landing thing, so I got busy on it and I studied it quite a bit myself. I used to work two days every day, you might say. I could do that because I only need four or five hours' sleep. I guess I inherited this. My father was the same way.

One of the things we did here was to try to design the LCIL in such a way that there would be very few parts in it, that the shape would be such that it was developable - so you didn't have to furnace any plates that you put on.

I talked to Tom Bossett from New York Ship. He was the manager of New York Ship. I talked to him about this boat that we were coming up with, and I suggested to him that he build the first one in his yard.

Q: Why did you select New York Ship?

Mr. N.: Because they were a big yard, and it was going into a small yacht-building yard. This was going to be a steel ship and I wanted to test it out in a ship yard that had good naval architects and draftsmen. And Tom said:

"Oh, John, where would I put it?"

"Well," I said, "find space in between the cruisers. You've got plenty of room there. There must be plenty of room for this little fellow. Just build one. Build the first one and then somebody else will get it."

I think they already had the yard picked out - Lawley's from Massachusetts was the prime yard. They built these.

So the hull form was developable. We developed the hull form, we sent the rough sketches. I got Captain Saunders in. He was head of the Taylor Model Basin. And Schoenherr came in. I wanted to talk to him about it. I wanted the self-propelled tests run and finished within a week. Could it be done? Towed tests and self-propelled tests.

They went away and we set up a paper model of it and tried to see whether we were getting it developable. We sent it down and the model basin finished all their tests on the LCIL in one week.

Q: This was admirable speed. Had you been told that these ships were needed for a particular operation coming up?

Mr. N.: Well, yes, we were told it was to carry the infantry and they put the two little bicycle ramps on the side. There would be no berthing.

Oh, yes, that reminds me. I put contour seats in these boats. I used to ride the Staten Island ferry a lot and I managed to get hold of a sketch or the design of the contour seats in the Staten Island ferries. I think I got it out of Simpson's handbook -

Q: All the comforts of home you wanted in it!

Mr. N.: Yes. I used to sit on those benches all the time and I knew they were comfortable, and so I went to work and did this. Thousands of these seats were built and they were very successful. These infantrymen who were supposed to go down the ramps had bicycles. I imagined they were going to be raiders going to different places and ride around and get confidential information from the natives in the places they would go to. And then also they were used on the Pacific coast. LCILs were used here on this thing, I think, and the LSMs were in there, and landing ship, docks. That's another thing we worked on around that time. The landing ship, dock, which was a great big ship originally designed to take two barges, maybe 150 feet long each, and then float them out. Then they could land ashore on a shallow beach. They never did carry the thing they were originally designed for.

That design was almost completed by the British. They did have a good design developed, but the stability was poor and we modified the lines of the ship, changed a lot of it, and adopted it for our own use. That's the same type that was built by Litton after five years of design work and building - LHG, or whatever they called it. They put decks over it, I think. These were like great big docks with no deck overhead. We used to sink the whole ship down. The water would be inside this dock and you'd haul the barge in and then you'd pump the water out again. There was quite a problem in stability but we worked it out.

Q: Is it true that once the principle of these landing ships had been established with the LST, the others came along much more readily?

Mr. N.: Well, they did, but they were all different. They weren't really related, but we were more aware of what it took to get on a beach because we'd already been having landing operations. I'd been there, anyway. I always was out in the field with somebody.

Q: Did you witness any landing operations in North Africa

or the Mediterranean?

Mr. N.: No. That brings up another thing that I did in connection with the LST.

After I came back to Washington from the trial landing operations attended by the Combined Chiefs of Staff - quite a lot of these LSTs had now been built and the British were to get the first fifty. They were coming in to New York and leaving New York for Europe. I came back to Washington and got the group busy on writing up an instruction book. I wrote up some of the particulars in connection with the landing, and they wrote an instruction book within the week. I arrived home probably on a Saturday or a Sunday, Monday they got started, by Friday the instruction book was written, and we sent fifty or so copies up to New York to leave with the LSTs when they left for Africa.

But I did something there that my guardian angel who I always carried on this shoulder tipped me off that I'd better tell somebody that we had these instruction books around. I may have given one to one of the Seabee officers that I knew very well - the Seabee who was the head lieutenant or whatever it was of the group that was going over to Africa. I told him about these instruction books and I probably gave him a copy and explained it to him. When they got over there -

Q: In Morocco?

Mr. N.: Well, all I can say is that it was Morocco then.

There was a big landing place there and Admiral Kirk was there. He was in charge -

Q: Probably Rabat.

Mr. N.: It might have been. It was very good that I had told this Seabee officer about this and he knew then how the ships had to be trimmed down by the bow to land at Sicily. They were getting ready for this landing operation in Sicily. He walked up and down the pier and he reported back to Admiral Kirk that they were not trimming the LSTs properly, that there must be instruction books around somewhere to tell these people how to do it. They hunted around. They hadn't given any instruction books out. They got lost somewhere but they found them packed away, I guess in a store room or somewhere, and they gave the books out, so all the LSTs that were going in to Sicily were properly trimmed to land on this beach. I'd been told how flat it was and the beach that I landed on up in Narragansett Bay was to simulate the beach that they expected to land on over there. That's how it went.

As I told you before, this was a kind of mixed-up story because there were so many things coming in there about these landing craft and, in addition, we had questions coming up in connection with the destroyers and escort vessels that had to be worked on and developed.

Q: And the cruisers?

Mr. N.: Well, we got in next to where the cruisers came in.

It wasn't very long after the creation or getting the idea and the plans ready on the LST when Pearl Harbor happened, December 7th, and by the end of the month, of course, as history has recorded - we were badly hit then - and by the end of the month a conference was called at the White House where Mr. Metten, who was president of New York Ship attended, and Admiral Howard, who was head of design. He was really Captain Cochrane's senior at this moment, but Cochrane and I were in the same boat together all the time.

I wasn't at that meeting because I was busy on some project. I don't think anybody else from the Bureau of Ships was there but Howard. We were running pretty thin with people.

Howard came back that evening close to quitting time. I was the only one who was left. In the meantime I had gotten a telephone call from Tom Bossett at New York Ship asking me what I knew about converting the cruisers into aircraft carriers, because the Cleveland-class cruisers were being built at New York Ship and it was the lead job there: I said:

"I know quite a bit about it," that's probably the way I put it because I didn't know the whole story, but we had done some work on converting the cruisers to carriers. I told Tom that I knew what to do, and he said: "When could we come?" Now it was New Year's Eve so I said:

"What about tomorrow morning? Why can't you be here tomorrow morning?"

He said, fine, "We'll be there tomorrow morning."

A few minutes after I got through talking to Tom Bossett, Admiral Howard came in and said:

"John, I've got another job for you."

I said: "It couldn't be converting the cruiser to the aircraft carrier?"

And he said: "How do you know?"

They'd had this top secret meeting over at the White House but evidently they called Bossett up right away to get ready and get in contact with me. Howard was coming in to tell me, I guess, that Bossett was going to call me up and so forth. Instead of that I told him, and he was surprised that I knew. I said:

"Well, Tom Bossett called me up and asked about this thing and I told him I knew what to do and to get his team ready. I told him he could be here tomorrow morning."

Admiral Howard said fine, then he turned on his heels and left. That's all he said.

The next day that team came in and they worked with my group. We hauled out our material and we turned it over to them, and they turned those ships into airplane carriers.

Q: How much of a job was this?

Mr. N.: It was quite a complete job because, after all, they became full carriers. The guns had to be left off, there'd be no gun foundations in them. The machinery was the same, but we had the study made and he knew what to do.

The main deck was left, they had to change that to a hangar deck.

Q: They had to install elevators, I suppose?

Mr. N.: Yes, they had to have those. They worked it out all right. This was on the 1st of January 1942, and about the middle of January 1943 the Independence was finished, she was commissioned.

Q: That was just about a year?

Mr. N.: Yes, and the Princeton was commissioned in February of 1943.

In connection with that job, I don't remember any problems that they had at all because as time went on New York Ship finished all nine of them in 1943, and they got out there and into the battle area. The Princeton is the one, I think, that had the most thrilling experience, but she lost her life in it around Manila there, Leyte Gulf. She was hit by a kamikaze and set on fire. The surprising thing about that was that she had a bad explosion but she didn't sink from any of the things that happened to her by the kamikaze or the fire. They had to go in and torpedo her and sink her. We had to knock her out ourselves. That was to me the sad thing about that.

When these ships got out there and in operation, for their part they were called light carriers. They had pretty lucky lives. I think the Princeton was the only one we lost of that group. Up until that time we lost others one after the other. We lost the Hornet, the Wasp, the Yorktown, the Lexington.

Q: Of course, the Japs concentrated on our carriers.

Mr. N.: Yes, they did, but I think that the big job that these carriers did was to trim down the aviation force of the Japs. Towards the end, they didn't have the flight crews any more to come in and sink them. So that's the reason, I think, that most of our aircraft carriers survived.

Also, the battleships played a part in there of being strong and well protected and really covered with all kinds of antiaircraft. They stayed close to the Big E, the Enterprise - that is, the original Enterprise.

Q: They, in a sense, served as escorts to the carriers.

Mr. N.: Yes, they did, and they provided an unsinkable island there. As a result of that, the record really doesn't give these young aviators a high enough place in the story about the Pacific war. I notice that when you read about it you find that the Enterprise would send out its flyers and half the crew would come back - half of the flight crew would come back. They really went out and did their stuff. This is a remarkable thing. People have written about the submarines and the individuals and we refer to the submarines as the silent navy. I think the flyers who were out there were the silent people in the Navy because I haven't seen the aviators getting as much historical comment.

Q: Tell me how these converted cruisers of the Cleveland-class differed from the Essex.

Mr. N.: They had the same speed but they didn't have the room in them and their decks couldn't handle the same size planes. The Essex could carry the largest planes available at the time. One of the last things we had to do was to provide a means of strengthening the flight deck of the Essex, which we did by calling for stronger steel, higher tensile strength steel, for all the structure. Later on, they even took heavier planes and they stiffened the decks up some more.

The Essex had a weakness forward. The forward end of the flight deck was propped up by stanchions because the planes were flying off the deck. The Bureau of Aeronautics wouldn't allow us to fill in the sides of the ship, but it was obvious that it would be better to fill in up to the flight deck but as a fighter would fly right off the ship the air currents that were formed around that forward end of the flight deck would be different if you filled it in.

Q: Why did they object to filling it in?

Mr. N.: There would be eddy currents of the air and they were afraid that the flyer - because he's reaching a point where he's got to have complete flight capacity, lift, and they were afraid he'd lose that. And, of course, what would happen as he went off into the space - they tried to keep the air over the flight deck just about the way it would be just forward of the flight deck. They didn't want them to nose down because that's what would happen, especially if the weather was a little rough.

Q: Was it not true that this extension of the deck was damaged in some of the typhoons that ships got in?

Mr. N.: Yes, but they really collapsed. They knocked the props out and the whole forward end of the flight deck fell down on the deck below. It would just bend down.

Q: Yes, but it was vulnerable in that sense, wasn't it?

Mr. N.: Right.

All during the time that we were getting these things ready and they were building, we were coming along with the modified destroyers. The Fletcher-class destroyer we kept modifying that class right through to the end. They were destroyer leaders in the beginning, but the succeeding Fletchers that came along that were strengthened would be the leaders. Quite a lot of changes were made.

Q: Did they maintain the same tonnage?

Mr. N.: No, they had to go up some. They changed the lines

as they came along.

Q: These changes that were made as you went along through the years, were they a result of feed-in from battle experience?

Mr. N.: I would say so, yes, because I imagine that the first Fletchers that went out were probably wetter than they wanted them, and some of the arrangements of our superstructure, you know - a destroyer depends a lot on the arrangement of the superstructure because their main deck is so close to the waterline. I was always surprised that they were able to do what they did. It was really tough going.

With the battleships one of the big things that always distressed me was the fact that before the war we went to work and built all these battleships and we only had a few airplane carriers. That was the big problem. Here, we had seventeen battleships and only seven aircraft carriers in 1941.

Q: Yes.

Mr. N.: What kind of thinking was going on there, I don't know. The Yorktown and the Enterprise were very good carriers. They were 20,000-ton carriers, and the Essex was about 27,000 tons.

Q: Wasn't the emphasis on the battleship a cary-over from earlier on, and some of the battleship admirals were still in the saddle? Is that not perhaps an explanation?

Mr. N.: Of course, that's right. That's true. The bomb came

along later and thinking about the take-off with these bombers and everything, we were playing around with airplanes, seaplanes. I remember talking to aviation about it. They would develop these seaplanes, they built a few, and they folded up. Remember the wind currents. They must have reached that critical -

Q: Speed of sound.

Mr. N.: Yes.

I think I should fall back here and explain a few points on those LCILs, which we mentioned before. I just had a thought that we ran into a considerable amount of trouble in getting engines for these little LCILs. We had trouble getting pipes and plumbing for them. The yards and the manufacturers were pretty well saturated by that time, and this was early 1942.

Q: This was just adding something.

Mr. N.: We were adding a bunch of new ships and they kept telling me the steel mills couldn't do it. And the same way with the LST.

In connection with the LST and these other craft, the LCIL, we started using the steel that they rolled for automobiles with the fast rolling mills that they had for that purpose. That steel was not considered very good because often you would get folds in it. The steel would be going through the mills and it would fold under ahead and there would be an overlap in it. The edges of these plates that they made were rather weak and they didn't think they could use sheet steel at first, but then they finally did use it by trimming the edges of all the plates that were rolled for this sheet stuff. The LSTs, LCIs, LSMs, LSMR, and LSD, I imagine, but I'm not sure about that because that was a big ship.

Then the plumbing. We couldn't get any plumbing to speak of. Just a few odd lots of plumbing on the LCILs. We had the fuel tanks in the ships all right, but we had to run hoses - we were able to get suction hoses, so suction hoses would be led to the manhole over a fuel-oil tank. They'd shove it in there and they'd pump the oil out of the tank into the reserve fuel tanks for the engines. Of course, you would have a certain amount of plumbing to get that fuel oil to the engines.

As far as the engines went, we had to use Gray diesels, little Gray diesels. We put four of them on each shaft. They had two shafts. We packed them well together and geared them to a shaft, and that's the way we engined the LCILs.

Q: What had been your original plan for engines?

Mr. N.: That was the original plan. We knew how much horsepower there was and then we had to try to get the engines, and the marine engineering people would have to go hunting around to see what they could do, and they came up with these Gray diesels. We put four on a shaft and it worked all right, and I was told later that anybody who had duty in that engine room couldn't hear for the longest time after he got out of it.

It was this sort of short-cutting and cutting of red tape that made it possible for us to get all those ships that I recited here that Admiral James had put together, this column of ships for 1941.

Q: Isn't that an American characteristic, the ability to adapt in situations where it's demanded?

Mr. N.: Yes, I think it was that way. I'm afraid now it isn't that way. I'm afraid that we're losing a certain amount of genius and I believe it's because we're depending on automation and the machine to do everything. So a large number of us are more and more robots. This is the way it is.

I just wanted to bring that in at this point. We've recited the story about all these landing craft, I believe.

During this war period, Admiral Beuret, who was a former chief of the bureau and was chief when I got down to the bureau in 1928, was now retired and he was on the Inventors' Council with Vannevar Bush. Bush was the former president of M.I.T. and he would sort out the inventions and suggestions that were coming in that were related to shipbuilding.

Q: I suppose they increased in number during the war years, did they?

Mr. N.: Yes, there were quite a few, enough to have a regular department that did nothing but that. Vannevar Bush, of course, was an idea man, too, so he felt that we shouldn't fail to be respectful to ideas.

However, Beuret would come to me about twice every week and this contact with him brought the two of us rather closer than we were when he was chief of the bureau. He didn't seem too satisfied with the idea that I came in from the field. I think I know why. Because it didn't sit too well with a lot of the other people there for engineers like myself to pick off a choice berth. But he finally decided that I had a pretty good way of getting at this thing. He told several people who later on came in to see me told me what Beuret had told them what my method was.

I'd say: "Let's see what's good about this." He thought that was pretty clever because most of the other people that he went to would always start from the other end of the scale to find out what's wrong with it. But I was short of time and I'd like to find something good first. I was never aware of this, so Admiral Beuret found that for me, and I was very glad to know that we had something that would bring us together.

Q: Did anything good come out of these schemes?

Mr. N.: That's the next point I want to make. Quite a number of ideas came along and some of them wound up being surface-effects ships, for instance. The idea of that came along at that time. A couple of British people came in and talked to me about the surface ship. They didn't really know what to call it at that time, but they had an air bubble that they'd talk about. I always wondered just what they did with that bubble. I couldn't see the use of it, and it seemed to me that we couldn't afford to stop at this point and take a long time to develop it to a useful thing, and the war was no time to do it. Later on, it did come in and, you know, they're still working on it. It's something like the hydrofoil. Bell thought of it around 1900 and we still haven't got a hydrofoil that is much bigger than maybe 250 or 500 tons. I don't believe we've got anything over 250 tons. There's a limit, I believe, to the size the hydrofoil will ever go to or beyond.

Oddly enough, my first contact with this was with Vannevar Bush in connection with a hydrofoil. Then later on with Ken Davidson from Stevens. Ken came in and was promoting a hydrofoil. He thought that a 3,000-ton hydrofoil would be the thing. We investigated that and found that we didn't have any engines, in the first place, that could be put in the hydrofoil. We had to have engines of 5 pounds per horsepower, or something on that order. And then if you had anything that could work, it could only carry the fuel oil to get there. It wouldn't have enough capacity to do anything else but carry fuel oil. I didn't realize at that time that 3,000 tons was almost impossible, and I realized then that we couldn't do it.

But, in connection with that, Vannevar Bush got the idea to force our hand on hydrofoils, and so he had his chief assistant coming around about hydrofoils. Now I'm touching on some postwar events.

Q: Yes, I know.

Mr. N.: But I think it's suitable to get there because I mentioned Vannevar Bush, and the war was nearing its end and we weren't adding any more ships. In fact, we were stopping the building of ships in the yards. We stopped one battleship that I know. She was building down in Norfolk, I guess. I think it was called the Kentucky.

Q: Stopped the Illinois, too, I believe.

Mr. N.: And others. Somehow, Vannevar Bush tried to force the chief's hand to go into hydrofoils because he built a hydrofoil and hooked it into a little sailing vessel that he had. He managed to ride on a hydrofoil for a little while that way.

He sent his chief assistant, who had done a great job in working out something on a heat-transfer job that they ran into in connection with some of the bombers that they had during the war. He solved that special problem for Vannevar

Bush. This aide came to me to talk to me about the hydrofoil and tell me about the lift to drag ratio that he thought we could get. He said that in a hydrofoil we certainly could get a lift to drag ratio of 250. I said:

"250? I don't see how you could ever get that much. Where did you ever get that from?"

He said: "I got it from a propeller." I think it was a propeller on one of our ships, maybe a propeller on our airplane carriers or something. It was a very good propeller, and a propeller blade works like a foil and it works exactly like an airplane wing. The lift is bigger than the push. I said:

"No. If you got 30 I think you would be doing well." But, no, he didn't want to listen to me, so they dropped me and the bureau and went out to the West Coast to hunt up people out there and get them interested in a hyrdoroil. And they bumped into some people who knew me. Vannevar Bush's assistant was out there talking to them and they said to him:

"Why don't you go back to Washington and talk to John Niedermair?" where he'd been before he went out there. Then he came back again and they took me out to dinner a few times. We finally settled the thing by the chief of the Bureau of Aeronautics, I think it was, and the chief of the Bureau of Ships - they have a certain amount of ready money that they can use for something experimental.

Q: A contingency fund?

Mr. N.: Yes. They put that together and gave Vannevar Bush a contract to build a hydrofoil over in Annapolis. And they built a hydrofoil.

In the meantime, they were also interested in a hydrofoil that an Englishman had built and they were running it in Annapolis. They wanted me to come over there to see it and I didn't want to go and see it.

Q: Why?

Mr. N.: Because I didn't think much of it, and I thought that they were out after publicity. In other words, this Englishman got Vannevar Bush to look at it in Annapolis. Now they wanted to bring it to Washington and run it and show it to me down there, but I put a condition on it. I would go down and watch it, provided they wouldn't mention my name in anything in connection with it, that they wouldn't tell anybody that I went down to see it.

And, behold, it wasn't very long after I went down there to see it - a lot of people were anxious to ride on it, but I wouldn't go on it. I just watched it. I got a letter from a man over in France where they had told him that I was there watching it. I never even answered the letter.

So the hydrofoil has had quite a struggle. Bell discovered it in 1920 and they're still struggling with it. It's a highly sophisticated piece of equipment that has to have special treatment. You've got to get special steels, special procedures so that your ship is light, and it's pretty tricky on the foils. You've got to keep it clean. We lift ours out of the water in the Navy, lift the wings out, then we can run on the clean foils.

The Russians are using them on rivers, but on rivers you can use a surface-piercing foil, and it doesn't bounce around too much. But a surface-piercing foil when you get out into waves will chatter and knock your teeth together.

Q: They're using them commercially, the Russians, are they not, and also the Scandinavians?

Mr. N.: They've developed it, but they're in limited size. They're still not very big. They're around 250 or 300 tons. The smaller ones they're using now for ferries in the Hawaiian Islands. I think Boeing is interested in that development. They learned all they know about it from the Navy contract they had.

We've been talking about the hydrofoil and I've mentioned Vannevar Bush and his hydrofoil.

Q: What ever became of his?

Mr. N.: This is a sad thing that happened with his hydrofoil. It didn't do too well, and they were lifting it up out of the water one time or putting it into the water and the crane collapsed and the hydrofoil collapsed, and, as I understand it, that was the end of that hydrofoil. They didn't go back in it any more.

Q: And this was the collapse of Vannevar Bush's enthusiasm for it?

Mr. N.: Well, I guess he was getting old, too. He's gone now. He's not here to protect himself. The last time I met his assistant was down in Houston when I was working on the Mohole project down there.

This is now getting us into the postwar period, and in all our talks we haven't said a word about submarines.

Q: No, we haven't!

Mr. N.: There's a good reason for that, because we worked on submarines for a long time, the salvage of the submarines S-51 and S-4 that I talked about earlier in these tape recordings and that illustrated certain weaknesses that we had in our submarines. There were things that needed to be done. Especially after the S-4, we - not we - I wasn't concerned in it, I was off on other things - they developed a diving bell and lungs for saving people in submarines. I think all the ventilation valves and other valves were made so that they would be proof against the pressure inside the hull.

We had people like Captain Cochrane who was at the Portsmouth submarine yard up in New Hampshire. Then we had Andy McKee in submarines, Admiral Morgan, who was a captain then and was in submarines. We had a lot of good dedicated submariners.

In about 1937 or '38 I got one young fellow in, a Webb graduate, which I am also, Ralph Lacey. He came in and worked in preliminary design, and somehow or other Ned Cochrane sensed something in Lacey about submarines. Lacey had just graduated from Webb and worked in our group for a little while when Ned Cochrane came to me and said:

"I think every once in a while we ought to send some of our young people out into a yard where they can get some yard experience." And I said:

"Oh, no, I don't think we need to do that," and so forth, but he kept after me. Then he came up and said it again about Lacey. He said:

"I think we ought to transfer Lacey up to the submarine yard in New London and get him busy in submarines."

I said: "No, if you get him up there, we'll lose him." I tried to talk him out of it and he said:

"You're a fine one to be talking about not sending these young fellows out to the yards. Where did you come from?"

So I said, "Yes, I guess you're right."

So we sent Lacey up to New London and he hadn't been there very long when the war started and we didn't get him back into the bureau until the war was over. During that time he'd probably ridden in more submarines, different submarines, than anybody alive.

Q: He went into the submarine service, did he?

Mr. N.: No, he was up there working in the design department and the hull department but he was still on the Navy payroll but working as a civilian naval architect.

We lost him during the war but after the war, all of a sudden, I heard that Lacey was working in contract plans in the bureau. He never came in to see me. So I got hold of the officer in charge of contract design there and talked to him about it. I said:

"You've got Lacey over there and he really belongs to me. I don't know how he got in there. We sent him up to New London to get this experience."

Then he gave him up. He let me have him, and I got Lacey back into my group, and he's been in submarines ever since. He's there yet. All the postwar submarines he was working on and he rode in a lot of them up at Electric Boat. Then he came down to the bureau and he was connected with the development, as I said, of the postwar ones. Particularly when we got working on trying to use the hydrogen peroxide-catalytic system, where we could get a catalyst to break down this rich peroxide mixture and get superheated steam out of it. So Ralph Lacey is a product of the war. We made him into a person who is still with the Navy. Look at this Trident that they're talking about, and he's still at it.

Q: Did he work on the original Polaris?

Mr. N.: Yes. The Polaris came along about 1956 or '57. Captain McQuilkin came to me and told me what was up. It was a big secret, this Polaris thing, and he said:

"We've got to get a team together to design a guided-missile submarine."

So we got our heads together. Who would we pick to start if off? I said:

"Well, we'll put Lacey on it."

Then Captain McQuilkin told me we'd put Captain Jackson on it. He was a Michigan graduate, who was a naval officer. He was a reserve officer at first but I guess he was in the regular navy afterwards, and so we picked Jackson.

Then we gave them a free hand to pick whoever they wanted in the bureau to help them, to go over with Red Raborn and work on his team to develop the Polaris submarine. Red, McQuilkin, and I talked that one over, and I said to McQuilkin:

"The thing we've got to do is - they don't know anything about submarines. Any design development that Lacey and Jackson manage to work out should always come back to us here in the bureau for approval."

That is, Raborn's outfit wouldn't have anything to say about whether it was good or bad. They would try to work the thing out and we would approve it. That's why I always thought Raborn was a pretty smart fellow. He let us do that, because he really had the use of the bureau, too, when we said that.

Q: He was head of Special Projects.

Mr. N.: Yes, and that's what I wanted. I ran into trouble with Rickover on the business of developing these nuclear-powered submarines because I drew up an organization diagram and, of course, I wanted the nuclear-powered submarines that he was talking about always to come back to us for approval. But I never saw that organization diagram again.

Q: You mean he didn't send it back?

Mr. N.: No.

Q: He made the decision himself?

Mr. N.: Yes. I don't know why.

At this point now, as long as we are sort of putting together the beginning of the postwar period, some parts of it and some of the aggravations that came into it. We worked with hydrogen peroxide. Of course, the bomb had been dropped on Japan and the argument about nuclear power came up. Cochrane left the Bureau of Ships and Earl Mills was the chief of the Bureau of Ships.

And they had an Atomic Energy Commission. I guess they called it that from the start.

Q: And did, yes.

Mr. N.: Strauss was the head of it.

Q: Lewis Strauss.

Mr. N.: Then Mills decided that Rickover should do this.

Q: Should do what?

Mr. N.: He picked Rickover to go over and be liaison between the AEC and the Bureau of Ships, and Rickover didn't want to take it. He really balked.

Q: What was his objection?

Mr. N.: I don't know what it was, but I know that he didn't want it. I never was told the complete story. But Mills more or less forced him to do it.

Q: I didn't know anybody ever forced him to do anything!

Mr. N.: Well, he did. I think Rickover was a dedicated Navy man in his own way. Maybe he was playing hard to get because he knew how he was going to do it, so he probably knew that if he resisted it then they'd have to take him the way he was, which is a fact. That's what he was. He was Rickover.

Q: He wrote his own terms.

Mr. N.: And Rickover one day during the war came to me and said:

"Niedermair, could I ride in your car, with your driving group?"

I had a choice parking space in Washington.

Q: You had a car pool, did you?

Mr. N.: No, I didn't really have a car pool but I took people, anyway, and he asked me if I had room, and I had room all right, so I said:

"Yes, that's OK with me. I think so. I go down Connecticut Avenue. Where do you want me to pick you up?"

He said he'd be standing on a certain corner right across the street from where I lived, and he said:

"I'll do it on one condition, and that is if you're coming down Connecticut Avenue and I'm in the middle of Connecticut Avenue and I'm not across the street standing there waiting for you, keep right on going. I don't want you to wait for me ever. If I'm not there, that's my fault."

Q: He said that?

Mr. N.: Yes.

Q: What was the reasoning back of that?

Mr. N.: He didn't want to put me out. I thought that was very good. It was a condition he was putting on himself. He wasn't putting any conditions on me, in a way. That settled it, and so for a long time during the war I took him down.

I used to go down Connecticut Avenue lots of time when Rick wouldn't be around, because I would go to work at two o'clock in the morning quite often. I got a ticket one morning, going to work at two o'clock, in Washington.

Q: Suspect!

Mr. N.: Yes. For driving too far to the left.

Q: Did you get to know Rickover pretty well?

Mr. N.: Fairly well, yes. He confided in me about a number of things that he did and he'd always be so happy about what he was doing, but as the war came along it changed what I was doing. I was preparing myself already with regard to personnel and then when the rules were changed I still fitted in and Rick didn't. Now he had a hard job to keep his people. I already had faced the problem.

Rick wouldn't hire anybody under thirty or something like that, and I took whatever I could get - if I could get the star, the top guy, I'd take him if he was only twenty-three. I didn't care how old he was and so I had whatever hardship there was to give. So it wasn't a problem for me.

Q: You mean you had a postwar personnel setup?

Mr. N.: Well, some good people were available and I didn't make age one of my requirements. Women, I had women.

Q: How large a staff did you have?

Mr. N.: Oh, I don't know. We never exceeded forty, in my knowledge. But that reminds me of another thing that happened on December 7th 1941.

Before December 7th, I had complained no doubt to Ned Cochrane that the people who were working on the theoretical damage conditions of ships –

Q: Damage control?

Mr. N.: – in the damage-control section would work these things up and I discovered that they didn't send them out to the ship, didn't give the ship the information that they would find out about the number of compartments that might cause the loss of the ship or how to save it.

Q: So the damage-control officer on the ship wasn't informed?

Mr. N.: He wasn't informed, and they said to me:

"We can't do that because we can't boss the captain around." It was so silly, and I evidently told Cochrane about this.

December 7th was a Sunday, just like it was this year.

Q: Thirty-four years ago!

Mr. N.: Yes. I got in the office and Ned Cochrane was there early in the morning to see me and he said:

"John, you're going to be handling damage control," just like that.

We were going to develop the damage-control group, damage stability, and all that sort of thing, on December 7th or December 8th.

Q: Timely!

Mr. N.: And I didn't take a single one of the people who were in the old damage-control group, not one.

Q: Your reasoning?

Mr. N.: Well, to start it off, I turned the job over to Ted Sargeant, who was a very clever fellow from the University of Washington - Theodore Sargeant. He was really good, and he worked up stability and all that sort of thing. He's written quite a number of papers on this sort of thing.

And another thing, in our preliminary design group there, we didn't use the Navy filing system. Our files were different than the regular filing system. And the way we marked our filing cabinets, you had to have the code to get in them.

Q: Oh, I see, it was for security reasons?

Mr. N.: We didn't tell anybody. We did that ourselves, and when the Secretary of the Navy got his engineers in from Chicago, efficiency engineers, to investigate all the Navy to see how prepared it was, getting ready for the war -

Q: When did he do this?

Mr. N.: He did it just about the beginning of the war, and they're still in Washington. They came into Washington then and the company is still there.

Q: Is that Boos Allen?

Mr. N.: Yes. Boos, Allen, in the first place, gave us a very good report and they were very interested in the way we did this. I had broken down our first few studies - in the first few studies you'd only do a few things. I already had a bracket in which you would do this. Then the next step, I'd have a few more things you had to do. The final stage would take in the whole study. They were always interested in these things. I turned this job over to Ted, and they gave us a superb statement in which they said that you had to be internationally famous, or something like that, but I was the only fellow that they could say that about. So they applied it to all the rest of them.

Q: In the field of damage control, this became of paramount importance with the operating forces?

Mr. N.: That became a very big thing. Bob Gooding, who is head of design now - he heads up the Navy design department and he's trying to move the gang over to Crystal City from Hyattsville. They'll be going over there next March. He was in the war-damage group. He came in and worked in our section. The last time I saw him, he said he didn't know whether I was working for him or he was working for me. "I never could figure it out," he said!

Q: Tell me about the development of this whole subject of damage control.

Mr. N.: The thing is, of course, you have to investigate the stability characteristics of the ship itself and find out how many compartments you could take without being lost. You made all these calculations and you'd make a report on it. It was a very long extended investigation which more or less indicated what it took to sink you.

Q: And this varied, of course, with different classes of ships?

Mr. N.: It also varied depending on which part of the ship you got hit on. If you got hit in the bow or hit in the stern or hit amidships, and you'd make these thorough investigations. But they also investigated all the damages that were done during the war. They were there during the war and ships were hit and worked on.

Then, after the war was over and the nuclear bombs were dropped on ships, the damage group went out there, when the cruisers and other ships were bombed. I went out to the West Coast and went down to the San Francisco yard and went on board to see what happened, and went through a cruiser that had radioactive water and the stuff that was in it with geiger counters and one thing and another in special suits. Then I went up to Puget Sound and went through a destroyer that was up there, not a destroyer but a cruiser that had been hit by an atomic bomb. There were all radioactive parts in it and the dust was radioactive. We had to wear gas masks and all that to go in.

Q: Tell me, did this section studying the whole problem of damage control in ships, did they go into the necessity for taking various spare parts and equipment and what have you when a ship sailed for the war zone? Was this a part of their study also? Did they help the damage-control officer on a ship in this way by advising him what it might be necessary for him to take with him?

Mr. N.: No, I don't think so. They might have talked about it just like I talked to the damage-control people in the field. I'd give them lectures about it. I gave some lectures on the history of damaged ships, merchant ships, and all that sort of thing. I lectured up in the Philadelphia yard and I gave the history of that up till 1950. Then they wondered whether I wouldn't write up for any future ships. I haven't done it, but maybe I'll give you a copy of that as part of your files.

Another one I put together had to do with the history of keeping the Navy seagoing from 1800 and something up to 1900 and something.

Interview No. 5 with Mr. John C. Niedermair
Place: His home in Stone Harbor, New Jersey
Date: Monday, 9 February 1976
Subject: Biography
By: John T. Mason, Jr.

Q: John, I'm delighted to see you, a picture of health, today.

Mr. N.: Yes, I feel very good, too. I try to keep myself in shape. I've had trouble with colds and everything, but this is the season for it.

I want to answer the question with regard to damage control.

We really didn't actually issue information to any of the captains, except we did this one thing. At Philadelphia we had a training center and any of the damage-control officers who were going off and going aboard ship would be trained at the damage-control center, where we would have not only damage control with regard to flooding but also primed them with regard to fires. So they would be pretty well primed by this. For example, the publication here that I showed you a little while ago. This is dated February 1944 and it consists of probably sixteen or eighteen lectures that went on by Richard Mandelkorn, a commander, U.S. Navy. He did it in collaboration with Robert Danse and Sol Kaufman. Kaufman was a naval architect and Danse was a lieutenant in the Naval Reserve and later on Kaufman was in the Naval Reserve also. By 1945 he was.

At the Naval Damage Control Training Center, Philadelphia, the damage-control school. In connection with that Admiral Cochrane was very much interested in this damage-control work and he came across the idea that the New York Fire Department was using fog nozzles to put fires out. He brought that into the Navy and had the people at Philadelphia who were working on the fire risks and the control of fires to get busy and become familiar with what the New York Fire Department was doing.

Incidentally, I tried to find out whether Sam Morison ever talked about Admiral Cochrane, who contributed so much in our naval construction and all the ships that were out there fighting the war, and I found that the only mention he made of Vice Admiral Cochrane in his history was that he had gone and made contact with the Fire Department in New York City and found that they were using fog nozzles to put out fires. And I was a little disappointed. That is one of the problems in this history. I checked up a number of things. I saw the fine Essex paper in the Naval Institute Proceedings recently, where they talked about the Essex class and really praised it for all the things that it was able to do and continued to do. But no mention was made of the basic design. The reason that they were able to use that Essex class and continue to use it for such a long time was the fact that naval architecture margins had been put into that ship, by design engineers.

I recall one of the things I did to provide the damage protection. I was afraid that maybe we would be faced with mine damage when the Essex class came up, and I did something that was a controversial matter and debated quite often later. I put two inner bottoms into the Essex class. I don't know whether they got eliminated later, but the original design had two inner bottoms. My idea was that it was the only thing you had between you, if you were in the engine room, and the water outside were two thicknesses of plating, maybe not more than a half-inch or an inch thick, and that was it, and a gap of probably 4, 5, or 6 feet of the inner bottom depth. I knew that a direct hit or a direct explosion right over a mine, there wasn't any kind of structure in there that would save you. But these magnetic mines could be set off if you were riding alongside of them, so I felt that this explosion would only damage the shell and the second inner bottom - the first inner bottom, I mean, the one just above the shell, and then the inner bottom above that would still be intact.

Q: A precautionary measure.

Mr. N.: So I put that sort of a safety feature into the Essex class.

There were many other things that got going but, towards the end there, the ships that were doing the job, the Essex class they were able to handle the big planes that we had at that time and they were ready. In fact, I don't know how many of them were finished by 1943. We had all the ones that were converted from Cleveland-class cruisers, the Independence class, all nine were ready, and probably nine or ten of the Essex class were ready.

These particular specific things are put into the ship and I find that fault of non-mention of the design input goes on throughout our industry, so that the Navy isn't the only one that doesn't do it.

Q: I suppose, in defense of Morison, one might say that he was dealing with operational things, an account of the operational activities of the Navy in World War II, and made no pretense of going into the background?

Mr. N.: That is true, but he had people on his staff like Admiral Furer, who was a naval constructor, and he was investigating management concepts and all that sort of thing. They did in a way deal with it but they didn't get it into the main history because, I guess, it's like anything else, it's a passive thing, it's not an active thing, you might put it that way. Really, you win the war with people and ships and command is very important and that's what you deal with, I suppose, when you write history.

We talked about this bridge across the Atlantic and I brought in the Delano-Burgess team. I mentioned that they had a private naval architect as an adviser but I couldn't think of his name. I have the name now. It's Eads Johnson. He was a naval architect from New York. He isn't here now, he's gone. He was an adviser to them and then he quit when he found that the concept was really way off base, and he made a public statement about it.

Then I mentioned that there was a naval architect who represented the Secretary of the Navy up at the first trials in Boston with the LSTs, when Schuyler Pyne came to me and said that there was a Gestapo on board and he was finding fault with the LST. It so happens that Eads Johnson was this same person. When I was talking the last time, I couldn't catch that name, but now we have it in the record. He was quite a prominent naval architect. Of course, I went on to say later how we handled him, so we understand who the person was.

We are now practically through the war. The bomb, I would say, had been dropped and so forth, and Admiral Spruance was one of the great advocates for getting busy to build a new carrier. Because of war experience, he felt we needed a larger carrier, and as a result of his early efforts we got busy very early in the game after the war in collecting information, and the General Board and Ships' Characteristics Board were busy collecting information on what the future carriers should look like. We wound up, of course, with the one that had the keel laid in 1950, I believe it was, and Johnson, who was Secretary of Defense at the time, stopped it.

But Spruance was the one who really got busy very early in the game to do this. Admiral King, Ernie King, was still Chief of Naval Operations and he was the one who advised the idea of creating a ships' characteristics board made up of younger officers than the officers that generally were on the General Board. The General Board officers originally were people who were getting ready to retire. They were rear admirals who were not going to sea again.

He did that and that meant that we had a great deal of contact with the various officers who had been to sea not only on the carriers, but we got into the submarines because submarine commanders had reported on some of the difficulties they had out in the China Sea area, off the Japanese coast, and how they fired their torpedoes and they bounced off the side of the Jap ship and didn't go off.

Also, in our last talk, we touched on submarines but didn't talk very much about them. I mentioned that the submarine was pretty well developed and standardized, beginning very early in the thirties, so that by the time the war came along we had very good submarines ready, especially in structural work. There were two or three civilians who were prime movers with regard to the structural strength of submarines. One was Charley Anderson, who was in the Bureau of C & R and in the Bureau of Ships for a while. He handled the structural strength problems in connection with submarines. Then there was a Dr. Wendenberg at the Taylor Model Basin, who was the research end of the deal. That was quite a team, a great creative team.

We had Wendenberg in the laboratories researching it, and Charley Anderson, the naval architect, who was interested in the structure. He became the specialist who went out to sea and actually took stress readings in the submarines as they went down. Wendenberg and Charley Anderson worked together on this thing. So due to their efforts, the structural side of the hull was pretty well worked out. There has been a lot of praise put on by commanders in the way of depth bombs and one thing and another in the war area, because they really praised the structure of the ship which saved their lives.

I've mentioned some of the other officers who were connected with it. There was McKee, and, of course, Cochrane was also a submarine man. He was a submarine builder. And Morgan. Then there was Admiral Leggett, who was later on chief of the bureau. When I mentioned McKee and Charley Anderson and people like that I was talking about hull but no mention of the machinery. A submarine is very dependent on machinery.

Q: Yes!

Mr. N.: That's why I'm bringing up Admiral Leggett. He was an engineering man, so was Earl Mills an engineering man. They're a different breed altogether, and I always got along very well with the engineering people, the engineering side. I tried to keep myself well informed in their area, too.

Leggett had been to sea in submarines in the engine room in his early days. Later on he was in charge of the work on diesel engines at various ports on land. Then he became the chief of the bureau. He succeeded Admiral Wallin as chief of the bureau. I knew Admiral Wallin from about 1924 or 1925 at New York Navy Yard until he left the Navy. He was a trained naval architect. So there's the team that we had with Leggett and Wallin.

Wallin was quite an expert on welding. He wrote one of the prize papers. He and Commodore Shade wrote one of the prize papers about 1930 in connection with the welding of a structure, a barge or something, and it was well publicized in those days because welding was just getting into the picture. The one thing that brought welding in more than anything else was the treaty limitations that we had on displacement. Welding led to being able to build a lighter hull because we eliminated rivets and seams and overlaps and so on.

Q: Were the other participants, the other signers of the treaty also involved with welding?

Mr. N.: I don't know how the other people did it, but we had people like Wallin and Shade and so on, who got into this thing very early in the game.

Q: No, but I meant the Japanese and the British and the other signers of the treaty, were they also using welding?

Mr. N.: They were coming along. I think we were ahead of them, though, for quite a while. I never knew too much about whether the Japanese were or not because we never could find anything out about the Japanese. We told them everything we did in one way or another, but I never was able to find any good concrete information about what they were doing. So you asked the question what they were doing, I say I don't know. They never told you anything. But we did. As a matter of fact, we told them all about it because when Wallin and Shade wrote the paper for the Lincoln Electric Company, they really told the world how we did it at the very beginning. It was a good idea, though, because they got busy then to get proper welding equipment.

You can talk about welding, but it was the backup stuff like the nozzles and so on and how you handled the air and one thing and another in order to weld. That's where the great techniques came in. Also the kind of rods that you used. If you didn't use the proper rods, the welds would become brittle, for instance.

Wallin was at Pearl Harbor when it was hit by the Japs,

and he's the one who really did great work in salvaging and floating quite a few of the ships that were badly damaged out at Pearl Harbor. As a matter of fact, he sent a telegram into the bureau asking the bureau to send me out there about the day after the 7th of December. But the bureau didn't do that. They decided that they'd keep me in Washington.

Welding came in very well in connection with our submarines later. Most of our submarines were welded later on, but it was a gradual process. Even when we designed the Essex class, I had to do some dodging around, as I mentioned before, in connection with connecting up the strength deck. The hangar deck was the strength deck on the Essex and the flight deck was not the strength deck.

That gives you some background of the sort of things that I was thinking about. I'm bringing that in because after Pearl Harbor Wallin did come east and he worked on the salvage and getting a ship that ran aground down in Norfolk, one of our big ships that had to be gotten off a sandbar or something. He was down there in Norfolk at that time and he handled that project. I don't know whether you have had a chance to talk to Wallin or not. He's out on the West Coast, up in Seattle.

There have been some articles about his salvage work in the Naval Institute Proceedings, so you could look him up that way to see what he did and what his reports are like.

As I said before, Spruance got us going on the carrier, but at the same time problems began to come up in connection with submarine designs. There wasn't very much talk in the beginning about nuclear power for submarines. What we were looking into more than anything else was the hydrogen-peroxide catalyst combination. The catalyst would get mixed up in there and the oxygen and the peroxide and so on would let go and you'd get superheated steam from that combination.

We worked on that and the first submarines were designed strictly in line with conventional diesel engines. I shouldn't say "conventional" because it wasn't very long before General Motors came up with the idea of what they called the "pancake engine."

Q: Pancake?

Mr. N.: Pancake, yes. Instead of the cylinders being in a horizontal line, they stood the thing up and piled one over the other.

Q: And the advantage?

Mr. N.: You didn't need so much length in the engine room. You had to have a certain diameter to carry the weight in the submarine, so you made the engine vertical and it was less long. That was one of the primary reasons for doing it, because diesel engines, in order to get power, have got to have very long engines. So the pancake engines came into the picture and the first postwar submarines were based on using diesel engines and we put pancake engines in them. But they didn't turn out to be successful.

Q: Why?

Mr. N.: Because of lubrication problems. They seemed to use up a lot more oil than a regular diesel engine. You can imagine trying to get oil in the top bank of these cylinders and it wound up that they had the wrong piston rings in there and they took the engine apart at the engineering experimental lab at Annapolis and set it up. Finally, they solved the ring problem, but it didn't solve all the other problems that they got into with these engines in the way of valves and so on. Probably, cooling was also a thing that was bothering them. They phased out and then Fairbanks Morse engines had to be put in. So the General Motors pancake engine was replaced by the Fairbanks Morse.

I've talked about the hydrogen-peroxide idea and the reason is that these investigations to try to build in more submerged endurance. By using the hydrogen-peroxide and the catalyst, you could run the engines submerged because the hydrogen-peroxide was furnishing you with the oxygen that you needed, so you could run the diesel engines submerged, especially in the higher powers was the idea.

I made some investigations in the early days in that connection, and I came up with a figure of about 15,000 shaft horsepower for the early classes of these early submarines. The Albacore finally got into the picture around 1947 or

1948 or something like that, and that had General Motors diesel engines in it. That had a 15,000 shaft horsepower in it.

Q: Was this known as a fleet submarine?

Mr. N.: No, the Albacore was a test submarine, an experimental submarine. It was testing out a hull form, an airship type of hull form. That's what it was testing out.

There's an interesting thing about that hull form. I was being bothered by quite a few people. Ken Davidson from the Stevens Model Basin, Ken and I were on a very friendly basis and what I mention wasn't a belligerency on his part, neither was it on mine. He suggested the streamlined hull form to me and to others just as though we had never thought of it. So in the process of following up this influence of Ken Davidson, one thing he did anyway, he got the top guys to listen to us about this streamlined hull form. He did that, all right. But it's interesting to know, and I went up to Electric Boat Company about that time when I was under pressure, and I talked to the president. I was in the president's office at Electric Boat in Groton and I noticed a model there of the Plunger. It was in a glass case and I said to him:

"Could you send that model to me down in Washington? I need it. I want to put it in my office and when these people who are coming in to sell me on a streamlined-form submarine arrive, I would like to have that model and point to it to show that we already know about streamline."

He said: "No, I can't do that because this is a very valuable model of the Plunger. I'll do the next best thing. I'll take some pictures, photographs, and I'll send you a whole set of them."

I looked this up for you and I have here a set of those photographs. In that connection, I have a note here that those photographs, and I think there are four of them but I'm not sure - U.S. Plunger (A-1). That was a model that the Electric Boat Company made. These pictures were prepared for me, at my request, by the president of Electric Boat.

The interesting thing about this little model, as it turned out, was that the length over beam ratio, which is a critical ratio that you use in connection with these airship-type forms, came out equal to 5, because the length of that little boat was 22 feet and its beam, or diameter, was 4.4 feet, so that ratio is 5.

While we were working on the Albacore, I went down to Langley Field and I talked to them down there. Since we were using an airship type, I thought it would be a good idea to turn around and build the submarine and have it tested in the air tunnel first. First, have a nice smooth hull and test the resistance of it in there, because the only difference between air and water is the difference in density. So they did that, and they came up with the idea that you didn't have any holes or appendages on the hull, holes in it like we have to have in a submarine to get the ballast water in, why, these field tests indicated that the best hull form had a ratio of length over beam that was equal to 5. I didn't know that and I don't think Electric Boat knows it to this day, but I checked it out. I ran across one of my notes and I thought you would like to hear about this.

So about 1950 - this little submarine here, I don't know whether they have a date on there -

Q: 1903.

Mr. N.: 1903, so I tested it about 1953, fifty years later, and I found that it came out the same ratio, L over B was 5, fifty years later. And you know, every once in a while, you see somebody mention that the proper length-to-beam ratio is 5. I thought you would like to know that and you can have this note that I made up for you.

Q: All right, Sir.

Mr. N.: The Albacore was our research vehicle. It had no military equipment in it. It was done strictly to find out how that hull form would perform, and, of course, you had to learn how to control it for diving and so on, turning under water, and these things. Also, it only had one propeller on it. Up to that time nearly all submarines had two propellers, but now we only had one, which put the propeller directly in line with the nice streamlining. So the Albacore, the test vehicle, had one propeller and its horsepower was about 15,000. I keep emphasizing that 15,000 because submarine after submarine after submarine that went on to be built with nuclear power in it had 15,000 horsepower.

Q: The ideal -

Mr. N.: Yes, and somehow the horsepower is going to last us a good long time. This is the point I want to make, but this is so important because when you get enough experience of background in here, you have an insight on these things. This hidden little thing that you build up, you get these insights, and this is what controls your actions.

Q: Yes, I understand. In the case of 15,000 horsepower, is this designed for what kind of speed?

Mr. N.: Speeds that run you up in submerged speeds probably to around 30 knots. This is because you can pull full power out of it with atomic energy, where before you crept around in World War II submarines and they were lucky if they could make 12 knots for an hour. So you couldn't get very far away when they were dropping these depth bombs on you.

We proceeded along all through the postwar times there, but it's these early things that we had to work on that led to what you might call the postwar programs.

The <u>Forrestal</u> didn't come along until sometime in 1950. In the meantime, Cochrane had finished off, Mills became the chief. He was an engineering officer. And then Rickover got into it after Mills was the chief. I've forgotten now just when Mills became the chief. Yes, here it is. He became the chief about 1946, and it was during this period 1946-49 that he, of course, got interested in nuclear power and he picked Rickover to be liaison, as I mentioned before and we talked about it here.

It was a natural for Earl Mills to think that way because he was an engineering officer, not a naval architect. That's the way this thing sort of gets in there. Mills got along and he left in 1949, and he was followed by Admiral Clark.

Q: Admiral what Clark?

Mr. N.: He was Rear Admiral D. H. Clark. He was chief of the bureau from 1949-51. He was only there a short time. Then that's where Holmer Wallin comes in. We've mentioned him.

The submarine program had a lot of interesting facets to it, especially when we were getting into the streamlined or the airship type of form. It so happened that we had information on the hull form of the British airship. The British had an airship for a while that got into trouble. It didn't last very long. It was similar to the zeppelins. Probably it was a German zeppelin that was built for the British. I don't think that's right, because I had another odd thing in connection with that hull form, and that is that I was told that a woman was the one who developed the hull form for that British airship. Her name was Hilda Lyons.

Q: An English woman?

Mr. N.: An English woman. She had quite a lot to do with that hull form. Women's lib would like to know this! I'm not sure about this but I think Dr. Todd, who came over here from Great Britain, was the one who had the contact.

In any event, Captain Saunders was in contact with the British people quite a lot, so if it wasn't Todd it might have been Captain Saunders who led to the use of that British airship hull form for the Albacore. Of course, the things have been refined. But, you know, as you put holes and put appendages into these submarines, the least-resistance type is one that has an L over B ratio that's greater than 5. It sort of compensates for the holes that you put in it by trying to make it slimmer. I have a number on your note there that says L=8. We found out when we put the holes into the model of the Albacore, the best length to beam ratio was 8.

You could vary these things to suit so you'd get the least resistance and better control and so on. You tried to get the least resistance and tried to get the best flow because a lot of noise is developed by the water flowing over these, especially when they go fast under water. If any turbulence is developed it makes a noise.

I think that that gets us into submarines and -

Q: Let me ask how successful the Albacore proved to be?

Mr. N.: Very successful. I have a note here, but that's way, way along, that the hull form of the Darter, I think it was, had a streamlined, less noise, hull form. The last non-nuclear submarine was the Albacore hull form. All the rest of them were that form. I just wanted to bring that up to show. The Skate was the first production type nuclear submarine, but there was a terrific amount of field work that you had to do. I had to go over to Annapolis and have demonstrations made for me to show how this hydrogen-peroxide explodes. When you were through you'd have a little cupful of hydrogen-peroxide and you'd have the catalyst and you'd try to toss it into the cup and the thing would go zoom and it would explode. The catalyst would set it right off. I'm glad we didn't get into that sort of thing.

Q: It sounds rather dangerous.

Mr. N.: I thought it was more dangerous than nuclear.

Here's another thing in connection with this question of trying to run a submarine and be able to run it at high speed for greater periods of time submerged. We had all kinds of suggestions coming up. One of them was to carry liquid oxygen in the submarine. I made an investigation of how to carry liquid oxygen in a tank in the submarine. I tried all kinds of ways. I finally came up with the idea of suspending the tank inside the submarine on a system that looked like the spokes of a bicycle wheel, because it was in contact with the outside and the water was cold to you but it would be hot to the liquid oxygen and would expand it.

Then, in the end, we found out we really couldn't keep this liquid oxygen a captive. No matter how you tried, it would try to leak out. So by the time they came to the development of the Polaris submarines, they were trying to put missiles into those early missile submarines based on the Redstone missile that had liquid oxygen in it. We already knew that oxygen had all kinds of risks and you never knew whether the thing would take off, because with this escaping oxygen it would always condense any moisture that was around the mounts of the valves. They had a lot of trouble down on the launching pads. They had to postpone the launching for a day or two because of difficulties with freezing up.

That was another angle. The risks involved with the hydrogen-peroxide, the thought was to carry liquid oxygen instead, carry fuel oil and a liquid oxygen and you would have the oxygen right there. That was another way of doing it but we never did it. It was impossible to work it that way.

The trend, however, as I pointed out, while Mills was there until 1949, during his time Rickover got started on the idea of nuclear power, and that meant that we could drop the idea of anything but nuclear power. So they're all nuclear-powered now.

Around that time, in those early days, I already sensed that the submarine would be the - I somewhere have a note of mine here in which I looked into the future and decided that the backbone of the fleet would be nuclear-powered submarines. I see now the debates that are going on for the carriers. They're phasing out the big carriers because of the problems with the missiles that are coming out - that is, missiles that can destroy the surface ship. The carrier will be phased out as the backbone of the fleet, and I still think that the submarine will be it.

There has been much talk about how to destroy the submarine. A lot of work is going on to find out some way of destroying a submarine, and we had that same problem when we were working with the submarine. In fact, preliminary design worked with all types of ships. We'd be designing a submarine on one end and a ship on the other end that was supposed to go out and get a submarine and drop a depth bomb on her. That's why I'd get these ideas, because I'd have both ends of them in the same shop!

In any case, that I saw just recently, and I have a paper here somewhere clipped out of The New York Times about the debate that's going on with regard to the aircraft carrier and its future.

Q: It has been for a number of years.

Mr. N.: Yes.

Of course, we weren't standing still just working on submarines. We were also working on new destroyers because the

World War II destroyers were all little fellows. I have here a little check-up I made at one time and I came across it.

The Fletcher class was the basis. The Sumner class came in later and finally wound up being 476 feet long in 1963. But it started with the Fletcher class, which was only 376 feet long. The demands of the war started making these ships longer and longer. The first postwar destroyer was the Forrest Sherman class and that wound up with a length of about 407 feet on the DD.

We finished our design on the first one. Cochrane was still in the bureau when we started our studies. I had finished a study and I found that, no matter what I did, this thing kept getting bigger and bigger all the time.

Q: What were some of the new requirements that made it get bigger?

Mr. N.: Well, the missile armament that had to go on it. They took up more room. And the accommodations - people didn't want to be packed into the same space any more. They had to have more endurance. The speed was about the same. But it's like everything else. It never gets smaller. It keeps getting bigger and better, they say, but Cochrane used to worry about that and he'd always take length out because he'd say even if it was only a couple of feet he'd like to get it out, because the shorter, the smaller, the less work you had to do.

Anyway, the Sherman wound up being about 407 feet long,

but the DDG, which was the guided-missile ship - you see, the postwar Sherman still only had guns on it, but when you got into a guided-missile ship the length jumped up to 476 feet, and the horsepower jumped up to 80,000, while the Forrest Sherman had 70,000. That's how these things were jumping.

They were very anxious to get this destroyer into contract design phase and get started on building the new destroyers. The yards were crying for work, actually.

Q: So that was one of the factors?

Mr. N.: That was one of the factors. So I had to turn it over to contract design. I felt that I was still not sure of the weight. I felt that it could increase another 100 or 200 tons of weight. No, they said, turn it over to contract design and they'll find the weight. But my experience had been that they never found weight, they always added weight to it. And so the first postwar destroyer went into contract design, they started making the DD contract design, and it got heavier and heavier and heavier, and finally it was decided to turn it back to us, which I wanted to do in the first place. I told them:

"Now, I've finished this, I think I ought to start all over again."

But they said, no, we'd better get going on it. So it came back and it wasn't until 1952, the 1952 to 1956 era, that the Forrest Sherman was really finished. That was eight to ten years.

Q: And what was her length then?

Mr. N.: It was 407 feet long, which wasn't too bad, but still we couldn't put a guided missile in it. This was the problem. They wanted to get a guided missile in it. So we finished the Forrest Sherman up and that class were shorter than the DDGs. The DDGs, the 927 class, which came out ahead of the Sherman, was 476 feet long and their horsepower was 80,000.

I just bring this sort of thing up to give you some idea of just how you struggled around with the war there and we finished up our carrier in time. By about 1950 the carrier had been finished that Spruance was interested in.

Q: It was called the United States?

Mr. N.: Yes, but it wasn't really. I don't see how you could call it the United States because the keel was only laid. It never was christened. It would have been the 49 or 48 or something like that. But it was supposed to be the United States.

The interesting thing about that United States was that it had an angled deck on it. We had the angled deck to get the fighters off, so fighters could take off while the bombers were sitting on the catapult side. Fighters could take off from the angled deck, which was on the starboard side, as I remember, and the takeoff was on the starboard side. The island was on the port side, as I recall it.

When we come in now the angled deck — on the Forrestal it was a landing angled deck, and I think that's where the British got the idea. When they saw the original sketches of the United States, they thought that's what it was. They never said so. I don't know why BuAir didn't get the idea first, but they didn't. The first angled deck was on the United States. That was to let the flyers go off.

Q: Was there a feeling of shock in the Bureau of Ships when this was cancelled?

Mr. N.: Oh, yes, the shock was terrific. That's a good question. Actually, the shock was so that Secretary Johnson ordered that all information on the United States should be rolled up and put away and not another minute's work was to be done in connection with carriers. That was a military order, but it didn't apply to me. None of the officers or the chief of the bureau came down to tell me what to do. So I didn't abide by that restriction. I had my chief surface-ship man, George Dankers, button up everything we had in connection with the United States.

Another interesting thing on the United States, I was also afraid of the increased power of torpedoes. So in the design of the United States I increased the torpedo protection, the depth of the torpedo protection 25 per cent to take care of what I thought would be the more powerful torpedoes, and they are more powerful. I know that. That was long before they did any work in underwater explosion laboratories down in Portsmouth. They tested for years and I think they kept the same depth that I took. They kept working on it and I noticed - I have a note here where Captain Evans, who wrote to the Naval Institute Proceedings about the short time it took us to build the LSTs, we mentioned that, I think, before, he was down at Newport News during the time that the Forrestal was building down there. Newport News wanted to take the extra depth out of the ship to save weight, but I told Captain Evans:

"No, you won't save weight. You actually will increase weight because it's part of the torpedo-protection system. They could save weight and also get more room inside for the machinery."

You see, both things, but I said:

"No, you can't save weight because you'd have to make all the other things heavier against the bigger torpedo that I'm thinking about."

So they didn't change it, and when we designed the Forrestal we kept that same depth. With all the research that had gone on in the meantime, it never got changed during my time. I understand now that most of the big carriers are Forrestals and there are one or two nuclear-powered carriers.

The big quarrel that's going on is that the Navy wants to phase out the Forrestal types and come in with all nuclear carriers, because they got better endurance that way. But they're not smaller and they're more expensive. According to the original estimates that I worked on, the Forrestal would cost about $300 million, and the Enterprise, which we got into later, couldn't do anything else except it had more endurance than the Forrestal, cost twice that, $600 million. Now, I think they cost a billion for one ship.

Q: Yes, the Nimitz, I think.

Mr. N.: And I don't blame them for worrying about spending that kind of money on a ship that maybe could be knocked out with a missile, which is a lot worse than a torpedo. It's more like a kamikaze airplane coming down on you.

I'm keeping myself up-to-date on this thing because I'm still very much interested in what's going on.

I put an escalator in the Forrestal. I put it in and nobody took it out. I mentioned, I think, the Franklin had a kamikaze and they lost a lot of people in a space between the flight deck - between the hangar deck and the flight deck there were the ready rooms, right under the flight deck, in the Essex class. And when the kamikaze hit, the ready room was wiped out. It killed all the pilots who were in there. So I wanted to have the pilots stay down below and then put escalators in so the ready rooms would be below, and on the Forrestal they are below and they come up on the escalator from the ready rooms. It's safer. And the Forrestal, as compared with the Essex class, the flight deck is built into the strength of the ship. There are no expansion joints in the Forrestal, but the flight deck on the Essex had an expansion joints.

All these different things that you see there were done and decided by 1956 or 1958. I retired in 1958. It was also during that time, of course, that I received all kinds of honors in connection with this sort of thing.

Q: By that time, all the lessons of the war had been absorbed, hadn't they?

Mr. N.: To a certain extent they had, yes, but the lessons from that war - one of the risks of learning a lesson from a previous war is the probability that the next war won't be the same. Unless you have imagination and this insight that I'm telling you about, it's not going to work. You know that your enemy is going to study what you have. If he's wise, he's going to find out where your weak points are and he'll decide to hit your Achilles heel. That's all there is to it. All you need to do is read your Greek mythology to find out how to do it!

In the same period after the war, the Army transportation service was asking us to make designs for them.

Q: MSTS?

Mr. N.: Yes. We developed the first roll-on/roll-off ship design for the MSTS.

Q: This was quite innovative, was it?

Mr. N.: Yes. The nearest thing we had to it was a ship that was designed by Seatrain people. You know, trains would go down to Panama and so on on Seatrain ships. In a way, they were roll-on/roll-off but not the same as these. These were trucks and craft of that kind.

We also got busy trying to come up with designs for making LSTs faster because the speed of the LST was a little over 10 knots, and of course, in the modern age 10 knots is like standing still. They worked on that and came up with solutions on how to design them with more speed. We did build faster ones and streamlined them and so on. But we kept the same slope on the bottom that I picked out in the early days, 1 in 50, which Professor Hovgaard didn't agree on. That is still the basic slope of these LSTs and any of these fleet landing ships.

The landing ships, dock, came in during the war, and the landing ship, dock, was really designed by the British. They came up with almost a complete concept. They carried long barges in it during the war. The Marines liked that LSD very much. We had an open deck, like having half of the ship look like a dry dock, with boxy wings on the sides and a big tank in the middle, and a big gate on the end.

Q: What is the length of the landing ship, dock?

Mr. N.: It would be somewhere around 500 or 600 feet long. They could carry long barges in there, a couple of hundred feet long each. They were designed to carry two barges around 200 feet long, but they never carried them. They were much better for everything else. At the landings in Okinawa, they used the LSDs, and the Marines used a lot of their smaller amphibious craft. They'd carry them in the LSDs and then they'd float out of the LSD, you had to sink the LSD down, put the gate down, and you'd fill the compartment with water, the central compartment, you let the water run in there. And you put water into the side tanks to increase the draft of the ship, and these things could float themselves out.

That was a great idea and we used it in many ways. The Marines really latched onto that. Then they wanted a deck put over to close the compartment off so they could land helicopters on the deck. And then they came up with a later design.

We put that thing together. In fact, we had to redesign the British LSD because it didn't have enough stability.

Q: When you begin to build all that superstructure, of course, it doesn't.

Mr. N.: And the gate was very heavy. It had to be worked out. It had to be very wide. Gibbs and Cox did that. We did put a deck over on the later models. Various things were done to the LSDs. Until just lately, they worked about ten years on getting out the LHD, or whatever it was, down at Litton, for the Marines. It was an offshoot from the LSDs.

Q: LHD.

Mr. N.: I don't know what they called it. They had a design contest back in the sixties on those, and they just recently launched them and put one into service. In the wartime you can't sit around and wait that long.

The problem of how to catch the submarines is still before you. They haven't really solved that problem. In order to solve it, we're coming along with the SES type designs, fast surface ships.

We just recently have had this Guatemalan earthquake thing and I got thinking of that in my mind, and I got thinking again, really a naval architect is the only one who can design something against disaster, like that, because what does he do? He designs a structure that goes out on a liquid base when the stormy weather comes around there's an earthquake every day. The base that the ship is going on and the thing that's destroying these houses is the shock wave that comes along. The Japanese have designed a certain proper base for structures to withstand a certain amount of earthquake destruction.

So I got thinking, well, gee, a naval architect is always working with earthquakes - seaquakes, if you want to call them that! What led me to that idea was that this is what these different little gadgets are faced with, the SES, or any one of these little things. It would be very difficult to have them be out at sea, whereas the submarine doesn't have to worry about this. It's submerged. Not only that, one of these submarines, the Skate, I think it was, ran submerged all the way across the ocean, then it went under the north pole.

Q: Yes.

Mr. N.: I guess I was at Groton, Connecticut, when I got these pictures of the Plunger #1 in connection with the Skate. It takes a long time before you arrive at the Skate. The Albacore was the preceding thing, and because of that interest, I was right up at Electric Boat there and I got these pictures.

But the submarines have to be designed against pressure and they're limited in the depth they can go to, but we can go much deeper than the World War II submarines. World War II submarines could only go down a couple of hundred feet.

Q: Which wasn't safe really because they could be reached by the depth bombs?

Mr. N.: Yes, in a very short time. And another thing is they could only travel twelve miles or so. They could creep at a creeping speed and go probably thirty miles, they'd have enough juice in the battery.

These are the problems so now the backbone of the fleet, I think, is going to be the submarine, if you're going to have a navy. They'll be the infantry. No matter how many bombs you have or how many missiles you have, you can't get control of the sea without having a ship on it of some kind. The submarine will be the one that will have to do it. Submarines can't screen a carrier against a missile, a submarine can't do that, so we have destroyer screens around to screen against any ships. They forewarn the fleet that the enemy is coming, where the fleet would be.

Now, we're getting into the age when maybe that's not the way to live. I don't know.

Interview No. 6 with Mr. John C. Niedermair
Place: His residence in Stone Harbor, New Jersey
Date: Monday afternoon, 19 April 1976
Subject: Biography
By: John T. Mason, Jr.

Q: You were about to describe a folder that you gave me with some enclosures.

Mr. N.: That's right. First, I furnished you with copies of McQuilkin's letter and so forth. Then an index to the damage-control book by Mandelkorn. And the other is the Geographic picture of the Plunger, which was Holland's design, and this memorial with the Plunger in it is in Jersey.

Then there are a few corrections that I want to bring out in the last recording, that is, the February 9th recording. I was fumbling around on the United States with regard to her number. I believe I said it was 48 or 49. It was really 58. Now, the Forrestal's number was 59.

Q: You had not attempted to give me that number. That's 59.

Mr. N.: 59, yes. Then I said that the test lab in there with regard to torpedo protection and one thing and another was at Portsmouth, and that isn't correct. It was Norfolk Naval Shipyard where that's located.

Somewhere along the line in the last talk I said something about the oxygen tank, liquid oxygen tank, that we were considering to be put into the submarines. I mentioned that the contact of the oxygen tank with the sea water - that statement is wrong, because that wasn't our problem. Our problem was that we had to keep the side of the oxygen tank clear of anything else. It had to be an independent structure so that you could always examine it for leakage. We couldn't integrate it. We tried that originally and I shouldn't have mentioned that we hooked it onto the hull, because we soon found out that we had to make an individual tank, and that's why I had to suspend it on these bicycle rods so that it was a floating tank, really. It didn't touch anything around.

I support that tank like you do a bicycle wheel, but we never used it.

That takes care of the notes that I made with regard to our last talk. Now, as we agreed before we wanted to do, I want to get into some management considerations here. I was particularly thinking about the reason why the Navy yards were started in the first place. Now they're phasing out Navy yards, and I know why. Because private industry was always anxious to get that much more business, which is logical, it's all right.

Q: It was too great a competition.

Mr. N.: The original need for the Navy yards was, first, to build up a system of training for the members of the Construction Corps, and especially since submarines and things like that were getting in the picture and one thing and another. The other need for having ships built in Navy yards was that when they were building some of the ships, it was very hard to get them out of the private yards, first, because they dragged out the building of the ships in the yard; and, second, was that often the private yards were really not doing very good work.

Q: They were heavily unionized, weren't they?

Mr. N.: In those early days they were not, really. Not back when they got going on some of these yards. For instance, my Professor Cathcart, he was a commander in the Navy, was telling me while I was a student at Webb what happened to him when he was on a trial trip on a ship that was built at the Cramp yard. It had reciprocating engines in it and so, in order to find out how much indicated horsepower the engine was putting out, you had to get indicator cards which depended on a spring that was inside and the area of the indicator cards was a function of the indicated horsepower. So if they had the wrong spring tension in there, it could come out as having a nice big indicated horsepower.

Well, Cathcart let them go on their trials, as he told me, and when he got back from the trial trip he said:

"One of the things I want to take with me are the springs that were in the indicator device."

Then they knew the jig was up!

They tried to hire him but he wouldn't do it.

I was on the Nevada in 1915, my first summer job - Webb had a system of 10 weeks of summer work. I went up to the Fall River Yard and worked on the Nevada. She was the first Navy, or really the first big ship, that I'd ever been on. My experience on that ship indicated, too, that you had to be pretty foxy. In fact, the shipfitters told me about some problems in the framing, where the framing missed the side of the ship and they filled out the distance with wood. I believe I mentioned that in a passing sort of way once before, but it did have something to do with the kind of troubles that the constructors were getting into. In the early days of building submarines, the Portsmouth Naval Shipyard got in there as a submarine-building yard so that the constructors could handle that and know how to judge the construction and the work that was going on in other yards. This increased the expertise of our naval Construction Corps and also made a wonderful esprit de corps in the Construction Corps.

The Philadelphia yard was a great yard and the New York Naval Shipyard was one of the greatest, but that's phased out.

I feel in the modern time it's in the wrong place.

That's one of the problems of management that we got into. We were constantly under pressure because one of the things was that we didn't have insurance fees the same as private yards had to carry and so our costs would be always compared back and forth.

Q: Are you going to talk about the value of the Navy yards in World War II?

Mr. N.: In World War II, of course, the Navy yards were really very great. The Boston yard was filled with work. Charlie Brand was commander of that yard, in charge of that yard, during the war, during part of the war. The LSTs were built there and escort vessels. It was a terribly busy yard. I used the Boston Navy yard when I was demonstrating the LSTs, and they furnished me with transportation and everything and we really got things done in a hurry by the work that the Boston yard did for me. All I had to do was to get sketches for them. And then when the Combined Chiefs of Staff came up to see the first trials of the LST, they accepted it and they knew then - at least they thought they did - that they could land on Sicily or wherever they were going.

The Philadelphia yard was always a very good yard and a fine design organization. They built practically every type of ship there. Later on, when they needed to develop boiler-testing stations, they had one in Philadelphia. The Air Force had a base at Philadelphia, that is, the Navy air people.

Then the Norfolk Navy Shipyard certainly proved itself to be a very capable yard. It's still a great yard and it's in being.

Then there's the Charleston Navy Yard. That still has quite a record.

They've all kept up-to-date in their technical things. I know when I was in the New York Yard - I really got started at the New York yard. Whatever part of my career amounted to can be traced back to the freedom that I had at the New York yard. That led to my coming to the bureau and contacting people like Admiral Rock and others, Admiral Wallen and so on. My whole career got started up there. As a matter of fact, I had ten years of field work at the New York yard before I got to Washington.

Q: Yes. You made that very clear that this was of immense value in the development of your career.

Mr. N.: As far as I was concerned, I couldn't have had this and it became very valuable during the war. Apparently, my contribution during the war has been considered as quite a worthy one.

Q: It causes me to ask, with the phasing out of some of these naval shipyards, diminishing the number, what happens in case we get into another real conflict?

Mr. N.: That is still a question. The Philadelphia yard is

still functioning, Norfolk Naval Ship Yard is still functioning.

I went to Washington in March and I met Vice Admiral Gooding and had a chat with him, and they're making great efforts to break away from this package system of awarding contracts that McNamara instituted, and they're trying to develop their in-house design. I do want to say that our naval Construction Corps was based on the British experience. The British didn't have a construction corps in the early days and the line officers ran the show in Great Britain. Then around the Civil War days or after the Civil War days, they built some Monitor-type ships there and they were really handled by line officers. The line officers wanted to keep control of this thing and the constructors really didn't have a say on how unseaworthy these monitors would be.

The line officer and his aides and all went off on the trials with the monitors that had been finished and were going off to sea, and they were all lost. He was lost with it. That was quite a disaster. Then they passed a law in Great Britain that made it so that the Construction Corps would be in charge of shipbuilding and ship-designing.

Q: Based on that disaster?

Mr. N.: That and similar cases. That was a very important one, but there were other disasters, where the Camperdown, in turning, was in a collision and capsized.

The result of all that was that the independent Construction Corps was organized at that time and their word was law. The only one who could change their decision was the king, so they told me.

Taylor was one of the stars who were trained over in Great Britain, at Greenwich, and Admiral Rock was in the British shipyards up in Scotland. I don't know whether he went to Greenwich or not. He never told me. Maybe he went to the University of Glasgow, up on the River Clyde, because he told me about that. He learned shipbuilding there.

Then some of our constructors went to France and learned how the French were doing their building. This gave us an advantage on what other countries were doing. Captain H.T. Wright was French-trained.

Q: Williams was also.

Mr. N.: Williams probably, yes. He came at that time. I didn't know, though, that he went to France.

Q: He told me he did.

Mr. N.: Did he? And I think Leslie Kniskern went to France - Admiral Kniskern - Leslie, to me. And so it went, and they brought this expertise back.

Admiral Taylor went over there and he went into the naval Construction Corps. He came out on top. He had the highest marks of any naval constructor over there. There he came in contact with Froude's Model Basin and he came back to the United States and an experimental model basin was built at the Washington Navy Yard. There's where Taylor got started on working out a series of experiments that resulted in a very famous book Resistance and Propulsion of Ships. I used to know that so well that I could imagine the diagrams and the pages they were on. I could even visualize the shape of the diagrams, which helped me a lot.

Later on, I became fairly close to Admiral Taylor. One of the honors that I received was in the way that he consulted me, and it upset other people in the bureau because I was a new guy down there and Admiral Taylor had been chief of the bureau and they didn't like him coming in to see this new guy. No one ever talked to me about that, how come Taylor came to see me. They kept that pretty quiet. Anyway, Admiral Taylor used to talk to me about these things.

Later on I met quite a few people who worked with him. There was one named Phillips and Hewins who worked at his experimental model basin and part of the work that resulted in this book. So Admiral Taylor, who was really a genius, learned that by going over and working with the British constructors.

All this great work helped us through World War I. Taylor was the chief of the bureau then. And then by 1928, when I arrived in Washington, George Rock was the assistant chief and Beuret was the chief of the bureau. There again, I had met Admiral Rock up at the New York yard. He knew then when I had gotten in touch with Admiral King on the salvage of the S-51, when these letters of commendation came into the bureau recommending me for promotion and so on, there was no problem because Rock knew me right away, and he wrote to me about how pleased he was to hear that I had been successful.

So, you see, the tie-in there with the people who had the contact and understood the kind of person I was, they already had been working like that and were trained to understand it, whereas a line officer wouldn't be able to understand it. However, I got support from line officers, also, because I worked with them and I answered their questions and never violated any confidence that they had put in me when they exhibited what they didn't know about something. This sort of thing was appreciated.

Rock then became chief of the bureau and then Jerry Land became chief of the bureau. There were others in there - Clark. I was very close to Jerry Land. I don't know where he got his training, but he must have gotten it in Great Britain because during World War I he was over there, working very closely with the British, and he got involved in submarines then - Jerry did. Again, Jerry Land could understand me. He tried to hire me for BuAir when he heard about me. He tried to get me into the lighter-than-air side and he tried to convince me:

"Don't worry about going into lighter-than-air, naval architecture isn't too far away from that."

But you see the understanding that he had of these things and that helped me again. So you can see why I was a great believer in the Construction Corps and how these men were trained. A lot of great work was done by them. Quite often they came up with ideas that became a fundamental part of our business. Wallen, for instance, he's one of them. He got into the welding. This intense feeling for these technical things. No line officer will ever do that, unless he's trained that way. Not only that, but they spent years of service in the shipyards where they were building the ships. Now, it's too bad because the Construction Corps was eliminated about 1939. That came about when Charlie Edison was Secretary of the Navy, Rear Admiral Harold G. Bowen was chief of engineering, and Rear Admiral W. G. DuBois was chief of the Bureau of C. & R.

They got into trouble with destroyer stability and one thing and another, which I told about before, but really that wasn't the reason for the whole thing. It was really mostly personality.

They combined the Bureau of Engineering and the Bureau of C & R. The engineering officers were usually line officers. They had been seagoing officers who worked in the engine room. Constructors very seldom had that kind of duty, although they could become the first lieutenant, as they called them. That is, I think, what they called the construction officer on the ship, for some reason.

Q: But the engineering officer was an EDO, wasn't he?

Mr. N.: The engineering officer was not an EDO.

Q: He was not an EDO?

Mr. N.: No. Some of them were interested in design, like Mike Robinson - Sam Robinson. He was greatly interested in design. The EDOs came in afterwards. All these people who became head of the engineering lab or became important in the bureau were officers who had served as an engineering officer running the machinery on the ship. They became familiar with the way the machinery was working and actually were the chief engineers of the ships. But a construction officer, a first lieutenant, who was on a ship wasn't running the ship. There was quite a difference.

However, I got along very well with these people, too. As it turned out, the engineering officers, Bowen and later on Mills - Earl Mills, who was an engineering officer, and Leggett was an engineering officer. He was in command of a submarine at one time and he also was the engineering officer on a submarine. But no construction officer would have commanded a submarine.

When they combined the Bureau of C & R with the Bureau of Engineering it was almost settled that that was the end of the Construction Corps, because now these line officers, the engineering people who were the chief engineers of ships and seagoing in their own field - as a result of all that and Charlie Edison and the other difficulties, by 1939 the thing was consolidated, and it wasn't very long after that, about 1942 - I have here an organization diagram that shows the organization that came into being when Admiral Van Keuren was chief of the Bureau of Ships. Robinson had been chief of the bureau for just a little while - Mike Robinson.

Q: You called him, Sam, too?

Mr. N.: Yes.

Q: Mike was a nickname?

Mr. N.: Yes.

Q: Sam was his given name?

Mr. N.: It was his given name. I don't know how he ever got Mike. I knew him very well because he became head of Webb at one time. I might tell a story about Mike.

When the war was over, I never had met him. He sent his aide up. He had a paper to write about the future of shipbuilding. His aide gave me a few minutes and I said:

"Yes, I know. You go back and tell Admiral Robinson to take a look at the ships that were built in 1900. Our ships that we have today will look just as bad thirty years from now."

Then Mike Robinson called me on the phone and said he'd like to see me in his office, and he congratulated me for that suggestion. He said:

"Now I don't have to write a speech."

It was just little things like that that I could think of in a split second, which was helpful. It's like a joke. If you tell it tomorrow, it's too late!

Anyway, I regretted to see the Construction Corps go because that expertise, I was afraid, would disappear. This experience in the yard, the handling of the men working in the yard, and so on - and Admiral Julius Furer, who was one of the people in the Construction Corps and he became a rear admiral, he was a rear admiral in about 1915. And Taylor became a rear admiral because he was chief of the bureau. I don't think Furer was in the Bureau of C & R during World War I.

Furer opposed this thing, the elimination of the Construction Corps.

Q: What was his reasoning?

Mr. N.: Because of just what I was telling you. The spirit of the corps would be lost, it would disappear, because it had quite a reputation and lots of power. Anyway, so was Jimmy James opposed to it, he told me many times. Furer was working with Morison - Samuel Morison, the historian, at the time, and he came to me to talk about organization and the new organization under the new system and what would happen to the expertise, and the clamor for top promotion. This was a thing that he was worried about. Of course, he got to be a rear admiral, all right, but I think we lost some good men who left because they couldn't get to that position. The highest rank an officer in the Construction Corps could really hope to get was captain.

Q: Oh, really?

Mr. N.: Yes. I don't think that they even made a commodore, although in World War II Shade became a commodore - Commodore Shade, who's a professor out at the University of California - Packy Shade. I know Packy very well. He handled the carrier desk when he was in the bureau for a while.

So Furer was opposed to the idea. I was, too, and I felt that the system of promoting these officers should be changed. But, you see, we were taking in regular line officers now, who were alternating at being chiefs of the Bureau of Ships with the old engineering officers who came in now, former heads of the Bureau of Engineering. They alternated. Cochrane, a constructor, was chief of the bureau, and Mills was chief of the bureau next, and he was an engineering man. Wallen got in there, and Leggett, an engineering officer, came in next. So it went.

I don't know just whether that system kept up, but it seemed to be rocking back and forth.

The result was that we lost the Construction Corps, and we began to get a scramble for choice billets so they could always qualify for the next grade. Even in preliminary design, even though I was there and was still carrying on, they would make up these design arrangements - I gave you a set of early ones - for preliminary design. I also included in the data one arrangement on the record - and here's some more rearrangement, bringing in billets. Then along came Captain Romberg, and he redrew the thing. What did he do? He didn't have an assistant head of preliminary design, so he created a vacancy for another fellow to get in there.

Q: I see.

Mr. N.: Then they would draw the diagrams and I would be in the middle and they'd draw all kinds of lines all around us, so that I could get anywhere I wanted to get, but that was simply a play at making up an organization diagram to find billets for these people.

We did finally get quite a few officers in there. When I first started there was no officer in preliminary design. Jimmy Bates was a civilian and I was selected to relieve him. And we didn't have any contact with the experimental model basin because the officer in charge there refused to come up to the bureau. For some reason or other, he didn't like the bureau system, and so Admiral Rock brought a young officer in, Leslie Kniskern, to be liaison between preliminary design and the model basin. So Leslie Kniskern came in and worked in our group as a liaison officer, and gradually, when things started to get fixed up, a billet was established for him to be in preliminary design when Bates left.

From a military standpoint, you have to have contact with other military people. I can understand that, but I never could understand trying to do it this way. There's a limited number.

I'm giving you this bunch here and included in this group are the early attempts at building up an organization diagram for preliminary design. I included a position description because I created this job, in a way, of the position that I finally arrived at as technical director of preliminary design. You have a copy of this in there, plus two position descriptions - one long one describing the thing in great detail, and then my original comment on an organization that was being attempted. You have this on the advantages and disadvantages of some reorganization they were trying to make. I included that in there so for the record you have the problem of rearranging and rearranging and rearranging.

Romberg came into our section as a captain and usually the people who came in here wound up later on being a rear admiral, but Romberg wasn't. He never became a rear admiral.

He left and he remained a captain. He was in there in 1951. He worked very hard at this but somebody caught him, I guess. He was always a little bit afraid of Armand Morgan. I won't tell you who told me that, but it was a very high-ranking officer who told me, and he was also afraid of me, this high-ranking officer. He confessed it to me not too long ago. He said: "You know, John, I was always afraid of you."

I said: "You don't really mean that. You had no reason to be afraid of me."

But I was so close with everyone up at the top that any young officer who came into my group tried his best to be a very good fellow.

So, poor Romberg, he never made it. He didn't make it for a lot of good reasons.

That brings us along quite a way here in this story about organization. The consolidation was effected in 1939, and Admiral Cochrane became chief of the bureau in about 1942.

You don't have a copy of this that I call No. 1 on my talk sheet, which is the organization of the Bureau of C & R under Jerry Land shortly before it was consolidated. It was signed by Jerry Land on July 1, 1935. I don't know how I can duplicate that, but I do have it, so if there's any demand for it, maybe I could find some way to copy it. That's No. 1.

No. 2 of the organization diagram made up by Van Keuren for BuShips on October 23, 1942. Now it's BuShips. That's the first inkling I have of an organization and that was drawn up during Van Keuren's short time. That, I suppose, can be copied because it's a black and white sort of thing. I'll try to work up some copies and put them together for you. I think, for the record, you ought to have copies of these.

Now, then, there's another one that gets into the picture and it's connected with Admiral Cochrane. I call it No. 3 in my story here. It was gotten up by Admiral Cochrane pretty soon after he got to be chief of the bureau, on December 30, 1942. So you know what the organization looked like at the beginning of the war. That's why I was glad to have that.

You asked what are we going to do when the war comes, where will we get our talent.

Another piece of information in this organization business is a geographical list of shipyards that was made in the Bureau of Ships on 10 December 1943. This list includes private shipyards, Navy yards, building vessels for the United States Navy. It also lists the builders for the U.S. Army, Maritime Commission, Coast Guard, and it included Canadian yards. They had a list of the people and where they were, and I'll try to get you a copy of that. That's item No. 4.

As we said before, there were a lot of regrets about jumping from the Construction Corps to this new organization, but this new organization got busy pretty quickly, which you can see from all these shipyards that they could manage. A lot of that was because of the great expertise of the previous officers who'd been in the Construction Corps, like Admiral Haberle, Cochrane, and Captain Irish, for instance, who ran the New York office in connection with Gibbs and Cox.

Q: Also, the pressure of war, I would think, was a factor, wasn't it?

Mr. N.: Yes, but these people really were good. They knew this stuff so well that they could decide. They didn't always come back and have to see the chief.

Q: No, but the fact that they were working under pressure.

Mr. N.: I don't know. It does something to you. Really, you're a different animal altogether. Your mind is much quicker. I guess it's because a guy's aiming at you with bullets. You've got to be quick or you're dead. That's about what you mean, isn't it?

Q: That's what I mean, yes.

Mr. N.: Anyway, I have a list here that I call No. 5. It's the way when I got busy and began to take over I broke up the work of preliminary design into a sheet like this, which included three stages. There was the A stage, the B stage, and the C stage. The C stage was the final one. The B stage was what they call now the conceptual stage. The B stage is an extension of the conceptual. The A stage is over here. I just called it A. In the present way of looking at it, that's conceptual design.

Q: A is conceptual, and B is conceptual also?

Mr. N.: B probably is the second phase of the conceptual. And what I called the C stage is what they call the final preliminary design. So you can list that among the things that you should be getting.

Then, for the record, I decided that you ought to know what the Ships' Characteristics Board looked like shortly after the war.

Q: Indeed, yes, I'd like to.

Mr. N.: And the officers who were on it.

Q: Is that No. 6?

Mr. N.: That is No. 6. It is the Ships' Characteristics Board roster of officers. See what it says on top, in pencil.

Q: July 1950, yes.

Mr. N.: Now, to continue this thing and give you a further idea of how we tackled preliminary design and the way we looked upon our contact, you'll find that in a paper that you have in there that's entitled "Preliminary Ship Design." It's already marked 7a, 7b, and 7c in your folder. In here we have a diagram, a very simple diagram, that shows the way - my concept of how quickly I could step right from here to there. You have a copy of that.

Then, to continue this article I wrote at the time, I believe this was a lecture that I probably gave some of the officers of the Navy, or it might have been given at the postgraduate school, I don't know. I continued this and I wrote down what I called a mission, the tasks and the characteristics list. That's given on page 3. Page 2 has a little diagram that shows things flowed between us and the Ships' Characteristics Board, and from us down to engineering, contract design, and the code desks, and so on. Further, I list the immediate job and the different things that we had to do, which would be judged by item No. 6 that I told you about.

One of the important things that's in here is a list - this was written on 12 June 1954, that is No. 7a - that includes, as I said, an indication of the broad field we worked in, as given by the following partial list of ships we have studied since World War II, and then I give a list running all the way down from airplane carriers, landing ships, minesweepers, hydrofoil craft, oil tankers, refrigerator ships, icebreakers, and so forth, which I think you'll find very useful as a reference.

Q: Yes. In the previous taped interview you talked about some of that.

Mr. N.: But not completely.

Q: No, no, no.

Mr. N.: Then again, in the same period, I list submarines, the different types that we worked on, and so forth. I thought that I should include this for you because it completes the story that you will have in your appendix and I think would be a fine way to refer to that one, which will be a very important item in this thing.

Then there's an item that you have in your folder called 7b, which discusses the problem of personnel with regard to preliminary design and the type of people that we think we need and how we never would have enough people, the kind of people, and the training that was necessary after the war ended. We had to continue getting more people and training them because we felt that we would be busier than ever after the war than we were before, and it turned out that way.

Item 7c, of which you have a copy, was the Boos, Fry, Allen, Hamilton report to Secretary of the Navy Knox about the preliminary design branch and what they thought of us.

Q: Their report to the Secretary of the Navy?

Mr. N.: Well, they originally were doing this for Secretary Knox. He was the fellow who brought them in from Chicago. He wanted to know whether we were ready. We certainly were ready, according to this. They say here, "They are men of worldwide fame," but it so happened that I was the only one who could fit that description. People knew that I became that way, anyway, and they got to be known, too. It rubbed off on them.

So there you have these specialty things that I made up related to the way we were managing because I'll be drifting in to some things of interest later.

Included further, I have a thing that happened July 11, 1949, which I call item No. 8 here.

Q: Do I have a copy of that?

Mr. N.: No, you don't because I haven't had time to do any of these things.

Item 8 is entitled "Provisions of HR 1689," which is a congressional thing, and (Calendar No. 641 in the U.S. Senate, July 11, 1949). It lists the proposed salary schedule for U.S. government officials between $25,000 to $10,000 annual salary. About that time I became technical director and I was included in this sort of thing in another bill, but this is the only record of this sort of thing I have. If you think you want that part of my story, I'll get a copy of 8 for you.

Q: All right.

Mr. N.: Because you should have the story.

That completes the enclosures or whatever you call them, appendixes, because now I'm coming to the point - we talked about the elimination of the Construction Corps and now, in this management procedure, I have hit the point where we're going to eliminate the Bureau of Ships.

It's been a long life, hasn't it?

Admiral Brockett was the chief of the Bureau of Ships until 1965, and shortly after Brockett's resignation - I must have a statement here. Yes, I was a little ahead of myself. 7a and I gave you No. 8. I retired November 1, 1958, and so these design procedures that I mentioned here and organization continued to about 1962, with modifications brought about by the effects of systems analysis and the impact of project management. These were brought to the fore by the Polaris Special Project under Rear Admiral Raborn, with the PERT charts and all the fancy names. But, you know, systems analysis was really invented by General Electric. They finally decided they had to put their refrigerators through this to be sure they were going to make the best refrigerators, for example. So they had a systems analysis.

So, now, I retired in '58 and I worked with Raborn to get the Polaris started. That was one of the last projects I was on. I helped to build up the team that was responsible, and I mentioned that before, and it resulted in Raborn's great success. In fact, we not only designed the submarine, but we forced the rocket that Werner von Braun wanted to put into the submarine out of the picture. Solid-fueled missiles came into the picture at that point. The missile was developed in parallel with the development of the submarine that was to carry it, a very unusual procedure. This had everybody thinking, now, that's the way to do a job, to put it into a project.

Q: A special project?

Mr. N.: Yes.

Q: But you can only have one special project going at a time.

Mr. N.: We knew with that oxygen tank that I was trying to get into the submarine and the oxygen leaking out of it, you couldn't use the Redstone missile, which was another oxygen tank, sixteen of them. It could have only carried about two of those on the ship. They were too big, in the first place.

Q: So was the Jupiter too big.

Mr. N.: Was that the Jupiter?

Q: Jupiter was the Army's, yes. Redstone was the Air Force's.

Mr. N.: I thought it was the Redstone missile because it was a missile that Werner von Braun had something to do with. In any case, we wiped that out of the picture, and I left. And I've been told that the retirement party I got finished all retirement parties. People came from all over the United States. Admiral Cochrane came down and brought his son, and all the shipyards sent their people down, Bethlehem, Newport News.

I have loads of pictures in here that illustrate that. It was really a wonderful party. It was so good that I hated to leave! For my wife and me that was a great experience.

But, anyway I went off and by 1961 Robert S. McNamara became Secretary of Defense. That's why I said about 1962 they began to modify the system. They gave him a chance to get in there. He brought about the so-called total package procurement system, which included naval ships. You could see package stuff for an airplane, maybe, or smaller things, but a ship is quite a complicated thing. It's the biggest man-built structure ever, actually.

Rear Admiral William Brockett, chief of the Bureau of Ships, strongly opposed the adoption of what he called the package award system - that is, Brockett called it that. He resigned as chief of the bureau and his assistant resigned with him. The two left. Fortunately for me, being a Webb man and the people who were looking for somebody to head up Webb and friends of mine came to me and asked me what I knew about Brockett. Of course, I knew a lot about Brockett. So he became head of Webb.

As I say here, "Shortly after Brockett's resignation, the Bureau of Ships was phased out, and the Naval Ships Systems Command was phased in." I don't know of any better way than that to say it, because it had to be done something like that. Rear Admiral Nathan Sonenshein was appointed commander of the Naval Ships Systems Command and held that position from 1965 to 1972. And here's where I got in on this thing.

I met Sonenshein in New York at a meeting of naval architects and I advised him that the package system - or the package winner take all, as I called it - would be a failure, especially during war emergency. I told him that in 1965, when he first got the job. Then I met him again in his office in June 1972, when I discussed the 2,000-ton surface-effects ship design, because I was asked to take on the job by Aerojet, as a consultant for them in connection with the SES. So I went to his office and talked about this idea because I wanted to find out just how serious the Navy was about the surface-effects ship. We talked for about an hour, and one of the things was that Sonenshein wondered whether a smaller SES should be tackled, so now he was consulting me. I told him I thought not. I said:

"No, you might as well find out the limitation of the SES."

I knew you could make the little ones go and they're still trying to come out with a big one.

I say here that I had arranged this meeting with Sonenshein to find out how serious the Navy was about the SES. This was a very fortunate meeting for me because now I met Bob Gooding and, that same day, he was going to take over Sonenshein's job.

Q: Oh, I see.

Mr. N.: Bob Gooding, incidentally, had worked in preliminary design under the war damage group when I was there. He is a vice admiral now. I said to him:

"Gee, I'm glad to see you because I want to break into the Pentagon today."

He asked me why, and I said: "I want to see an admiral over there," I can't think of his name now, "and I want to talk to him about SES because some project management group of his is working on the SES. I'd like to meet him."

I remember Bob Gooding calling him up and saying:

"A friend of mine is here, John Niedermair, and he'd like to see you. He's forgotten more than we'll ever know."

So I had a date with him that day and that's the last I saw of this person.

Then I studied further into this question of what was happening in this management system, and I found that Leopold wrote quite an article in the U.S. Naval Institute Proceedings and the Naval Review of 1975, in which the article was entitled "Should the Navy Design Its Own Ships?" He gives a rather complete discussion of the present design and procurement procedure, and he also refers to how the organization appeared before 1966, but he doesn't say too much about that.

Then there was another article - and this one was really an eye-opener - by Ken B. Spaulding, Jr., and Anthony F. Johnson. It was in Naval Engineer Journal, that is, the naval engineers' journal, of February 1976, quite recent, entitled "Management of Ship Design at the Naval Engineering Center." This gives a very complete insight into what this new procedure looks like. I looked it over and I decided that to me the entire method appeared too dependent on design teams systems approach. The long time lapse from the time that there is a need for a new type of ship to completion of the preliminary design and contract design is entirely too long and complicated, with management methodology. This systems approach, again.

Interestingly enough, I'm a Webb man and I found out that Ken B. Spaulding, who wrote a very good paper on how they're doing it, told me all about it, is a Webb man. I only found that out by trying to find out why he could write such an article. Now I know.

Q: Now you're going to talk about some of the recognition that you received in the postwar era as a result of what you did during World War II, particularly.

Mr. N.: Yes, I'll try to get into it in sort of a chronological way.

Around November of 1945 I received the Navy's Distinguished Civilian Service Award, which is the first one that I got. The next thing that happened to me was that I became the president of Senior Engineers, an engineering organization. I was their first president, by the way. I helped put this organization together and that organization presents an award every year, which is called the J. C. Niedermair Award, for the best paper that's presented at their symposium.

Q: And is there a monetary award as well as -

Mr. N.: It's just an award. You get a plaque with my name on it. It's a beautiful plaque. I have one that they gave me and I'll show it to you next time, if I think of it. I've got it in the same package it came in.

Anyway, then I became chairman of the local section of the Society of Naval Architects and Marine Engineers. I was their second chairman because I recommended that Bates, who had been my previous boss and went with MARAD, become the first chairman of that section. We were the second district section that was established by the society. Now, of course, the Society of Naval Engineers has that same system. They have a special name for their local sections.

In 1956 one of the more astonishing awards came to me when I was picked as one of the top ten Civil Service people in the United States. I received a lot of publicity from that and the Navy seemed to feel quite honored by it, that I had been selected, and they sent a bulletin around to all the naval stations in the whole United States and abroad, too.

Q: Who makes this selection?

Mr. N.: The Civil Service League. This was the second year that they did this, and I was on the second one. Quite a lot of people went to this meeting and they made a particular effort to get the governor of New Jersey to attend this meeting because I was considered a native son of Jersey. I left Jersey when I was four years old, my father took me away.

Q: But here you are back again!

Mr. N.: The governor came and he made the principal address.

Q: Who was that, Meyner?

Mr. N.: No. I can't think of his name now. He was quite a prominent governor but it's too far back for me to pick up his name. I'll look it up later.

These things have a way of being like fire, you know, you set the grass on fire and it keeps spreading. So that year I also received the honor of becoming an honorary member of the Society of Naval Architects, and also a council member of the Society of Naval Engineers about the same time. In 1958 I received the Society of Naval Architect's top award, which is the David Taylor Gold Medal - a solid gold medal that weighs about eleven ounces - ten ounces, or something like that.

Somewhere along the line in there I received the William S. Owen Award from my alumni association - the William Selcock Owen Award - which commemorated my contributions and what I did for my alumni and for Webb.

About two years ago, in November, the society also made

me a fellow of the Society of Naval Architects, so I've had about everything that they can do for me. I presented two papers before the society. They both had to do with the stability of ships. After I came back from the Safety of Life at Sea Conference in 1929, Admiral Rock, who considered me the top expert in that field, wanted me to present a paper, which I did around 1932 or '33. Then a couple of years later I wrote another one.

In 1950 or '51 I went over to the 100th anniversary of the Royal Institute of Naval Architects, and Jimmy James went over there, too. I presented a paper before the Royal Society and he presented a paper, also.

Q: Cochrane did, too, did he not?

Mr. N.: No, he didn't. He was knighted, but he didn't present a paper at that time. He was so busy with other things he could only stay one day. He flew in and left the next day. But he really received quite a bunch of honors that day. I've forgotten what they were all about.

I received a sort of a small award for my paper from the society.

Then I made some presentations at the University of Michigan, at Webb Institute, and also at the postgraduate school at Annapolis, at Philadelphia at the damage-control school there. I spent quite a bit of time doing that sort of thing.

So much for these honors. I've been honored, I believe, very generously, but as it goes, you know, none of us do these things alone. I would say that I have been given credit for having put together the best technical team in my field. The British naval constructors when they came over here during the war went back home and tried their darnedest to do the same thing the way I'd worked it out, and they never succeeded. I went over particularly to see the chief constructor over there, but they never could undo. This is what I'm afraid will happen here because we've undone a good working arrangement. They had a working arrangement of sorts before for a long time and they couldn't undo that one to go to work and do the one that I had, which was really better than what they had, but they couldn't undo what they had.

They'll find trouble with this organization they have now, with all the different groups that they've built up.

Q: You mean our people?

Mr. N.: Yes. There'll be a lot of resistance against this project manager system for a long time. It takes ten years to build up a good football team and you can lose a good football team in the same time, if you're not careful.

Q: Faster than that!

Mr. N.: Yes. So it's going to be a hard job.

I also co-authored the first chapter in the society's

<u>Principles of Naval Architecture</u>, which is a worldwide basic textbook on naval architecture. I co-authored that because this William S. Owen Award that I mentioned that I got, he was a professor of naval architecture at Webb and he was the author of a previous article, or chapter, in a book of naval architecture. Now the book is going to be done over again and he was going to be working on it, but he died before he could do anything, so I took it over. I used some of his material but I changed the ship he used and all that sort of thing. Anyway, I'm on that and the society said they couldn't do anything for me. They gave some of the authors a life membership and one thing and another, but Holden said to me:

"John, we can't do anything for you. You already have it." So I told him not to worry.

Then I was a chief consultant for Gibbs on a limited-time basis. I wouldn't give them any more than about a third of my time. They didn't like that very much.

Q: You mean this was in retirement?

Mr. N.: Yes. I felt I didn't want to be a fulltime consultant. I wanted to be free to be on other committee types of work, so while I was not more than a third of my time consultant to Gibbs, in the meantime I was also on committees for the Mohole Project with the Academy of Sciences committees in connection with the Mohole Project, which was to drill a hole through the mantle somewhere where the sea was 25,000 feet deep.

With the Academy of Sciences or the Science Foundation, I was on the advisory committee to CNO Arleigh Burke regarding the selection of advanced ideas. Arleigh said, "I don't know anything about this stuff. You people pick it out." And no sooner did we come around with our report when all the professors on this thing found things in there that they wanted to write papers on, even on our recommendations to Arleigh. I wouldn't let them do it, so the academic people weren't very happy with me. That was that.

Then, again, I was on another committee in the academy, either the Science Foundation or the academy, an advisory committee to the Maritime Administration regarding the future of the merchant marine.

Q: In what period of time was this?

Mr. N.: These all took place between, I would say, 1960 and 1968. On top of that I was on the advisory committee to the Bureau of C & R. Rear Admiral Ralph James was there on hydrofoil designs and fast destroyer type designs.

So you can see I kept occupied.

The Bureau wasn't C & R really. That should have been Bureau of Ships there. I was an old hand so I called it C & R! My subconscious mind was rescuing the old C & R.

I was on the advisory committee to the Ships Systems Command. I got into that place. That happened to be through

Rear Admiral Frank C. Jones. This was a very interesting committee that I was on because it concerned personnel selection and policy questions. I liked Frank Jones quite a bit. That was around the time that the Ships Systems Command was under way, right in the very beginning, and they knew they had to get rearrangement in their organization, and one of the problems was the selection of the personnel. So from that standpoint, I had something to do with the people who were supposed to do it, but while policy questions came in they never brought up these other things. Maybe their bosses were bossing them around so there wasn't anything that I could advise them on because they couldn't tell the boss off! So there I was stuck with something I didn't like, but I did the best job I could in picking the things out for them. I've been over there and been in Leopold's office, talking to them, and they all want me around, which is very nice, I think. Regardless of whether I agree with them, they all want to see me.

By 1960 I was on a long job that started before I retired in preparation for a Safety of Life at Sea conference in London. Cochrane was the chairman of that committee. Of course, being in the bureau, I was appointed on the committee and now I was retiring, so I wrote to Admiral Cochrane and told him that I was leaving the bureau and I guessed he'd have to pick somebody else to represent the bureau. He wrote back and said:

"We didn't pick you to represent the bureau. We picked you as a person."

That was nice of him to say. I have a letter in which he says, "you weren't representing the bureau, you were representing John Niedermair."

Fortunately for me, I was walking through these spider webs. I was this female spider on this web and I wouldn't get caught!

Anyway, I finally wound up in London in 1960 as the industry expert, representing the industry for the Society of Naval Architects. By that time, the Coast Guard was responsible for safety of life at sea. In London I got very much upset by the system that the British representative was using to get the votes on his side. They had a secret code arranged, and it had to do with the way he held a card. He always had a card in his hand, and if he held it edgewise it would be the same as saying "down," no. If he didn't raise that card up, it was yes.

Q: How did you catch on to the system?

Mr. N.: Well, I watched this person and I noticed it corresponded with the way this group voted. I had talked to John Comstock - Cochrane had died now and John Comstock became the chairman of the committee. He was the naval architect for Newport News. We were sitting there in this big room and it occurred to me what the hell they were doing and I said:

"John, I've got it. You know I've been complaining about this voting and it's funny that these people are all voting against us."

The only people who were voting for us were the Russians, the Italians maybe, and so on, and I said:

"I know how they do it."

He said: "Shh, John, keep quiet. You're talking too loud."

I was all excited now that I had the answer and it was the code, yes. I was so damned mad when I came back here I had a heart attack.

Q: But it wasn't publicized there?

Mr. N.: No, we didn't do it. They asked me not to do it because what difference would it make.

Q: Tell me about the award that is still to be given you next Monday by the Academy of Sciences.

Mr. N.: Yes, at age eighty-two. I think we should put that in the record. It's very nice.

Q: You certainly should.

Mr. N.: This award will be given by the Academy of Sciences. It's the Gibbs Brothers Award. It's a sort of a great surprise to me. I was amazed to get the announcement of it on April 2nd. That was the first I knew of it. And it took from April 2nd until just last Saturday to find out just what kind of a suit I had to wear.

Q: Now you know it's black tie.

Mr. N.: Now I know. I think it's a very fine thing because I knew William Francis Gibbs quite well. He did some great work for the Navy. There was no question about that. He was a great organizer. I doubt very much whether anybody could beat him at that, because during the war he not only did great work for the Navy but he also did great work for the merchant marine, too. The Ugly Ducklings and all those ships, he organized. Now this medal is in honor of the Gibbs brothers.

Q: And it is for what kind of merit?

Mr. N.: I understand it's for my outstanding contributions in naval architecture and marine engineering, particularly in regard to my guidance, I believe is the way they put it, or direction of the basic designs of all types of Navy ships. I believe that's the way they worded it.

Q: That's quite a sweeping award.

Mr. N.: Yes.

Q: And it's a gold medal plus $1,000?

Mr. N.: And an illuminated plaque. I think it's a tremendous thing. They're giving me one minute and I could really talk for an hour!

Q: Well, this will cause you for a few days before the award is given to really choose every word.

Thank you very much, John.

APPENDIX

to

Series of Interviews

with

John C. Niedermair

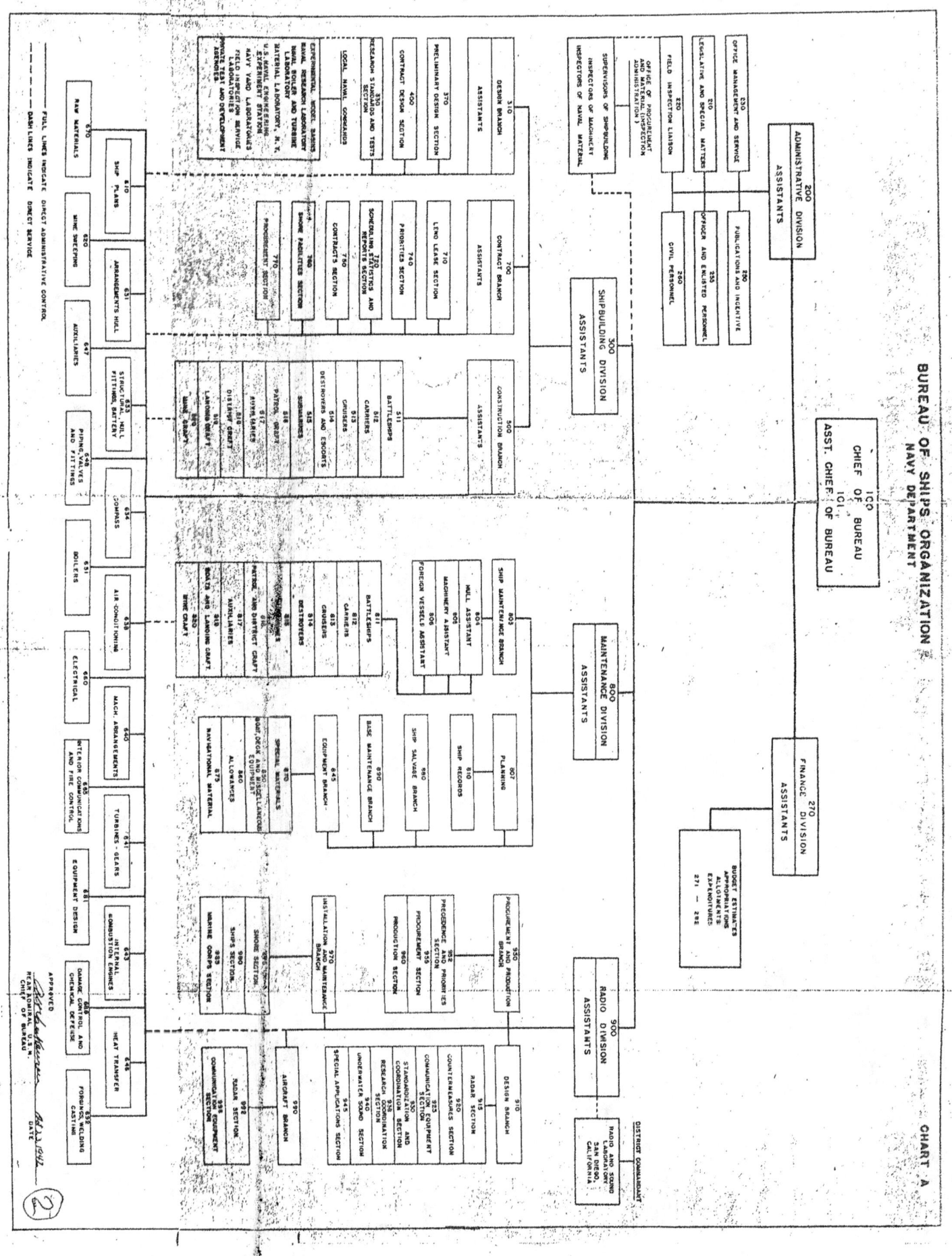

NAVY DEPARTMENT
BUREAU OF SHIPS
WASHINGTON, D.C.
10 September 1943

GEOGRAPHICAL LIST OF SHIPYARDS
NAVSHIPS (728)

This list includes all Private Shipyards and Navy Yards building vessels for the United States Navy.

These yards are arranged in geographical order by areas, with a number beside each yard indicating its exact location on the front cover map.

The main body of the report lists the builders alphabetically by company name.

There is added a listing of builders for the United States Army, Maritime Commission and Coast Guard.

NORTH ATLANTIC AREA
(From Maine through Maryland)

Geo. No.	Name of Company	Geo. No.	Name of Company	Geo. No.	Name of Company	Geo. No.	Name of Company
1.	Maine Bt. Yd. Associates, Ind., Ellsworth, Maine	27.	Baltzer-Jonesport Bt. Corp., Medford, Mass.	48.	Mystic Shipyard, West Mystic, Conn.	71.	Cons. S. B. Corp., Morris Heights, New York
2.	Mt. Desert Bt. Yd., Inc. Mt. Desert, Maine	28.	Simms Bros., Dorchester, Mass.	49.	Noank S. B. Co., Noank, Conn.	72.	Nassau Bt. Basin Inc., Freeport, L. I. N. Y.
4.	So. West Bt. Corp., Southwest Harbor, Maine	29.	Geo. Lawley & Sons Corp., Neponset, Mass.	50.	Electric Boat Co., Groton, Conn.	73.	Freeport Point Shipyard Inc., Freeport, L. I. New York
5.	S. B. Morton & Sons, Dark Harbor, Maine	30.	Beth. Fore River, Quincy, Mass.	52.	Saybrook Yacht Yard, Inc., Saybrook, Conn.	75.	Marin Bt. Wks. Inc., Arverne L. I. New York
7.	Bristol Yt. Bldg. Co., S. Bristol, Maine	31.	Beth. Hingham, Hingham, Mass.	53.	Eureka S. B. Corp., Newburgh, N. Y.	77.	J. K. Welding Co. Inc. Brooklyn, N.Y.
8.	Camden S. B. & Mar. Ry. Co., Camden, Maine	32.	U. S. Rubber Co., Woonsocket, R. I.	54.	New York Rubber Corp., Beacon, N. Y.	78.	Rubber Corp. of America, New York, N. J.
9.	Snow Shipyards, Rockland, Maine	34.	Walsh-Kaiser Co. Inc., Providence, R. I.	55.	Armstrong Rubber Co., West Haven, Conn.	79.	DeKoM S. B. Corp., Mill Basin, Brooklyn, N. Y.
10.	Waldoboro Shipyard Inc., Waldoboro, Maine	35.	T. B. Kingman Marine Constr., Cataumet, Mass.	56.	The City Lumber Co., Bridgeport, Conn.	81.	Dawn Cruisers Inc., Clason Point, N. Y.
11.	Bath Iron Works Corp., Bath, Maine	36.	R. Bigelow & Co., Monument Beach, Mass.	57.	The Boat Shop,	82.	Great Kills Bt. Yd.,
12.	R. G. Marr, Damriscotta, Maine	37.	Carl N. Beetle, New Bedford, Mass.	58.	Southold L. I. New York	83.	Beth. Steel Corp., Staten Island, New York, N. Y.
13.	Rice Bros. Corp., East Boothbay, Maine	38.	Palmer Scott & Co., New Bedford, Mass.	59.	Greenport Basin & Const. Co., Greenport, L. I. New York	86.	Great Kills, Staten Island, N. Y.
14.	Hodgdon Bros. & Goudy & Stevens, East Boothbay, Maine	39.	Martha's Vinyard S. B. Co., Vinyard Haven, Mass.	60.	Norwalk Tire & Rubber Co., Norwalk, Conn.	86.	Wheeler S. B. Corp., Whitestone, L. I. N. Y.
15.	Frank L. Sample Jr., Inc., Boothbay Harbor, Maine	40.	Herreshoff Mfg. Co., Bristol, Rhode Island	61.	Luders Marine Const. Co., Stamford, Conn.	87.	Trageser Copper Works, Maspeth, L. I. N. Y.
16.	Reed Brothers, Boothbay Harbor, Maine	41.	Warren Boat Yd. Inc., Warren, R. I.	63.	Walker E. Abrams Shipyard Inc. Malesite, L. I. N. Y.	88.	Peterson's Shipyard Inc., Port Washington, L. I., N. Y.
18.	A. R. True, Inc. Amesbury, Mass.	42.	Harris & Parsons Inc., East Greenwich, R. I.	65.	Wm. E. John & Associates, Milton Point, Rye, N. Y.	89.	Jakobson Shipyard Inc., Oyster Bay, N. Y.
22.	Quincy Adams Yt. Yd., Inc., Quincy, Mass.	43.	Perkins & Vaughn Inc., Wickford, R. I.	64.	Elscott Bt. Inc., City Island, N. Y.	92.	Ira S. Bushey & Son Inc., Brooklyn, N. Y.
23.	V. A. Robinson Enc., Ipswich, Mass.	44.	Anchorage, Inc., Warren, R. I.	65.	Robb. Jacob Inc., City Island, N. Y.	93.	Wheeler Shipyard Inc, Brooklyn, N. Y.
24.	Calderwood Yt. Yd., Inc., Manchester, Mass.	45.	C. Hiltebrant D. D. Co. Inc., Kingston, N. Y.	66.	United Bt. Ser. Corp., New York, N. Y.	94.	Sullivan D. D. & Repair Co., Brooklyn, N.Y.
25.	Hood Rubber Co., Inc., Watertown, Mass.	46.	Island Docks, Inc., Kingston, N. Y.	67.	Henry B. Nevins Inc. City Island, N. Y.	95.	Purdy Boat Co., Port Washington, L. I., N. Y.
26.	James Russel Boiler Wks., Boston, Mass.	47.	Franklin G. Post & Son, Mystic, Conn.	69.	Julius Peterson, Nyack, New York	97.	Electric Boat Co., Bayonne, N. J.
				70.	Bruns-Kimball & Co., Patchogue L. I., N. Y.	98.	Federal S. B. & D. D., Kearny, N. Y.
99.	Federal S. B. & D. D., Newark, N. J.
100.	New Jersey S. B. Corp., Barber N. J.
101.	Walsh-Steers Co., Jersey City, N. J.
102.	Jennings Yt. Bldg. & S. Yd. Inc., Keasbeys, N. J.
103.	Fairhaven Yacht Wks. Inc., Fair Haven, N. J.
104.	Zobel's Sea Skiff & Yt. Wks., Seabright, N. J.
105.	Irwin's Yacht Works, Red Banks, N. J.
106.	Hubert S. Johnson Bt. Mfg., Bay Head, N. J.
109.	Cramp S. B. Co., Philadelphia, Pa.
110.	John H. Mathis Co., Camden, N. J.
111.	John Trumpy & Sons Inc. Gloucester, N. J.
112.	New York S. B. Corp., Camden, New Jersey
113.	R.T.C. Shipbldg. Corp., Camden, New Jersey
114.	Penn-Jersey S. B. Corp., Camden, N. J.
115.	Chas. B. Leek & Sons, Lower Bank, New Jersey
116.	Ventnor Bt. Wks. Inc., Ventnor, New Jersey
118.	Dravo Corp., Wilmington, Delaware
119.	Am. Car & Fdy. Co., Wilmington, Delaware
120.	Delaware Bay S. B. Co. Inc., Leesburg, N.J.
121.	Berg Boat Co., Georgetown, Md.

-1-

NORTH ATLANTIC AREA (cont'd)
(From Maine through Maryland)

Geo. No.	Name of Company
123.	The Owens Yacht Co., Dundalk, Baltimore, Md.
124.	An Electric Welding Co. Inc., Baltimore, Md.
125.	Beth. Steel Corp., Key Highway, Baltimore, Md.
126.	Maryland D. D. Co., Baltimore, Md.
127.	Cape May Shipbldrs. Inc., Cape May, N. J.
128.	International Latex Corp., Dover, Delaware
130.	Oxford Boat Yard Co., Oxford, Maryland
131.	Modern Marine Serv., Severna Park, Md.
132.	Annapolis Yacht Yard Inc., Annapolis, Md.
133.	Vinyard S. B. Co., Milford, Delaware
134.	Seaford S. B. Co. Inc., Seaford, Delaware

SOUTH ATLANTIC AREA
(From Virginia to Miami, Florida)

Geo. No.	Name of Company
135.	Horace E. Dodge Boat & Plane Corp., Newport News, Va.
136.	Newport News S.B. & D.D. Co., Newport News, Va.
138.	Elizabeth City Shipyard, Elizabeth City, N. C.
139.	Barbour Boat Wks., New Bern, N. C.
141.	Charleston S. B. & D. D. Co., Charleston, S. C.
142.	Higgins Ind. Inc., Savannah, Ga.
143.	Savannah Mach. & Fdry. Co., Savannah, Ga.
144.	Brunswick Marine Const. Co., Brunswick, Ga.
145.	Aetna Iron & Steel Co., Jacksonville, Florida
146.	Huckins Yt. Corp., Jacksonville, Florida
146.	Gibbs, Jacksonville, Florida
147.	Daytona Beach Bt. Wks. Inc., Daytona Beach, Florida

SOUTH ATLANTIC AREA (cont'd)
(From Virginia to Miami, Florida)

Geo. No.	Name of Company
148.	Pine Castle Boat & Const. Co., Titusville, Fla.
149.	Ft. Pierce Bt. Co., Ft. Pierce, Florida
152.	Miami S. B. Corp., Miami, Florida
153.	Prigg Boat Wks., Miami, Florida

GULF COAST AREA
(From Fort Myers, Florida to Texas)

Geo. No.	Name of Company
155.	Bushnell-Lyons, I.W. Inc., Tampa, Fla.
156.	Tampa S. B. Co. Inc., Tampa, Fla.
157.	Food Machy. Corp. Inc., Lakeland, Fla.
159.	Newport Ships, Walnin (near Tallahasse, Fla.)
160.	Charles W. Smith, Receiver for Pensacola Shipyard & Eng. Corp., Pensacola, Florida
161.	Gulf S. B. Corp., Chickasaw, Alabama
162.	Choctaw Boat Works, Mobile, Ala.
163.	Ingalls S. B. Corp., Pascagoula, Miss.
164.	Westergard Boat Wks., Biloxi, Miss.
166.	Canulette S. B. Co., Slidell, La.
167.	Jones & Laughlin Steel Corp., New Orleans, La.
168.	Higgins Ind. Inc., New Orleans, La.
170.	Cons. Steel Corp., Ltd., Orange, Texas
171.	Weaver Shipyards, Orange, Texas
173.	Gulfport Boiler & Welding Wks., Port Arthur, Texas
175.	Brown S. B. Co., Houston, Texas
177.	Rice Bros. & Co., Rockport, Texas

GULF COAST AREA (cont'd)
(From Fort Myers, Florida to Texas)

Geo. No.	Name of Company
179.	Remontis Mfg. Co., Corpus Christi, Texas

PACIFIC COAST AREA
(From California to Territory of Alaska)

Geo. No.	Name of Company
181.	San Diego Marine Const. Co., San Diego, Calif.
182.	Kettenberg Boat Works, San Diego, Calif.
183.	Campbell Machine Co., San Diego, Calif.
184.	Harbor Boat Works, San Diego, Calif.
185.	Lynch S. B. Co., San Diego, Calif.
187.	American Pipe & Const. Co., Southgate, Calif.
188.	North American S. B. Corp., Newport Beach, Calif.
189.	The Peyton Co., Newport Beach, Calif.
190.	South Coast Co., Newport Beach, Calif.
192.	Long Beach Boat Shop, Long Beach, Calif.
193.	Victory S. B. Co., Newport Beach, Calif.
194.	Lomax Boat Co., Newport Beach, Calif.
195.	Wilson Co., Wilmington, Calif.
196.	Western Pipe & Steel Co., Los Angeles, Calif.
197.	Robert V. Staats Co., Newport Beach, Calif.
199.	Wilmington Boat Works Inc., Wilmington, Calif.
200.	Fellows & Stewart, Wilmington, Calif.
201.	Cons. Steel Corp. Craig Yd., Los Angeles, Calif.
202.	Food Machy. Corp., Riverside, Calif.
203.	Al Larson Boat Shop Inc., Terminal Island, Calif.
205.	Beth. S. P., Terminal Island, Calif.

PACIFIC COAST AREA (cont'd)
(From California to Territory of Alaska)

Geo. No.	Name of Company
206.	Garbutt - Walsh, Inc., San Pedro, Calif.
208.	Ackerman Boat Co., Newport Beach, Calif.
209.	Harbor Bt. Bldg. Co., Terminal Island, Calif.
210.	Soule Steel, Los Angeles, Calif.
211.	Beth. S. B. & D. D. Corp., San Pedro, Calif.
213.	Food Machinery, San Jose, Calif.
215.	Soule Steel, San Francisco, Calif.
216.	Anderson & Cristofani, San Francisco, Calif.
217.	Beth. Steel Corp., San Francisco, Calif.
218.	Judson - Pacific War Ind., San Francisco, Calif.
219.	George W. Kneass Co., San Francisco, Calif.
220.	Dravo Corp., Alameda, Calif.
221.	Moore D. D. Co., Oakland, Calif.
222.	Kaiser Co. Inc., Richmond, Calif.
224.	Wm. F. Stone & Son, Oakland, Calif.
226.	Gen. Eng. & D. D. Co., Alameda, Calif.
227.	McDonough Steel Co., Oakland, Calif.
228.	United Eng. Co., Alameda, Calif.
230.	Pollock Stockton S. B. Co., Stockton, Calif.
231.	Stephens Bros. Bt. Mfg. Co., Stockton, Calif.
232.	Madden & Lewis Co., Sousalito, Calif.
233.	Calif. Steel Prod. Co., Richmond, Calif.
234.	Fulton Shipyard, Antioch, Calif.
235.	Sacramento S. B. Co., Sacramento, Calif.

PACIFIC COAST AREA (cont'd)
(From California to Territory of Alaska)

Geo. No.	Name of Company
236.	Colberg Boat Works, Stockton, Calif.
237.	Moore Equipment Co., Stockton, Calif.
239.	Basalt Rock Co. Inc., Napa, Calif.
240.	Kruse & Banks S. B. Co. Inc., North Bend, Oregon
241.	Gunderson Bros., Portland, Oregon
242.	Commercial I. W., Portland, Oregon
243.	Albina Eng. & Mach. Wks. Inc., Portland, Oregon
244.	Willamette Iron & Steel Co., Portland, Oregon
245.	Portland S. B. Co., Portland, Oregon
247.	Kaiser Co. Inc., Vancouver, Wash.
248.	Astoria Mar. Const. Co., Astoria, Wash.
249.	Harbor Plywood Corp., Hoquiam, Wash.
251.	Tacoma Bt. Bldg. Co., Tacoma, Wash.
252.	Western Bt. Bldg. Co., Tacoma, Wash.
253.	Mojean & Ericson, Tacoma, Wash.
254.	Seattle-Tacoma S. B., Tacoma, Wash.
255.	Nelson Boiler & Tank Co. Inc., Tacoma, Wash.
256.	J. M. Martinac S. B. Co., Tacoma, Wash.
257.	Shain Mfg. Co., Seattle, Wash.
258.	Seattle S. B. Co., Seattle, Wash.
259.	Seattle-Tacoma S. B., Seattle, Wash.
261.	Ballard Mar. Ry. Co. Inc., Seattle, Wash.
262.	Assoc. Shipbldrs., E. I. Seattle, Wash.
265.	Assoc. Shipbldrs., L. U. Seattle, Wash.

- 2 -

PACIFIC COAST AREA (Cont'd)
(From California to Territory of Alaska)

Geo. No.	Name of Company
264.	Olson & Winge Mar. Wks., Seattle, Wash.
265.	N. J. Blanchard Boat Co., Seattle, Wash.
267.	Washington Boat Works, Seattle, Wash.
269.	Puget Sound Bridge & Dredging Co., Seattle, Wash.
271.	Winslow Mar. Ry. & S. B. Co. Inc., Winslow, Wash.
272.	Lake Washington Shipyards, Houghton, Wash.
273.	Everett Pacific Co., Everett, Wash.
274.	Everett Mar. Ways, Everett, Wash.
275.	Reinell Boat Works, Marysville, Wash.
276.	Bellingham Mar. Ry. & Bt. Bldg., Bellingham, Wash.
277.	Northwestern S. B. Co., S. Bellingham, Wash.

GREAT LAKES AREA
(From Vermont to Minnesota)

Geo. No.	Name of Company
278.	Donovan Contracting Co., Burlington, Vt.
279.	Proctor's Yt. Works, Burlington, Vt.
280.	Hutchinson Bt. Works Inc., Alexandria Bay, N. Y.
282.	Richardson Bt. Corp., North Tonawanda, N. Y.
284.	Bison S. B. Co., Buffalo, New York
285.	Dunlop Tire & Rubber Corp., Buffalo, N. Y.
286.	Niagara S. B. Corp., Buffalo, N. Y.
287.	Erie Concrete & St. S. B. Co., Erie, Pa.
288.	Am. Boiler Works, Erie, Pa.
290.	Stadium Yt. Basin Inc., Cleveland, Ohio
291.	General Motors Corp., Cleveland, Ohio

GREAT LAKES AREA (Cont'd)
(From Vermont to Minnesota)

Geo. No.	Name of Company
292.	Am. S. B. Co., Cleveland, Ohio
293.	Am. S. B. Co., Lorain Ohio
294.	~~Firestone Tire Rubber Co.,~~ ~~Akron, Ohio~~
295.	Goodyear Tire & Rubber Co., Akron, Ohio
296.	General Tire & Rubber Co., Akron, Ohio
298.	B. F. Goodrich Co., Akron, Ohio
299.	Master Tire & Rubber Corp., Findlay, Ohio
302.	The Matthews Co., Port Clinton, Ohio
303.	Lyman Boat Wks., Sandusky, Ohio
304.	Am.Cruiser Co. Inc., Detroit, Mich.
305.	Fisher Boat Works Inc., Detroit, Mich.
306.	Graham - Page Motors Corp., Detroit, Mich.
307.	Chrysler Corp., Detroit, Mich.
308.	Chris - Craft Corp., Algonac, Mich.
309.	Gar-Wood Ind. Inc., Marysville, Mich.
310.	Defoe S. B. Co., Bay City, Mich.
311.	Eddy S. B. Co., Bay City, Mich.
312.	Foster Boat Co., Charlevoix, Mich.
314.	Victory S. B. Co., Holland, Mich.
315.	Borg - Warner,Corp., Kalamazoo, Mich.
316.	Truscott Bt. & Dock Co., St. Joseph, Mich.
317.	Robinson Marine Const. Co., Benton Harbor, Mich.
318.	Dachel - Carter S. B. Corp., Benton Harbor, Mich.
319.	Chicago Bridge & Iron Co., Jeffersonville, Ind.
320.	Seneca, Ill.
321.	Pullman Standard Car Mfg. Co., Chicago, Ill.
321.	Henry C. Grebe & Co., Chicago, Ill.

GREAT LAKES AREA (Cont'd)
(From Vermont to Minnesota)

Geo. No.	Name of Company
323.	Froemming Bros. Inc., Milwaukee, Wisc.
324.	Burger Boat Co., Manitowoc, Wisc.
325.	Manitowoc S. B. Co., Manitowoc, Wisc.
326.	Dunphy Boat Corp., Oshkosh, Wisc.
327.	Leathem D. Smith S. B. Co., Sturgeon Bay, Wisc.
328.	Peterson Boat Works, Sturgeon Bay, Wisc.
330.	Fox River Boat Works Inc., West DePere, Wisc.
332.	Walter Butler, Superior, Wisc.
333.	Globe Shipbuilding Co., Superior, Wisc.
335.	Marine Iron & S. B. Co., Duluth, Minn.
336.	Zenith Dredge Co., Duluth, Minn.

MISSISSIPPI VALLEY AREA
(From Alabama to Minnesota)

Geo. No.	Name of Company
338.	Firestone Tire Rubber, Memphis, Tenn.
339.	Pidgeon - Thomas Iron Co., Memphis, Tenn.
340.	Nashville Bridge Co., Nashville, Tenn.
341.	Mo. Valley Bridge & I. Co. Ind., Evansville, Ind.
343.	St. Louis Car Co., St. Louis, Mo.
344.	St. Louis S. B. Steel Co., St. Louis, Mo.
345.	Mo. Valley Bridge& I. Co., Leavenworth, Kan.
346.	Darby Products of Steel Plate Co., Kansas City, Mo.
347.	Kansas City Structural Steel Co., Kansas City, Mo.
348.	Jeffersonville Bt. & Mach. Co., Jeffersonville, Ind.
350.	Mt. Vernon Bridge Co., Mt. Vernon, O.
351.	Quincy Barge Builders, Quincy, Ill.

MISSISSIPPI VALLEY AREA (Cont'd)
(From Alabama to Minnesota)

Geo. No.	Name of Company
352.	Omaha Steel Works, Omaha, Neb.
353.	Dravo. Corp. N. I. Pittsburgh, Pa.
354.	Am. Bridge Co., Ambridge, Pa.
355.	Chamberlain Corp., Waterloo, Iowa.
356.	Cargill, Inc., Minneapolis, Minn.
358.	Durkee Atwood Co., Minneapolis, Minn.

NAVY YARD AND CANADIAN COMPANIES

Geo. No.	Name of Company
17.	Navy Yard, Portsmouth, New Hampshire
21.	Navy Yard, Boston, Mass.
76.	Navy Yard, New York, N. Y.
107.	Navy Yard, Philadelphia, Pa.
137.	Navy Yard, Norfolk, Portsmouth, Va.
140.	Navy Yard, Charleston, S. C.
238.	Navy Yard, Mare Island, Calif.
270.	Navy Yard, Puget Sound Bremerton, Wash.
359.	Navy Yard, Pearl Harbor Honolulu, Territory of Hawaii.
360.	War Supplies Ltd.
360(a)	Collingwood Shipyds Inc., Collingwood, Ontario, Canada
360(b)	Kingston S. B. Ltd., Kingston, Ontario, Canada
360(c)	Midland Shipyards, Ltd., Midland, Ontario, Canada
360(d)	Morton Eng. & D. D. Co. Ltd., Quebec City, Quebec, Canada
360(e)	Canadian Vickers, Ltd., Montreal, Quebec, Canada.
360(f)	Toronto Shipbuilding Co. Ltd., Toronto, Canada.

- 3 -

Bureau of Ships
Navy Department
Washington, D. C.
10 September 1943

ALPHABETICAL LIST OF PRIVATE SHIPYARDS

U. S. Navy

Building Yard	Builder's Code No.	Inspector
Walter E. Abrams Shipyard, Inc. Halesite, Long Island, N. Y.	001	SupShip, 11 Broadway, New York, N. Y.
Ackerman Boat Company (USA) Newport Beach, California	003	SupShip, San Pedro - Terminal Island Office Terminal Island, California cc: SupShip, Los Angeles S.B. & D. D. Co., San Pedro, California
Aetna Iron & Steel Company Jacksonville, Florida	004	Asst. SupShip, P. O. Box 5236, Jacksonville, Fla. cc: SupShip, P. O. Box 1921, Savannah, Ga.
Albina Engine & Machine Works, Inc. Portland, Oregon	005	SupShip, Willamette Iron & Steel Corp. Portland, Oregon
American Boiler Works Erie, Pennsylvania	006	Asst. SupShip, Erie Concrete & Steel Supply Co., Erie, Pennsylvania cc: SupShip, 1100 Chester Avenue, Cleveland, Ohio
American Bridge Company (USA) Ambridge, Pennsylvania	007	Asst. SupShip, Ambridge, Pennsylvania SupShip, Dravo Corp., Neville Island, Pa.
American Car & Foundry Company Wilmington, Delaware	008	SupShip, Dravo Corporation Wilmington, Delaware
American Cruiser Company, Inc. Detroit, Michigan - Trenton Plant	010	SupShip Fisher Boat Works Detroit, Michigan
American Electric Welding Co., Inc. Baltimore, Maryland	011	SupShip, Annapolis Yacht Yard, Inc. Annapolis, Maryland

(USA) Yard Building for U. S. Army also.
\# Lend Lease Program

Preliminary Design - Bu. C. & R.
Schedule of Calculations, Curves, Plans, and Memoranda Required for a Complete Design.

Design.
Authorization.
Characteristics, Tentative   ; Final

No.	Work.	Remarks
	"A" Stage.	
1	Dimensions	
2	Displacement Standard ; Designed	
3	Arrangement Sketches	
4	Coefficients of Form.	
5	Speed, Resistance & Power Estimates	
6	Weight Estimates, First Check of No. 1.	
7	Rough Body Plan	
8	Information Furnished to General Board	
9		
10		
11		
12		
	"B" Stage.	
1	General Arrangement Plan (Spring Style)	
2	Floodable Length Curve - Approximate	
3	Required GM, probable worst case of damage, turning, rolling.	
4	Protection Studies, Sketches, Weights, Etc.	
5	Midship Section with Tentative Scantlings	
6	Weights Revised with Approx. Vertical & Long'l Centers.	
7	Volumetric Study	
8	Advance Information for Bureau of Engineering.	
9	Information Furnished to General Board	
10	Speed, Resistance & Power Est., Tentative Propeller Calc.	
11	Cruising Radius, Fuel Requirements, Etc.	
12	Memorandum on Selection of Form, Etc.	

No	WORK	REMARKS
	"C" STAGE	
1	LINES & BODY PLAN	
2	MEMORANDUM TO MODEL BASIN	
3	E.H.P. CURVES, MODEL BASIN REPORTS	
4	S.H.P. " " " "	
5	SECTIONS & OTHER INFORMATION FOR BU. ENG.	
6	DISPLACEMENT AND OTHER CURVES	
7	CROSS CURVES OF STABILITY	
8	STATICAL STABILITY CURVES	
9	WEIGHTS, RECAST FOR LONG'L STRENGTH CALCULATIONS	
10	BONJEAN CURVES FOR STRENGTH, FLOODING, ETC.	
11	LONGITUDINAL STRENGTH CALCS, BENDING MOMENT, ETC	
12	" " " , " " CURVES, ETC.	
13	MIDSHIP & OTHER SECTIONS WITH SCANTLINGS	
14	INERTIA OF SECTIONS, STRESS CALCULATIONS & CURVES	
15	GENERAL ARRANGEMENT PLAN	
16	SHELL EXPANSION & PLATING PLAN INCL. WEIGHT & CENTERS	
17	DECK PLATING PLAN " " " "	
18	FRAMING PLAN, TRANSVERSE & LONG'L., INCL. " " "	
19	MISCEL. STRUCTURAL PLANS INCLUDING " " "	
20	PROTECTION STUDIES & CALCULATIONS	
21	PROTECTION PLAN & WEIGHT	
22	WEIGHT ESTIMATE WITH VERTICAL & LONG'L CENTERS	
23	WEIGHT SUMMARIES WITH GM, DRAFT, TRIM	
24	MEMORANDUM ON ARRANGEMENT, STRUCTURE, STRENGTH	
25	RUDDER CALCS, HEEL WHEN TURNING, TACTICAL DIA., ETC	
26	COMPARTMENTATION, FLOODABLE LENGTH, DIRECT METHOD	
27	" DAMAGED STABILITY WITH SKETCHES	
28	" MEMORANDUM	
29	GENERAL MEMO. COVERING HISTORY, DEVELOPMENT OF TECHNICAL FEATURES, ETC.	
30	INFORMATION FURNISHED TO FINAL DESIGN (INCLUDING ABOVE ITEMS MARKED Ⓕ)	
31	NATURAL PERIOD OF HULL VIBRATION	

SHIP CHARACTERISTICS BOARD ROSTER OF OFFICERS

1 July 1950

NAME	DESIGNATION			ROOM	PHONE
RADM I.N. KILAND, USN	Senior Member			4E-614	55183
RADM J.E. MAHER, USN	Alternate Senior Member			4B-486	56071

MEMBERS

CAPT G.G. CRISSMAN, USN	DCNO (Operations) Member			4D-524	73069
Appropriate Desk, Op-34	DCNO (Operations) Alternate				
RADM A. SOUCEK, USN	DCNO (Air) Member			4E-408	52629
CAPT L.L. KOEPKE, USN	DCNO (Air) Alternate			5D-642	74250
CDR F.M. PETERS, USN	BuPers Member	(Arl.Annex)		2601	7738
CDR E.W. ABBOT, USN	BuPers Alternate	"	"	2604	7205
CDR S.W. BROWN, USN	BuAer Member	(Main Navy)		2W-96	2692
CDR A.E. PADDOCK, USN	BuAer Alternate	"	"	2W-96	3066
RADM J.A. SNACKENBERG, USN	BuOrd Member	"	"	0301	2005
CDR A.F. GERKEN, USN	BuOrd Alternate	"	"	4222	2003
CAPT C.K. BERGIN, USN	BuOrd Alternate	"	"	0317	3662
RADM F.E. HAEBERLE, USN	BuShips Member	"	"	3026	3956
CAPT P.D. GOLD, USN	BuShips Alternate	"	"	3026	3956
CAPT A.M. MORGAN, USN	BuShips Alternate	"	"	4522	5073
CAPT W.L. HOFFHEINS, USN	Head Fleet Maintenance			4A-478	55326
Type Desk	Head Fleet Maintenance (Alternate)				
CAPT O.F. NAQUIN, USN	Executive Member (Op-04E1)			4C-459	53816

ASSOCIATE MEMBERS

CAPT R.C. SUTLIFF, USN	A	Head Electronics	4B-533	52252
CAPT E.H. PIERCE, USN	R	Head Electronics	4B-533	52252
CAPT T.B. McMURTREY, USN		Head Electronics (Alternate)	4B-545	52535
RADM J.R. REDMAN, USN		Head Naval Communications	4C-675	55982
CDR J.W. JONES, USN	A	Head Naval Communications (Alternate)	5E-785	53429
CAPT J.A. MORRISON, USN	R	Head Naval Communications (Alternate)	5E-785	53429
RADM F.A. BRAISTED, USN		President Board InSurv (T-3 Bldg)	2035	2269
COL W.A. KENGLA, USMC		U.S. Marine Corps Member	4D-516	72145
CAPT O.H. ALEXANDER, MC, USN		BuMed Member	PA Bldg 4 23	3038
CAPT R.L. MORRIS, USN		Ship Command Op-04E1C	4C-457	53756
CAPT F.C.B. JORDAN, USN		Ship Electronics Op-04E1E	4C-457	53706
CDR P. VAN LEUNEN, USN		Asst. for CIC Op-04E1E1	4A-542	52821
CDR B.P. ROSS, USN		Ship Engineering Op-04E1F	4C-457	53756
CDR F.G. BENNETT, USN		Ship Armament Op-04E1D	4C-457	53706
CDR J.L. COUNIHAN jr, USN		Ship Aviation Op-04E1G	4C-453	53658
CDR B.P. ROSS, USN		Asst. for I.C. Op-04E1C1	4C-457	53756
CAPT L.R. LASPIT, USN		Submarines Op-04E1H	4D-645	73589
CAPT A.G.W. McFADDEN, USN		A/S Warfare Op-04E1J	4D-636	75826
Mr. A.E. SWIM		Recorder Op-04E1B	4C-453	53658

A - Acting
R - Ordered to Report

(All numbers are in the Pentagon unless indicated otherwise).

To those of us who have spent the greater portion of our professional lives in this field, it has afforded a unique satisfaction, since we have enjoyed the feeling of being "Masters of Approximations".

Preliminary design is the first "basic design" work that is undertaken in the design of a new ship. Hence, it would be better to refer to the work as "Basic Ship Design". This would then draw attention to the important nature of the design problem which draws heavily on the fundamentals of Naval Architecture and the other branches of engineering. The work is creative, and hence is most stimulating to the engineering talents and imagination of the individual designer.

The Preliminary design Branch, Code 420, of the Bureau of Ships, where this work is done, fits into the Department of Defense organization about as shown in the following flow diagram:

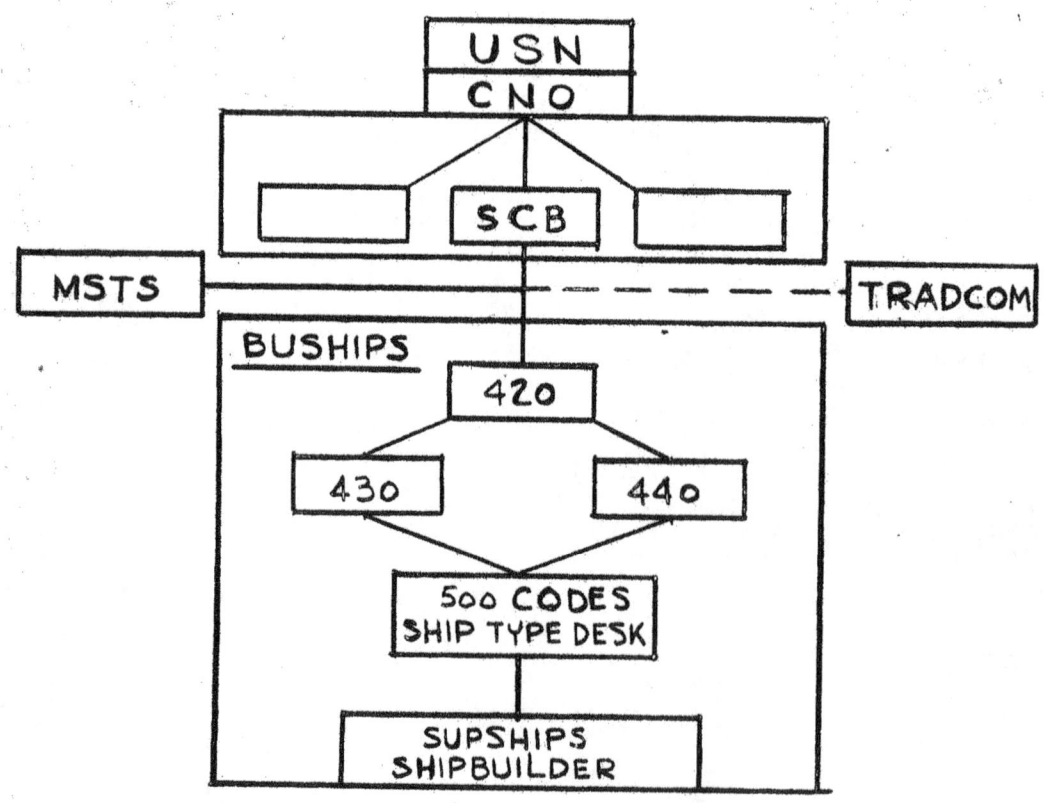

PRELIMINARY SHIP DESIGN

BY

JOHN C. NIEDERMAIR 4 June 1954

Since your are familiar with the application of the principles of Naval Architecture and Marine Engineering to the solution of a ship design problem, I will not take up the little time we have by dwelling on the detail attention which such a solution requires. The problem of ship design for all types of vessels whether they are large or small, for merchant or naval service, is basically the same. The main difference is that, in the case of naval ship design, the basic information on which to base a design is independent of Classification Society rules, or the U. S. Government regulations as administrered by the United States Coast Guard for merchant vessels. However, MSTS designs, which will be manned by civilian crews, must comply with Classification and Coast Guard requirements. Warship design is largely dependent upon the background information assembled by the responsible design agency, which, in the United States, is the Bureau of Ships.

The most appealing factor in preliminary design work is the lack of finality. There is no one answer to any one preliminary design problem. Given the same characteristics different naval architects will produce widely different designs. The personal view often seriously affects the final result. Long experience in this field has indicated that the path to success lies in the constant attention to the accumulation of basic data. Unfortunately, or fortunately, depending on the individual viewpoint, most of the fundamental problems which the naval architect has to deal with cannot be analyzed by applying simple engineering theory. Much of the work is based on empirical data. To the young naval architect this is a fortunate circumstance since this gives him many opportunities for further study and development.

This is an idealized "flow" diagram, in actuality there are many devious wanderings which are caused by the complications of administrative control of a shipbuilding contract. These are not shown as we are concerned at the moment only with the design of ships.

A ship design in the Bureau of Ships usually gets started by a request for a design study from the Chief of Naval Operations, or from ideas which originate in the Bureau of Ships, from a request by the Military Sea Transport Service, or from the Transportation Research and Development Command of the Army. In any case, the start is made by briefly listing the "characteristics" for the design in order to be objective in the design study. The "characteristics" list the mission, tasks and principal features of the ship under the following headings:

1. Mission and tasks
2. Displacement
3. Speed
4. Cruising Endurance
5. Armament and ammunition
6. Electronics
7. Protection
8. Aviation or other special features
9. Basic cargo

The immediate job we then have in the Bureau is to work out a design which meets the characteristics. And has —

1. A feasible arrangement
2. Adequate main machinery plant
3. Adequate stability and proper trim

4. Adequate strength

5. Good seaworthiness

6. Appropriate watertight integrity

7. Good maneuverability

An indication of the broad field we work in is given by the following partial list of ships we have studied since World War II --

Surface Ships -
1. Airplane Carriers
2. Anti-submarine ships
3. Destroyers
4. Escort Vessels
5. Landing Ships - Dock
6. Landing Ships - Tank
7. Inshore Fire Support Ship
8. Minesweepers
9. Patrol Craft
10. Mine Counter Measure Device
11. Hydrofoil Craft
12. Auxiliary Vessels - Oil Tanker
                 Attack Cargo Ship
                 Refrigerated Cargo Ship
                 Ammunition Ship
                 Vehicle Carrying Ship
                 Icebreakers and Vessels to operate in ice.

Submarines —
   a. Electric Powered
   b. Nuclear Powered
   c. Closed Cycle Powered
   1. Attack Types
   2. ASW or Killer Types
   3. Radar Picket
   4. Guided Missile
   5. Research
   6. Mine Laying
   7. Midget

STATUS OF THE BASIC DATA

At the present time a great deal of research work is being done in hydromechanics which eventually will improve our knowledge of hull form, resistance, and ship motions in rough water. Frictional resistance has received much special attention, since without accurate knowledge regarding the frictional coefficient for the model or the full scale ship little correct information can be derived regarding the residual resistance attributable to wave and form. At present the best information we have is the Schoenherr frictional formulation. To the C_f from the Schoenherr formula we add a roughness allowance which varies depending upon the type of surface roughness expected. The standard merchant ship allowance is .0004 while for Navy ships we allow .0008 or more depending upon the type of ship and kind of paint used.

The Taylor standard series is still a good basis for estimating the residual resistance. The David Taylor Model Basin has revised the standard series so that the residual resistance is expressed as a coefficient, C_r, plotted on a base of speed-length ratio. This method provides a coefficient which is directly additive to the Schoenherr frictional coefficient.

Ship turning has been receiving much attention but not much progress has been made in arriving at a good theory concerning ship turning. At present we still use approximations based on model tests to determine the turning characteristics of a design. The maneuvering of submerged submarines is also being studied and electronic computers are being used to solve the equations of motion and predict trajectories. This work has become more and more important as the speed of submarines has increased. A paper which was presented at the November, 1953 meeting of the Society NA&ME helps to clarify some of the problems concerning turning and the design of hull appendages.

Little progress has been made over the years regarding the prediction of speed loss and other performance factors in rough seas. Work is being done in this field but nearly all of our design work is based on careful comparison with existing ships. We know little more than R. E. Froude disclosed in an INA paper in 1905. It is fairly well known that the maximum loss of speed will occur in head seas when the wave length is in the zone of 0.75 to 1.25 times the ship length. Our studies to date seem to lead to these general conclusions:

    a. Main hull proportions may be more important than small refinements of the hull form.

    b. Narrow beam and deep draft appear to improve performance in rough water.

    c. There may be large differences in behavior between the performance in irregular seas and the performance in regular seas.

    i. That a fuller development of the analytical approach is required.

As a result of the failures of merchant ships, during and since World War II, a great deal of basic structural research has been devoted to the problem of notch sensitivity of ship structural steel. Considerable light has been thrown on the metallurgical requirements of steel for satisfactory notch toughness. These requirements are now appearing in commercial and navy specifications. The development of high yield strength hull steels has also advanced considerably and a new navy specification has recently been released for an 80,000 psi yield strength, low alloy steel. This material can be used to great advantage to save weight. The use of light alloys, such as aluminum, has also changed the "rules" for the designer and increased the efficiency of his design efforts.

Considerable attention has been paid to impact loads and vibration in recent years. We appear to be headed for dynamic rather than static structural design. The study of the dynamic loading of ships in a seaway is one phase of this development.

The living accommodations aboard ship are receiving a great deal of attention at the present time. The main effort is in the direction of more space and improved accommodations per person. This has been the trend in merchant ships since before World War II and in the U. S. Navy since the war. Air conditioning is being specified in some degree for nearly all major designs. Trends such as these are forcing us to much larger ships as compared with the pre-war designs.

Prior to World War II it was never realized that the training then received was all that would be available to carry on during the war. Furthermore it was also never realized that trained replacements must be near at hand for the key personnel of the section. ~~Naturally~~ Fortunately we went through the war with no casualties in the few civilians that were available. The small staff which has produced all of the preliminary designs of U.S. warships has never included sufficient personnel with suitable qualifications for understudy and possible replacement for the key individuals in the section. War experience and the post war work now going on has emphasized the need for a more complete organization. The main difficulty, however, has been the availability of suitably educated personnel with outstanding aptitudes which could be developed in the art of overall ship design. It has been found that personnel suitable for the work of the section can only be developed by a slow process of careful selection over a period of years. To attract outstanding personnel and retain them it is most important to give them every opportunity to develop on the job.

The preliminary design of all types of naval vessels is largely original in character in all stages of the shaping necessary to produce a given design. The opportunity for individual growth is almost unlimited. Therefore, in the several particular subdivisions of the work, it is inevitable that expertness will develop as time goes on providing suitable individuals were selected to handle these special subdivisions of ship design. In addition to being capable of carrying on the specialty it is also necessary that the specialist understand the other phases of the work and be capable of carrying a design along as a whole. As all of the factors involving an efficient overall design are almost infinite in scope, it is necessary to simplify the approach to a design by dividing the responsibilities with regard to expert knowledge into certain groupings which cover the basic essentials. It has been found that these essentials are covered by the specific work classification to which individuals were assigned who appeared to have the aptitude and education to develop the assignment to the full.

This system of developing the design talent and knowledge of the preliminary design group has been the recognized policy since 1940. This policy was ably summed up by the Bureau's Personnel Utilization Analysis report of Sept. 1944 which agreed that, "the accomplishment of this objective requires the development of a group of men who can take the desires of the General Board and carry them through the pre-characteristic development of any class or type of ship. This development includes the determination of whether all of the requirements of the Board are possible of accomplishment and in addition the many compromises that may have to be accepted. Each of these several men must also be able to develop "post-characteristics" upon reaching agreement as to specific requirements with the Board. Both of these stages of development involve the application of all those factors of speed, weight, strength, balance, stability, form, arrangement and resistance to damage which must be completely understood individually and as a whole in the preliminary design considerations. Furthermore, there must be allowance for the development of individuals to the point of being accepted as the expert in specific fields of endeavor, i.e., the expert in hull form as it relates to any class or type of ship. The report stated further that a distinct set of standards be established for the preliminary design naval architecture and restrict the application of those standards to that work. These standards included P-2 for learner grade, P-5 for full grade preliminary design naval architecture, P-6 for experts.

In accordance with this policy the outstanding individuals in the section were developed as specialists in certain fields of preliminary design in addition to being capable of understanding the preliminary design as a whole. Where, however, that development is definitely limited in scope and the degree of expertness is not outstanding the grade level is limited to P-5.

[Handwritten at top: SecNav Knox requested — Study Navy Dept Organization — Booz-Fry-Allen and Hamilton Efficiency Experts from Chicago — this is their report on —]

2. The Preliminary Design Branch

Beginning in Preliminary Design, a ship is ordinarily nothing more than a proposed solution to a set of military problems. These problems may be posed by the General Naval Board or by high ranking officers. But before the design of a ship can even be started, the ship's general feasibility must be determined. When the feasibility and effectiveness of a proposed ship is approved here, naval architects in this Branch block out the general outlines and contoures, the masses, weights, and stability of a ship. The basic character throughout is determined and established. Thereafter, these preliminary plans are turned over to the Contract Design Branch.

Upon the men of this department rest the hopes and plans for a great ship. They are men of world-wide fame, great skill, and high professional standing. The work of the branch is almost exclusively professional and technical. The Branch has very little correspondence and most of that is with the General Board covering discussion of proposed ships. The unit is highly self-contained and of necessity maintains its own files. Its work is in current condition.

A ship protection section of the Branch is engaged in fundamental study of the military damage of various forms to which men-of-war are exposed. It collects, studies, and analyzes the reports on actual war damage and on the extensive experimental research which the Bureau conducts. It keeps in convenient form for reference and ready use the data necessary to the design of protective features for new ships and to the planning of changes in existing ships.

NAVY DEPARTMENT
BUREAU OF SHIPS

ROUTE SLIP
Code of Originating Section _____

| Section Code | ACTION TAKEN || DATA REQUIRED OR INFORMATION OBTAINED |
	By	Date	
			Write-up given Preliminary Design Branch by Messrs. Booz - Fry - Allen and Hamilton, Efficiency experts.

JCN
Not one answer in the bunch. You should have taken up ____. See if Webb can't change ___. — DB

Provisions of H.R. 1689
(Calendar No. 641, in U. S. Senate, July 11, 1949)

$25,000 for
1. Head of each executive department
2. Secretary of Defense

$20,000 for
1. Administrator for Economic Cooperation
2. Comptroller General of the United States
3. Chairman of the Council of Economic Advisers
4. Director of the Bureau of the Budget
5. Chairman of the National Security Resources Board
6. Federal Security Administrator
7. Administrator of Veterans' Affairs
8. Administrator of General Services
9. Each Under Secretary of an executive department
10. Assistant to the Attorney General
11. Solicitor General of the United States
12. First Assistant Postmaster General
13. Two from the following, as determined by the President:
    a. Administrative Assistant to the President
    b. Executive Secretary, National Security Council
    c. White House secretary or staff assistant

$18,000 for
1. Housing and Home Finance Administrator
2. Chairman of the Atomic Energy Commission
3. Chairman of the Munitions Board
4. Chairman of the Research and Development Board
5. Deputy Administrator for Economic Cooperation
6. Assistant Comptroller General of the United States
7. Assistant Director of the Bureau of the Budget
8. Deputy Administrator of Veterans' Affairs
9. Three from the following, as determined by the President:
    a. Administrative Assistant to the President
    b. Executive Secretary, National Security Council
    c. White House secretary or staff assistant
10. The President authorized to fix at $18,000 the salary of a chairman or head of a board or Commission who receives the same salary as other members of the body under H.R. 1689 but who has important duties or responsibilities not imposed upon other members.

$17,500 for
1. Public Printer
2. Librarian of Congress
3. Members of the Council of Economic Advisers
4. Director of Central Intelligence
5. Federal Mediation and Conciliation Director
6. Assistant Federal Security Administrator
7. Director, Federal Bureau of Investigation

- 2 -

$16,000 for
1. Members, Board of Governors of the Federal Reserve System
2. Director of Aeronautical Research of the National Advisory Committee for Aeronautics
3. Members, Civil Aeronautics Board
4. Chairman of the Board of Directors of the Export-Import Bank of Washington
5. Members, Federal Communications Commission
6. Members of the Board of Directors of the Federal Deposit Insurance Corporation (including Comptroller of the Currency)
7. Members, Federal Power Commission
8. Members, Federal Trade Commission
9. Members, Interstate Commerce Commission
10. Members, National Labor Relations Board
11. Members, National Mediation Board
12. Members, Railroad Retirement Board
13. Chairman of the Board of Directors of the Reconstruction Finance Corporation
14. Members, Securities and Exchange Commission
15. Members, Board of Directors, Tennessee Valley Authority
16. Members, Civil Service Commission
17. Chairman of the United States Maritime Commission
18. Members, United States Tariff Commission
19. Members, (other than Chairman) Atomic Energy Commission
20. General Counsel of the National Labor Relations Board
21. Architect of the Capitol
22. Deputy Administrator of General Services
23. Seven from the following, as determined by the President:
    a. Administrative Assistant to the President
    b. Executive Secretary, National Security Council
    c. White House secretary or staff assistant

$15,000 for
1. Director, Administrative Office, U. S. Courts
2. Housing Expediter
3. Director of the Bureau of Federal Supply
4. Director of Selective Service
5. Archivist of the United States
6. Assistant Architect of the Capitol
7. Members, Displaced Persons Commission
8. Members, Indian Claims Commission
9. Members, War Claims Commission
10. Members, Philippine War Damage Commission
11. Each Assistant Secretary of an executive department (including the Fiscal Assistant Secretary of the Treasury)
12. Each Assistant Attorney General
13. Assistant Solicitor General of the United States
14. Counselor of the Department of State
15. The Second, Third and Fourth Assistant Postmasters General
16. Associate Federal Mediation and Conciliation Director
17. Deputy Director of Central Intelligence
18. Philippine Alien Property Administrator
19. Chief Assistant Librarian of Congress
20. Deputy Public Printer

- 3 -

$15,000 for 21. Members (other than Chairman), Board of Directors of the
(Continued)   Export-Import Bank of Washington
22. Members (other than Chairman), Board of Directors of the Reconstruction Finance Corporation
23. Members (other than Chairman), United States Maritime Commission
24. Administrator, Production and Marketing Administration
25. Commissioner of Internal Revenue
26. Director of the Bureau of Prisons
27. Commissioner of Public Roads
28. Commissioner of Public Buildings
29. Commissioner of Community Facilities
30. Commissioner of Immigration and Naturalization
31. Administrator of Civil Aeronautics
32. Administrator, Rural Electrification Administration
33. Commissioner for Social Security
34. Commissioner of Reclamation
35. Chief, Soil Conservation Service
36. Commissioner of Customs
37. Commissioner of Narcotics
38. Governor of the Farm Credit Administration
39. Chief Forester of the Forest Service
40. Administrator of the Farmers Home Administration
41. Manager of the Federal Crop Insurance Corporation
42. Three Special Assistants to the Secretary of Defense
43. Governors of Alaska, Hawaii, the Virgin Islands, and the Panama Canal

$12,000 for 1. Legislative Counsel of the House of Representatives
2. Legislative Counsel of the Senate

$10,330 for 1. Legal Adviser, Department of State

$10,000 for 1. Assistant Director, Administrative Office, United States Courts

THE SHIP OF THE FUTURE

BY DAVID R. LINDSAY

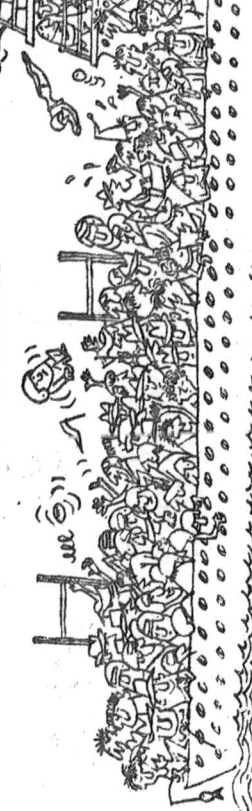

Man-made islands carrying 20,000 people and equipped with tennis courts and football fields may be our future homes

■ IN A SPRAWLING building on Washington D. C.'s Constitution Avenue is a small office, its metal door equipped with a vault lock and an electronic alarm system. Behind this fortified door sits John C. Niedermair whose main concern is to be at least 20 years ahead of everybody else.

Niedermair's picture of the future includes a solution to the earth's pressing population problem: The world's population is growing faster than ever. One proposed solution: to colonize the moon and Mars. But, Niedermair believes the answer lies closer to home.

His solution is a logical outgrowth of his present job as head naval architect of the U.S. Navy: chief of what is often called the Navy's dream department—the preliminary design section of the Bureau of Ships. Little known outside his field, Niedermair has guided the design of more ships than anyone who ever lived. Almost all of the thousands of vessels in America's World War II and post-war naval fleets started in his office. Because ships are supposed to keep up with the times during a useful life of at least two decades, Niedermair has to work in the future. Not surprisingly, his answer to the world's population problem is to have men move out onto the oceans.

Four-fifths of the earth's surface is water, Niedermair points out, so why try to lick the fantastic problems of interplanetary travel when people can find plenty of space by living on the sea? They'll be able to get more of their food from the sea, also. Furthermore, it won't simply be a matter of taking what nature provides, but of cultivating the ocean the way land is cultivated today. Fish will not simply be caught; they'll be raised as cattle are. Minerals and perhaps even fuel can also be taken from the water. When power from nuclear fusion becomes a reality, there will be an endless supply of hydrogen in the oceans.

When I visited him recently, the Navy's chief dreamer spoke of the future of the oceans with the warm affection a farmer might have for his own parcel of land. He finds it difficult to understand why young men in vast numbers crowd into aviation and practically none want careers in marine engineering or naval architecture. The great future of mankind, he believes, is in the hands of the marine designers.

When Niedermair first came to the Bureau of Ships nearly 30 years ago, he was asked to work out a prediction curve to show the gradual growth in the size of ships. The huge supercarriers of today, which are over 1000 feet long, fall right on his curve. Unfortunately, he didn't carry the predictions beyond the mid-century mark, but he sees no reason why ships shouldn't get to be twice as long, roughly two-fifths of a mile. It won't happen over night, though, as it normally takes five years to turn an idea into a ship.

Naturally, certain structural problems must be overcome before a

2000-foot ship is feasible. But, as Niedermair likes to point out, Naval experts once said that the 400-foot battleships of the early 1900's represented the ultimate in length. Actually, their over-all length and general proportions were roughly the same as those of Noah's Ark—if Biblical descriptions are accurate.

The 2000-foot ship of the future would have several disadvantages as well as advantages. On the debit side would be the gigantic investment involved and its inability to enter most of the harbors of the world. Instead of landing at docks, these man-made islands would have to load and unload in open roadsteads, transferring passengers to tenders or ferries to go ashore. Some ships are already too big for most ports. There are tankers in service from the Middle East to the oil refineries outside Philadelphia which draw so much water that they have to transfer part of their cargo to smaller ships before they can go up the Delaware River.

The reason ships continue to grow despite their inability to enter many ports is that the bigger they are, the more cargo and passengers they can carry per dollar of fuel and maintenance. A 2000-foot ship would be able to accommodate 10,000 to 12,000 passengers in comfort as compared to 2000 on the largest liners in existence today. Since waves would hardly affect her she'd be practically as steady as a floating island. Her exposed decks would cover around 10 acres of space, enough for several tennis courts and swimming pools plus a full-size football field if desired. Above all, she'd be far safer than any ship yet built.

Future ships will probably have a much smoother, less cluttered appearance than those on the seas now. For one thing, they won't need smoke stacks if nuclear fuel dis-

places oil. But they won't suddenly look like ocean-going rockets either, Niedermair explained. For a long time—until they can create their own artificial atmospheres—ships will need large openings to take in air for ventilation and cooling.

Passenger ships probably won't go a great deal faster than they do at present, unless some radical, unthought-of discoveries in propulsion are made. It would take 1½ million horsepower to drive the Queen Mary at 60 knots (68 m.p.h.), which is about normal turnpike driving speed. Now, the Queen has 150,000 horses to drive her at roughly 30. The fuel consumption at 60 would be five times as great per mile as at 30. So much space would be taken by machinery and fuel that there wouldn't be much left for passengers or cargo. Even nuclear power is unlikely to solve this problem.

Right after the first atomic bombs were set off, however, there were some people who thought that almost anything was possible. Niedermair told me that just after the news of the bomb, a high official rushed into his office and asked him what he could do with engines which turned up 5 million horsepower. He replied that if he were given six months notice he'd design a ship to take it. So far, he hasn't heard any more of the idea. Naval ships will probably go faster than at present, but how much faster is in the realm of classified information. There is a reason, of course, for that combination lock on Niedermair's door.

In his years in the Navy, Niedermair has spanned the changes from coal to oil to the atom. The first

bomb, he said, "blew the dust off everybody's brains. From that time on you no longer had to worry that someone would say you were a crackpot if you came up with something new."

The changes in ship design have been coming fast and furious since then. Already several nuclear-powered surface vessels have been worked out, including a guided-missile cruiser. Almost everything today is controlled electronically. Soon a captain will need eyes only to read gauges and radar scopes. Not too far away is the completely push-button operated ship with navigation handled automatically by star-trackers and gyro position-keepers more accurate than any sextant-using navigator.

Niedermair bubbles with enthusiasm when he is thinking about the future, but he is likely to bring himself quickly back to reality and explain what a tough place the surface of the sea is. It's so rugged that no animals, fish, or birds live there naturally. The fish which sometimes come to the surface dive below to avoid rough weather. Birds which occasionally land on water, fly away to avoid being swamped by breaking waves. Accordingly naval architects have had to use their own imaginations in designing ships—they have no natural prototype to copy. This, Niedermair says, is not the case with other engineers.

The closest a ship came to copying nature was the new super-streamlined submarine *Albacore* which was, according to newspaper reports, modeled after a whale. But Niedermair, who should know better than anyone else, claims that the sub is not a "mechanical whale" at

A SHIP IS BORN

In 1941 the British Navy sent a dispatch to Washington describing a ship capable of transporting 40-ton tanks across the open seas and then landing them on a flat shallow beach. Royal Navy engineers were unable to design one. But 30 seconds after he saw the message, Niedermair had come up with the solution. A ship with ballast tanks which are flooded to give stability at sea and pumped out to float the ship for landing. Less than 24 hours after Niedermair's brainstorm, a sketch (see below) of the first of W.W. II's famous LST's was sent to London.

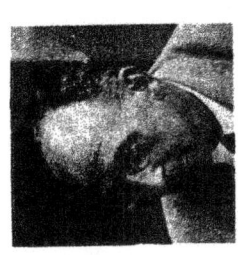

all but a seagoing airship. Its shape is partly a modification of an airplane design worked out by a British woman engineer. The use of an aircraft form under the sea is not surprising, he added, because water is a fluid just like air, only denser. Actually, many naval designs are tested in wind tunnels.

Niedermair is obviously fascinated by the whole subject of the oceans and ships. It's been that way ever since he first met salt water. Born in Union, N. J., in 1893, he moved to Staten Island, N. Y., when he was young. There he very often went to the hills overlooking New York Harbor, to watch ships come in and out of this busy port. From the very beginning, Niedermair insists, he has been exceedingly lucky. Until just before he was born there was no place to study naval architecture in the United States; you had to go to Europe. The way he tells the story, it sounds as if the first American school of naval architecture had been founded practically at the behest of a guardian angel. At any rate, the school, Webb Institute, was started by one of the country's leading shipbuilders, William H. Webb, who endowed it so that none of its students have to pay tuition, room, or board.

Because of the First World War there was a tremendous demand for naval architects when Niedermair was finishing at Webb. While still a junior, he went to work in the Brooklyn Navy Yard and was fortunate in working under an officer named Captain H. T. Wright who believed in giving youngsters a lot of responsibility.

Niedermair's big break came when Cpt. Wright assigned him to the salvage of the S-51, a submarine which had been sunk at sea in a collision. At the time, Niedermair knew absolutely nothing about salvage work, but he approached the job with an open mind and the theory that by using engineering techniques and calculations, he could do it. He did. In describing this first scientific salvage job, one high-ranking Navy man said that Niedermair had raised the sub "with a lead pencil."

Very soon, Niedermair had such a reputation that the Navy Department wanted him down in Washington, where he's been ever since.

Just about everything Niedermair does, he does a little more intensely than almost anyone around. For example, though he certainly hasn't been paid a grandiose amount in the government (he's had several outside offers which would have doubled his income), he raised a family of eight children. "It's just as easy to raise a big family as a small one," he commented and added after a pause, "if you have a good wife." When his doctor ordered him to take a rest after the war, he ended up by building himself a seaside house—not a cottage, but a two-story house which he put up with his own hands.

As one of the outstanding men in his field as well as one of the leading civil servants in the United States, Niedermair has received many commendations and citations. The most recent was the National Civil Service League's Career Service Award. To Niedermair these honors are the equivalent of a bonus given a kid for eating an extra portion of ice cream. He stuck with the government for his whole career, he explained to me, because he couldn't honestly imagine a job he would enjoy more. The Bureau of Ships is the biggest ship designing and building organization the world has ever known, he said, and naval architecture is a succession of intriguing challenges and surprises. That's why he can't understand why youngsters today don't go into it.

With most of the earth's surface to work with, naval architecture, in Niedermair's opinion, should be the most popular field of design. "Life started in the sea and it's inevitable that man will return to the sea more and more," he told me with great concern. "If the United States doesn't think this is important and train the necessary technical people, someone else will." ■

TABLE OF DAMES

One woman + one left turn = confusion
Two women + one secret = excitement
Three women + one bargain = bedlam
Four women + one lunch = chaos

—Henry Marble

Bureau of Ships Daily Administrative Bulletin

WEDNESDAY
27 JUNE 1956

John C. Niedermair
Technical Director of
Preliminary Ship Design

Top BUSHIPS Designer Receives National Honors

Mr. John C. Niedermair, Technical Director of Preliminary Ship Design, Bureau of Ships, has been selected by the National Civil Service League to receive one of its Career Service Awards for outstanding public service, the first Navy candidate to be so recognized. The Navy's chief naval architect since 1938, Mr. Niedermair has guided the basic designs from which some 8,000 combatant and auxiliary vessels have been constructed. He has been called the father of today's modern Navy, for almost all the proud ships that won World War II at sea as well as the mighty units joining the fleet today bear the stamp of his genius.

The Niedermair award is one of ten granted nationally each year by the National Civil Service League as a part of its efforts to enhance the prestige of public service.

Born in Union Hill, New Jersey, in 1893, Mr. Niedermair attended grade and high schools in Staten Island, New York. He won a scholarship to the Webb Institute of Naval Architecture and Marine Engineering from which he graduated at the head of his class in 1918. That same year he began his remarkable career as a ship draftsman in the New York Navy Yard.

Mr. Niedermair's stature permeates the entire field of naval architecture. His work on watertight integrity and ship stability has left a lasting imprint on practically every merchant ship constructed since 1929. He served as a consultant to a Senate Subcommittee investigating the "Mohawk" and "Morro Castle" disasters. In the course of the construction of the liner "America", Mr. Niedermair was appointed by Admiral Emory S. Land as technical conciliator between the design agent and building yard.

Despite his impressive contributions to commercial naval architecture, Mr. Niedermair's first love and the field of his greatest triumphs has been combatant ship design. Besides the direction and inspiration his leadership has provided BUSHIPS naval architects, Mr. Niedermair has originated many critical design innovations. His conception of the high tensile steel flight deck structure combined with his idea of building ballistic decks in layers to compensate for the then existing limitations in welding techniques, made possible some of the most valuable military characteristics of the ESSEX class aircraft carriers. Again, on the afternoon of November 4, 1941, in response to a British requirement received that day, Mr. Niedermair made a small pencil sketch and calculated the basic characteristics of an entirely new and radical ship which became the workhorse of World War II. Less than a year later on November 2, 1942, LST-384, first of a class which eventually totalled more than 1,100 ships, was commissioned, a feat of ship design and construction rarely if ever equalled.

Perhaps Mr. Niedermair's greatest contribution to his country will be realized through his efforts on behalf of his profession and through the young engineers he has trained and developed. He has been very active in professional circles and particularly in the Society of Naval Architects and Marine Engineers. He has fostered a high degree of technical excellence and professional pride in the men he has worked with and has done much by precept and example to inspire them and instill excellence into their work. He has wisely counselled two generations of naval officers. Almost every high-ranking officer of the Navy now engaged in ship design work has learned the fundamentals from "Johnny."

Mr. Niedermair's award will be presented to him at a banquet in Washington, D. C., on July 2. Principal speakers will be Governor Robert E. Meyner of New Jersey and Senator Frank Carlson of Kansas. Present to join the Nation in honoring Mr. Niedermair and his fellow awardees will be Rear Admiral A. G. Mumma, USN, Chief of the Bureau of Ships and many other top officials of the Bureau and the Navy.

REAR ADMIRAL EDWARD ELLSBERG
WINDSWEPT
SOUTHWEST HARBOR, MAINE 04679

Feb. 14, 1975

Dear John:

Many thanks for your remembrance of me in your Christmas letter. For myself, I recall vividly our first joint venture on the Leviathan and almost on the heels of that one being thrown together again on the S-51.

If, as you say, I helped put your foot on the first rung of the ladder upward, you did as much, and even far more, for me. Aside from all else, it took your technical skill, imagination and (in the case of the S-51), your loyalty and persistence in the face of disaster to result ultimately in success. And those qualities you provided quietly and unemotionally when all seemed lost,

I felt deeply in your debt for what you did for me and I still do. What little help I could give you on your way up later was gladly given. But I have never doubted that all your successes thereafter in the technical field, as well as this last one — as a Fellow of the Society of Naval Architects and Marine Engineers — came to you richly earned by your own abilities and by the wholeheartedness with which you applied them.

In my lifetime (I am now eighty-three) in many fields, in war and peace, three men stand out in my memory from the thousands with whom it has been my good fortune to have had Fate throw me into contact. They are — a strange trio, perhaps — Captain Kenny T. Wright, Fleet Admiral Ernest J. King, and John C. Niedermair.

Most sincerely,

Ned Ellsberg.

The instant it happened...

USS Squalus tears from the depths during salvage off Portsmouth, N.H. (Photo by Jimmy Jones)

Launched eight months earlier, the USS Squalus, America's newest and most modern submarine, was 12 miles off Portsmouth, N.H operating in 240 feet of water inside the Isle of Shoals. She was making practice dives in preparation for final testing. The date was May 23, 1939.

Six civilian navy yard workers were among the 59 aboard at 8:40 a.m. as Squalus made what was to have been her final dive, one that was to have lasted an hour.

During the descent, water poured into the after section of the craft sending it to the bottom and drowning 26 men. The 33 survivors were brought to the surface by a newly-devised rescue chamber — a diving bell — resembling an electric light bulb in shape.

Divers sped to Portsmouth by air, sea and over the road to participate in rescue and salvage operations. The Squalus, with 25 of the 26 bodies — one apparently had been carried to sea — returned to Portsmouth. Repaired and recommissioned the USS Sailfish, the vessel later served in the Pacific fleet during World War II, and was credited with sinking a Japanese carrier, among other targets.

Globeman Ne A. Barrows, covering the salvage operations from aboard the salvage ship Falcon, described the first attempt to raise the Squalus on July 13, 1939 as follows:

"A warning surge of green water, a tremendous upheaval of boiling white froth... and the bow shot out remaining for three or four seconds. Her number — 192 — stood out, white and distinct, in that terrible 10 seconds of disorder and dismay."

"Like a fearsome monster gone berserk, the sharp bow... leaped wildly out of the ocean...hung up right for a few seconds and slipped back to the bottom in a shambles of broken pontoons, torn lines and other wreckage.

The late Globe photographer Jimmy Jones, then with the old Boston Post, caught the action with his camera. He alone had it.

JC Wiederman walking B1st at Stan A Harbor July '75

Rhyme of the RR-66

KENTUCKY (Iowa Class)

THE NEW YORK TIMES MAGAZINE, DECEMBER 7, 1941.

WAR DEPARTMENT
OFFICE OF THE QUARTERMASTER GENERAL
WASHINGTON

MEMORANDUM TO

December 10 1941.

Dear John,-

Here is a poem I liked. Its from Sunday's N.Y. Times.

Best wishes, etc.

Cough
C. H. Rough.

Rhyme of the BB-66

The following poem was read recently over the Treasury radio hour.

By HERMAN WOUK

It is the BB-66
That they launch today at three.
The mighty BB-66
That was built to keep men free
And the people's roar wells up from shore
As she slides into the sea.

And when this ship goes down the ways
There's more on her ribs than steel;
The hope and love of a thousand men
Are built into her keel.
There's a nation's pride in her iron side—
And Liberty's at the wheel!

High in a tower on New York isle
There burned a lonely light;
And ship-designer William Lodge
Worked late into the night,
Sketching the BB-66
In penciled black on white.

Sprung from a strong New England line
Of clear-eyed men o' the sea,
This William Lodge put heart and soul
In the ship to keep men free;
Lovingly placed each giant gun.
Carefully placed each giant gun.
His pencil dropped; his work was done.
"I think she'll go," said he.

And when this ship goes down the ways
There's more on her ribs than steel.
New England's love of the rights of man
Is shaped into her keel.
There's tyrant-hate in her armor-plate
And Fear of God at the wheel.

The welding flame burned acrid blue,
Too strong for human eyes;
The welders wore weird iron masks
Like creatures from the skies,
But they worked as human beings work
For things that all men prize.

The welding flame moved straight and true
In the hand of Scott MacBride,
And Big Jake Lesnevic, the Pole,
Worked strongly by his side.
And the growing BB-66
Was all their joy and pride.

And there was Otto Peterson,
Of Norway's stock was he.
He thought of men betrayed, in chains,
Far, far across the sea,
And his jaw set tight as he worked by night
On the ship to keep men free.

Oh, when this ship goes down the ways,
There's more on her ribs than steel.
The brotherhood of kindly men
Is welded in her keel.
There's the Christian dream in her metal gleam—
And Tolerance at the wheel.

Then came the riggers, muscled men
To swing the guns in place.
The best was colored Dixie Joe
With smiling, gold-toothed face.
Five tons of bulkhead on a crane
He could swing with catlike grace.

And, as he worked he sang a tune
He learned when still a boy
Of Lincoln setting black men free—
And his body hummed with joy;
And he tossed a cannon mount around
Like a fragile Christmas toy.

Then came machinists, engineers,
A hundred more like these,
And filled her length with pounding strength
To drive her through the seas,
To defend the sod where men serve God
In any church they please.

And last came Captain Paul deVries
To explore from stem to stern;
And, like the Dutch, he spoke not much
On shore, at his return.
But the light of freedom in his eye
More brightly seemed to burn.

Oh, when this ship goes down the ways
There's more on her ribs than steel.
The hope and love of a thousand men
Are built into her keel.
Strong with the blood of the free and brave.
Ah, but proud she will ride the wave!
For her high, clear destiny is to save
Her land from a tyrant's heel!

It is the BB-66
That they launch today at three.
And the people's roar wells up from shore
As she slides into the sea;
For the ship will ride on the first flood tide
And sail to keep men free!

Jen - Onboard the Falcon about 1928
P. 151
P S-4 Salvage

Salvage Hatch - S4 at Boston Yard March 192

THE SECRETARY OF THE NAVY
WASHINGTON

18 JUL 1956

My dear Mr. Niedermair:

I would like you to know the pleasure and pride I felt when I learned that you had been selected by the National Civil Service League to receive one of their Career Service Awards. This is a very high honor and reflects great credit on you, the Bureau of Ships and the Navy.

In selecting you, the League made a very wise choice. You have rendered distinguished public service with the Navy since 1918. As the Navy's Chief Naval Architect and as Technical Director of Preliminary Ship Design of the Bureau of Ships, you hold one of the most responsible and demanding positions in the Department. You have carried those responsibilities with competence and have met those demands with ingenuity and vision. You are a renowned member of your profession and an admired and respected member of your community. Your kindness, dignity and sincerity have won you the friendship of your associates.

Please accept my congratulations on your award and my wish that you will enjoy many more years translating "a gleam in someone's eye" into better ships for our Navy.

Sincerely yours,

Charles S. Thomas

Mr. John C. Niedermair
6116 - 32nd Street N. W.
Washington, D. C.

MR. JOHN CHARLES NIEDERMAIR

Mr. John Charles Niedermair was born November 2, 1893 in Union Hill, New Jersey. During his youth he lived in Staten Island, New York where he attended grade and high schools. He was selected for a scholarship to and entered Webb Institute of Naval Architecture and Marine Engineering in 1914. He graduated at the head of his class in 1918.

After a brief period of duty in the Navy during the first World War as an officer candidate, he commenced his active career in the shipbuilding industry in December 1918 by accepting a permanent appointment as a ship draftsman at the New York Navy Yard. He remained at New York until April 1928 when the Navy Department requested his services in Washington in the Preliminary Design Branch of the Bureau of Construction and Repair. Ten years later, he rose to the position of senior civilian in this Branch and still holds this distinction. His present title is "Technical Director of Preliminary Ship Design" and he is the highest ranking naval architect in the U.S. Navy, as well as the highest ranking civilian in the Bureau of Ships.

Mr. Niedermair has attained international stature and recognition among members of the naval architectural profession particularly in the fields of salvage, stability, and basic design. While employed at the New York Navy Yard, Mr. Niedermair was instrumental in the prosecution of a number of special projects, the scope and variety of which attest to his versatility as an engineer. One of these was the design, planning, and active supervision of the construction of the battleship building ways laid down in the early 1920's. However, his most significant work during this period was in connection with the salvage operations of the ill-fated submarines, S51 and S4. In each of these instances, he provided on the spot technical direction of salvage procedures which he himself had devised. In recognition of these services, which were so vital to the success of these operations, he was highly commended by the Secretary of the Navy and received a special promotion. Since that time, he has served in a consultant capacity on many other salvage jobs.

Mr. Niedermair's transfer to the Bureau of Construction and Repair in 1928 was occasioned by the fact that his talents were needed in connection with preparations for the forthcoming International Safety of Life on Sea Convention. Mr. Niedermair attended the convention, which was held in London in 1929, as the Navy's technical expert, and was one of the signers of the resulting agreement. He was personally instrumental in securing the adoption of the United States' proposal that every passenger ship be inclined upon its completion, and that operating personnel be supplied with information regarding the stability necessary to permit efficient and safe handling of the ship. For his services on this occasion, he received a letter of commendation from the Secretary of State. Again during the Senate Investigation of the "Mohawk" and "Morro Castle" disasters, Mr. Niedermair served on the Subcommittee concerned with the Watertight Integrity and Stability of passenger ships. As a direct result thereof, in 1935, Mr. Niedermair's services were loaned by the Navy to the Department of Commerce where he established the Technical Division of the Bureau of Marine Inspection and Navigation, an activity designed to safeguard the public's interests against further such catastrophes. Mr. Niedermair's contributions in the field of ship stability are marked by many milestones not the least of which is his co-authorship (with Vice Admiral E.L. Cochrane, USN (Ret.)) of Construction and Repair Technical Bulletin No. 8, "Sub-division, Stability and Construction of Merchant Ships" (1935), a document still considered the basic primer on this subject.

In the field of basic design, Mr. Niedermair occupies a pre-eminent position and might well be termed the father of today's modern United States Navy. In addition, he contributions to the merchant shipbuilding field are also substantial. In the course of the design of the liner "America", Mr. Niedermair was appointed by Vice Admiral Emory S. Land, USN, to act as technical conciliatory between the design agent and the building yard. His contributions have left a lasting imprint on practically every merchant ship constructed since 1929.

It is in the field of naval ship design, however, that Mr. Niedermair has made his greatest contributions. As the civilian chief and Technical Directory of the Preliminary Design Branch of the Bureau of Ships for almost 20 years, Mr. Niedermair has been primarily responsible for the basic design of all types of naval ships during this most trying and critical period. This includes Battleships, Aircraft Carriers, Cruisers, Destroyers, Submarines, Patrol and Mine Craft; Auxilaries such as Tenders, Cargo Ships, and Tankers; Landing Craft including LST, LSD, and other special craft types. The designs which he guided from conception through construction became the ships which contributed so greatly to the winning of World War II and which excited the world by their performance. Worthy of particular mention is the part he played in the design of the LST. This ship, which was in large measure the product of Mr. Niedermair's originality and fine engineering judgment, was known as the work horse of World War II. Over 1,000 of these versatile craft were constructed, a memorial of which few, if any, other Naval Architects can boast. To date, approximately 8,000 ships, a staggering number, have been built from designs originated under Mr. Niedermair's guidance. It is improbable that a record such as this will ever be equaled. For his outstanding services to the Navy both prior to, and during World War II, Mr. Niedermair was presented the Distinguished Civilian Service Award, the Navy's highest honorary award, in 1945.

It is of particular note that Mr. Niedermair's genius has spanned the coming of the atomic age. The past few years have witnessed the advent of the first nuclear propelled ships. The NAUTILUS needs no introduction; SEA WOLF and other submarines to follow will in turn be followed by the nuclear carriers and cruisers now on the drafting boards. FORRESTAL, SARATOGA and their sisters are other mighty milestones of this newer Navy. The basic designs of all of these vessels were made under Mr. Niedermair's direction and exemplify the versatility and scope of his ability as a Naval Architect.

Mr. Niedermair has always been active in the work of the professional technical societies. In 1932, he presented a paper "Stability of Ships After Damage" before the Society of Naval Architects and Marine Engineers (SNAME). In 1936, he presented a companion paper, "Further Developments in the Stability and Rolling of Ships" before the same group. In 1951 he presented a paper on "Ship Motions" before the International Conference of Naval Architects and Marine Engineers in London under the auspices of the Institution of Naval Architects. Local Sections of the SNAME have also heard Mr. Niedermair on several occasions. He addressed the Chesapeake Section in 1950 on the subject of his own design experiences, and the same year presented a paper before the Philadelphia Section of the "Subdivision, Stability, and Damage Control of Merchant Ships." Mr. Niedermair has been a regular contributor to the discussions of technical papers presented before the Society. In addition to such technical activity, Mr. Niedermair has contributed his services on many occasions to the Society's work. He has served as a member of the Local Sections Committee since 1949. Currently he is a member of the committee engaged in revising the Society's book on "Naval Architecture." He has served as the Chairman of the Chesapeake Section (1946-1947), and has since served on the Executive Committee of that Section.

One of Mr. Niedermair's greatest and perhaps most lasting contributions to his profession lies in the interest he has always displayed in the younger engineers. Vitally interested in the future of the profession, he has fostered a high degree of technical excellence and professional pride among young Naval Architects and has done much by precept and example to inspire them and instill excellence into their work. He has constantly looked toward the future and his insight into it has led the way for many who follow. He has wisely counseled two generations of Naval Officers. Almost every high ranking officer of the Navy now actively engaged in ship design work has learned the fundamentals from "Johnny". A gentleman, a scholar, a man beloved by all with whom he is associated and finally as well as first and always, a Naval Architect, he has added a considerable lustre to an already honorable profession.

DEPARTMENT OF THE NAVY
BUREAU OF SHIPS
WASHINGTON 25. D. C.

IN REPLY REFER TO

BUSHIPS 12087
Ser 267-2412
26 June 1956

BUSHIPS NOTICE 12087

From: Chief, Bureau of Ships
To: Commanders, All U. S. Naval Shipyards (w/encl (1) and (2))
      Commanding Officer and Director (w/encl (1)):
         David W. Taylor Model Basin
         U. S. Navy Electronics Laboratory
         U. S. Naval Engineering Experiment Station
      Commanding Officer (w/encl (1) and (2)):
         U. S. Naval Repair Facility, San Diego
         U. S. Naval Submarine Base, New London
      Supervisors of Shipbuilding, USN and Naval Inspectors
         of Ordnance (w/encl (1))

Subj: National Civil Service League Career Service Awards

Ref: (a) NCPI 87.9-7

Encl: (1) Suggested item for local publication
      (2) Photograph of Mr. John C. Niedermair

1. **Purpose.** To inform addressees of the granting of one of subject awards to Mr. John C. Niedermair, Technical Director of Preliminary Ship Design, Bureau of Ships, and to make available enclosures (1) and (2).

2. **Background.** Subject awards are described in reference (a). They are presented annually by the National Civil Service League, as a part of its efforts to increase the prestige of public service, to ten men and women selected nationally whose accomplishments and services demonstrate and emphasize the primary characteristics of the career service -- competence, efficiency, character and continuity of service. The announcement of Mr. Niedermair's selection on 26 June 1956 reflects great credit on him, the Bureau and the Navy and should be given appropriate publicity.

3. **Action.** The enclosure(s) are forwarded for optional use in local publications and other appropriate communication media.

4. **Cancellation.** This Notice is cancelled 20 July 1956.

A. G. MUMMA

DISTRIBUTION LIST:
(See page 2)

BUSHIPSNOTE 12087
26 June 1956

Enclosure (1)

J. C. Niedermair, Top BUSHIPS Designer, Receives National Honors

Mr. John C. Niedermair, Technical Director of Preliminary Ship Design, Bureau of Ships, has been selected by the National Civil Service League to receive one of its Career Service Awards for outstanding public service, the first Navy candidate to be so recognized. The Navy's chief naval architect since 1938, Mr. Niedermair has guided the basic designs from which some 8,000 combatant and auxiliary vessels have been constructed. He has been called the father of today's modern Navy, for almost all the proud ships that won World War II at sea as well as the mighty units joining the fleet today bear the stamp of his genius.

The Niedermair award is one of ten granted nationally each year by the National Civil Service League as a part of its efforts to enhance the prestige of public service. The League is a non-partisan citizen organization founded in 1881 concerning which President Eisenhower recently stated: "Through the indispensable understanding, cooperation and constructive criticism of organizations such as the National Civil Service League, our efforts to improve the federal service are greatly aided."

Born in Union Hill, New Jersey, in 1893, Mr. Niedermair attended grade and high schools on Staten Island, New York. He won a scholarship to the Webb Institute of Naval Architecture and Marine Engineering from which he graduated in 1918. That same year he began his remarkable career as a ship draftsman in the New York Navy Yard. Largely as a result of his success in the raising the ill-fated submarines S51 and S4, the Navy Department called Mr. Niedermair to Washington in 1928.

Mr. Niedermair's stature permeates the entire field of naval architecture. His work on watertight integrity and ship stability has left a lasting imprint on practically every merchant ship constructed since 1929. He served as a consultant to a Senate Subcommittee investigating the "Mohawk" and "Morro Castle" disasters. In the course of the construction of the liner "America", Mr. Niedermair was appointed by Admiral Emory S. Land as technical conciliator between the design agent and building yard.

Despite his impressive contributions to commercial naval architecture, Mr. Niedermair's first love and the field of his greatest triumphs has been combatant ship design. Besides the direction and inspiration his leadership has provided BUSHIPS naval architects, Mr. Niedermair has originated many critical design innovations. His conception of the high tensile steel flight deck structure combined with his idea of building ballistic decks in layers to compensate for the then existing limitations in

Enclosure (1)

Index to

Series of Interviews

with

John C. NIEDERMAIR

AIRCRAFT CARRIERS: Niedermair in 1931 begins his study and interest in aircraft carriers, p. 139 - 140; interest of the General Board in subject, p. 140; Adm. Spruance interested in new design for post WWII era - resulted ultimately in plans for UNITED STATES - whose contract was cancelled in 1950, p. 280;

USS ALBACORE: an experimental submarine with an airship type hull, p. 287-91; use of British hull form, p. 292-3; the last non-nuclear submarine hull form, p. 294;

SS AMERICA: arguments develop between Gibbs and Cox and Newport News shipyard over design - Niedermair sent by Adm. Land as go-between, p. 174-5; Newport News designs ship to fit their drydock, p. 178; they finally agree to accept Gibbs and Cox design, p. 179; AMERICA serves as troopship (WEST POINT) during WWII - converted back at Newport News after war, p. 180;

ANDERSON, Charles: Naval architect, interested primarily in submarines, p. 282;

ANGLED DECK: the origins of the idea, p. 184; p. 186; p. 299-301;

BATES, James L.: top naval architect in Bureau of C and R (1929), p. 131; Niedermair becomes his understudy, p. 131-3; p. 138; p. 162-4; goes with Adm. Land to Maritime Commission (1938) - becomes head of design division, p. 181; p. 324-5;

BB's: Niedermair begins work on designs for BBs (1933), p. 156-8; Secretary of the Navy's special board, p. 161-2;

BEURET, Rear Admiral John D.: Chief of Bureau of C & R (1928) p. 122-4; member of Wartime (WW II) Inventor's Council, p. 256; p. 318;

BOWEN, VADM Harold G.: Chief of Bureau of Engineering - his ambitions clash with Bureau of C and R, p. 188; debate on stability of DDs enters picture, p. 188-191; p. 195;

BRAND, RADM Charles Lees: p. 197; p. 236;

BROCKETT, RADM Wm.: Chief, Bu Ships - resigned over reorganization plan - becomes head of Webb Institute, p. 335;

USS BROOKLYN - CL: p. 151-2; Niedermair acts as agent of Bu of C and R with N.Y. Ship, p. 151-3;

BROWN, Ray: Naval Architect, gets the job with lighter-than-air project in Washington, p. 91-2;

BUREAU OF CONSTRUCTION AND REPAIR (C&R): Niedermair accepts appointment in Washington (May 1, 1928), p. 113-114; p. 120; Niedermair changes from draftsman to Naval architect, p. 122; Niedermair begins to get experience in Bureau, p. 137-139; Niedermair opposed to practice of putting airports on decks of naval vessels, p. 142; Niedermair prepares paper for Admiral Rock on education of naval architects, p. 143; Niedermair prepares paper for Admiral Rock on education of naval architects, p. 143; Adm. Land becomes Chief (1932) - Niedermair involved with studies on BB's - ultimately resulting in construction of NORTH CAROLINA and WASHINGTON, p. 156-8; cooperating with BuOrd, p. 158-9; assumption of Niedermair Naval Architect has responsibility for whole ship; 160

BURGESS, Starling: yacht designer whom FDR sponsored in Bushlps for a time p. 206-7; his interest in designing a sub-chaser, p. 207; work on Delano's idea of a ship bridge across the Atlantic, p. 207-8;

BUSH, Dr. Vannevar: p. 256-7; his interest in hydrofoils, p. 259-61;

BUSHIPS (Bureau of Ships); process of amalgamation - Bureau of C & R with Bureau of Engineering, p. 193-4; p. 196-7; p. 319-20;

CHANTRY, RADM Allan J. Jr: p. 161-2; officer in charge of design for MIDWAY (1937-8), p. 182; his estimate of the struggle between Bureau of Engineering and C & R, p. 189; goes to command Philadelphia Navy Yard, p. 189-90

CLARK, RADM D.H.: Chief, BuShips (1949-51), p. 292;

CLEVELAND Class: p. 204; class converted to carriers (INDEPENDENCE, PRINCETON, etc.) p. 247-51;

COCHRANE, VADM Edward Lull: Niedermair co-authors with him on bulletin #8 - subdivision, stability and construction of naval vessels, p. 148; p. 163; p. 193; his interest in wooden minesweepers, p. 214-5; conveys British need for Landing Craft design, p. 225-7; p. 234; p. 263-4; p. 267; turns over damage control details to Niedermair in Dec. 1941 p. 271-2; uses experience of NY Fire Department in damage control school, p. 277; p. 282; p. 297-8; p. 327; p. 334;

COHN, Jake: ship ventilation expert - works on problem with SS LEVIATHAN, p. 51 ff; p. 59; p. 64-5;

COST ESTIMATES: Niedermair's concern in this area when designing a new ship, p. 192-3;

CRAMP'S SHIPYARD; p. 9 ff;

CROUCH, George: Professor of Naval Architecture, Webb Institute, p. 5; p. 19-20; p. 22;

DAMAGE CONTROL: Niedermair complains to Chief that damaged control was not given to individual ship captains, p. 271; Cochrane turns problem over to Niedermair, p. 271-5; Navy provided training center at Philadelphia for damage control officers, p. 276;

DIEHL, Captain Walter: p. 146; p. 185;

DU BOSE, Adm. Laurance Toombs: becomes head of Bureau of C & R after Adm. Land, p. 182; p. 186;

EDISON, The Hon. Charles: Secretary of the Navy, p. 194-5;

ELLSBERG, RADM Edward, USNR (Ret.): works a problem of ventilation in LEVIATHAN, p. 51 ff; p. 71; he learns to dive, p. 75-6; gets in trouble with salvage crew of S-51, p. 77-78; writes story of the salvage of S-51 for New York papers, p. 85-6; p. 88-89; p. 118-9; p. 121;

ESSEX Class: p. 186-7; more on early design problems, p. 197-200; p. 251; p. 277-8; p. 285;

USS FALCON - Salvage Ship: p. 68; p. 70; p. 74; at site of S-4 sinking, p. 103; p. 110;

FARRAGUT Class - DDs: Bureau of R and D begins studies, p. 141; Niedermair designs ship with intent of using stainless steel, p. 153-4;

FIVE INCH GUN: p. 220-221;

FLETCHER, H.C.: Chief Draftsman, New York Navy Yard, p. 22; p. 28; p. 118;

FLETCHER Class DDs: p. 252; problems in accommodating new armament, p. 297-8;

USS FORRESTAL: p. 203; p. 300-3; p. 310;

USS FORREST SHERMAN - DD: p. 297-9;

USS FRANKLIN: p. 199; p. 201-2;

FURER, RADM Julius: opposed to amalgamation of the Bureau of C and R and Engineering, p. 322-3;

GENERAL BOARD: their early interest (1931) in study of the aircraft carrier, p. 140; p. 160;

GIBBS BROTHERS AWARD: Niedermair gets the Award (1976) at the Academy of Sciences, p. 347-8;

GIBBS, Wm. Francis: Naval architect, p. 51; p. 55; p. 125; p. 162; p. 164; p. 177;

GOODING, VADM Robert C.: head of Navy design (1975), p. 273; succeeded Sonenshein as head of the Naval Ships System Command, p. 336;

USS HENDERSON: troopship, p. 12;

HYDROFOILS: beginnings in WWII, p. 258-60;

JOHNSON, Eads: Naval Architect - consulted with Delano and Sterling Burgess on their idea of a merchant-ship bridge across the Atlantic, p. 280; represented SecNav at initial trials of the LST, p. 280;

KING, Fleet Admiral Ernest J.: at scene of the S-51 accident (1925) p. 68 ff; permits Niedermair to take short diving cruise on S-50 at site of lost S-51 - to learn about SS operations, p. 79; p. 80-81; p. 84-5; p. 102-3; p. 109-110; p. 119; p. 124; p. 148; p. 195-6; p. 238;

KIRK, ADM Alan Goodrich: p. 246;

KNISKERN, RADM Leslie Albert: p. 316; p. 325;

LACEY, Ralph: Graduate of Webb Institute - Cochrane sends him to New London to acquire experience, p. 264-5; comes back to design section of BuShips after WWII, p. 265; works on POLARIS, p. 266;

LCI (L): p. 240; Niedermair gets New York Ship to build the prototype, p. 242; difficulty in getting engines, plumbing, etc. p. 254-5;

LAND, VADM Emory Scott: (Jerry): offers Niedermair job in Washington in connection with development of AKRON and MACON, p. 90; p. 132; p. 137; becomes Chief of Bureau of C and R (1932) p. 156; p. 174-5; becomes head of Maritime Commission (Feb. 1, 1938) - takes Vickery and Bates with him from C and R, p. 181-2; he guards closely the innovative designs of FDR, p. 204; p. 318-9;

LEGGETT, RADM Wilson Durward Jr.: a naval engineer - becomes Chief of BuShips, p. 283;

SS LEVIATHAN (ex German VATERLAND): seized in Hoboken, 1917 - Niedermair asked by CDR Wright to inspect ship and give estimate of troop carrying capacity, p. 15-16; p. 18-19; p. 50-51; Niedermair assigned to ship to help solve ventilation problems, p. 50 ff; problem with boilers, p. 53 ff; items to be corrected when she went into drydock in Boston (1925), p. 57; Niedermair makes six round trips in her across North Atlantic, p. 58-65; trouble with her again in 1929, p. 134-6;

LEWIS, Frank M.: Professor at M.I.T., p. 173-4;

LS, Dock: p. 304; later version of the earlier British design, p. 305-6;

LSTS: in post war period BuShips designed models with great speed, p. 304;

LST: Niedermair's story of the design development, p. 225-9; loading experiment on beach in Virginia, p. 230-1; the landing operation on a New England beach, p. 231-2; Naval Architect representing SecNav objects to ship's design, p. 231-5; a landing operation in Narragansett Bay with Combined Chiefs present, p. 235-9; first 50 turned over to the British - preparation of the Instruction Book, p. 245;

MANDELKORN, RADM Richard Shai: his lectures on damage control problems, p. 277;

SS MANHATTAN: Ernest Rigg designs, p. 147; Niedermair works on stability, etc., p. 147;

USS MANN - DD: assigned to take Niedermair from Boston Navy Yard to site of S-4 sinking, p. 103;

McQUILKIN, RADM John H.: p. 266;

MERRILL, Ambrose M.: Assistant Chief Draftsman at New York Navy Yard, p. 22; p. 117;

MERRITT, CHAPMAN, SCOTT: in charge of salvage operations for S-51, p. 69 ff; leave the job - Navy takes over, p. 79;

USS MIDWAY: Niedermair and the design section work on plans for MIDWAY, p. 182-3; Chantry has boilers designed outboard, p. 183-6; her contrasts with ESSEX class, p. 200-1;

MILLS, VADM Earle W.: p. 193; becomes head of BuShips (1946), p. 267; picked Rickover to be liaison with BuShips, p. 292; succeeded in 1949 by RADM D.H. Clark, p. 292;

MINESWEEPERS - Wooden: p. 214-5; Niedermair designs one - Cochrane brings back design of a British type, p. 216-9;

MOMSEN LUNG: SS rescue device, p. 110-111;

MORGAN, RADM Armand Malcolm: p. 263-4; p. 282; p. 326;

SS MORRO CASTLE: she sinks off Atlantic Coast (Sept. 1934) - Niedermair sent to reorganize Technical Division of Steamboat Inspection Service as result of this sinking, p. 167-ff; Adm. Rock and Niedermair on committee to come up with Senate Report 184 on Morro Castle, p. 170-1;

NAVAL CONSTRUCTION CORPS: early constructors like Admirals Taylor and Rock had training and experience in British and French yards - p. 315-6; they had regular experience of sea duty, p. 320;

NAVAL SHIPS: statistics for 1941 and 1945, p. 223-4;

NAVAL SHIPS SYSTEM COMMAND: p. 335 ff; p. 345;

NAVY YARDS: Niedermair talks about the U. S. Navy Yards - their reasons for being, training for members of the Construction Corps, etc. - p. 311 ff; use of the Navy Yards in WWII, p. 313-4; p. 327;

USS NEVADA: p. 6; p. 8; p. 10; p. 14;

NEWPORT NEWS SHIPBUILDING CO: works on plans for SS AMERICA (WEST POINT) p. 174-5 ; p. 178; p. 180;

NEW YORK NAVY YARD: p. 15; German ships (WWI) there, p. 18; Niedermair elected to head ship committee, p. 32-33; indiscriminate layoffs, p. 33-40; launching of USS PENSACOLA, p. 43-4; cost over-runs, p. 46; Niedermair undertakes specialized work on LEVIATHAN, p. 50 ff; bid on the proposed AMERICA of U. S. Lines, p. 176;

NEW YORK SHIPYARD: taken over by Cord, automobile manufacturer, p. 151-2; Niedermair works with NY Ship on plans for BROOKLYN Class cruisers, p. 151-3; charged with converting CLEVELAND Class cruisers to aircraft carriers, p. 247-9;

NIEDERMAIR, John C.: Naval Architect; personal data, p. 1; his marriage to Ethel Irwin (Apr. 22, 1923), p. 46-9; his promotion as result of work on S-51, p. 88-89; accepts bid to Bureau of C and R in Washington, (May 1, 1928), p. 113-4; p. 120; his series of post retirement awards, p. 338-9;

PANCAKE ENGINES: a design of General Motors for vertical diesel engines - to eliminate need for longer hulls, p. 286; replaced eventually because of lubrication problems with the Fairbanks-Morse engine, p. 287;

USS PENSACOLA: p. 43-5; launching from the building ways used for battleships, p. 92-3;

PLUNKETT, RADM C.P.: p. 36-7; his annoyance with publicity dealing with S-51; p. 86; his exploits in WWI with a Navy 14" gun, p. 87; calls Niedermair in on the sinking of S-4 (Dec. 17, 1927), p. 95 ff; his advice to Niedermair over request for duty in Washington, p. 112-133; p 116-7;

POLARIS: Niedermair makes a contribution to Special Project of RADM Raborn, p. 333-4;

USS PLUNGER: Electric Boat's design of a streamlined submarine hull, p. 288-9;

PT BOATS: Bureau of C and R instigates a design competition (1936-8)
- Prof. George Crouch of Webb wins for small PT boat
- Higgins wins the large one, p. 211; adoption of
the British Scott-Paine design, p. 212;

PYNE, RADM Schuyler: p. 231-2;

RABORN, VADM Wm. F. Jr.: his use of design facilities of BuShips in
development of POLARIS, p. 266;

RICKOVER, ADM. Hyman George: p. 267; rides with Niedermair in carpool,
p. 268-9; p. 292;

RIGG, Ernest: Naval Architect for New York Ship, p. 125; designs
SS MANHATTAN and the SS WASHINGTON, p. 147; p. 152;

ROBINSON, RADM Samual (Mike) Murray: p. 194; becomes first head of new
BuShips, p. 196; p. 301-2;

ROCK, Rear Admiral George: Chief Naval Constructor at New York Navy
Yard (1917), p. 19; p. 22; p. 33; p. 24-25; p. 29-31;
p. 40-42; his letter of commendation of Niedermair
for success with S-51; p. 88-89; invites Niedermair
to transfer to Bureau of C and R, p. 112-3; p. 115;
p. 124; p. 132; p. 137; p. 144; p. 147-8; p. 156; p.
168; p. 170; p. 316;

ROLL ON/ROLL OFF SHIP: p. 303;

ROOSEVELT, the Hon. Franklin D.: p. 149; has BuShips begin work on
6" cruisers, p. 149; his penchant for adding to design
of ships he sailed on, p. 204; sends his friend,
Starling Burgess to BuShips to help p. 206-7;

S-4: sinking off Provincetown, p. 96 ff; Niedermair plan for salvage
operation based on experience with S-51, p. 97-9;
Plunkett sends Niedermair to Boston for salvage job,
p. 100 ff; initial contacts with crew broken off by
stormy weather, p. 104-5; lack of cooperation from
Boston Navy Yard, p. 106-8; raising of S-4, p. 109-110;
as result of this work research continues on diving bell
and Momsen Lung, p. 110-111;

USS S-51: collided with CITY OF ROME (Sept. 25, 1925), p. 67; Ellsberg
and Niedermair assigned to salvage job, p. 68 ff;
problem with pontoons, p. 71 ff; raised and towed to
Navy Yard - hits a rock outside yard, sinks again,
p. 82-4; Niedermair writes report on salvage operation
stating what would be needed for another such operation
- refused permission to send to the Bureau in Washington
p. 94-5;

SAFETY OF LIFE AT SEA: work in preparation for the international convention, p. 122; the use of British Board of Trade rules, p. 124; the Convention in London (April, 1929) - Niedermair one of delegates, p. 125-8; Niedermair gets a provision on stability of ships, p. 128-130; p. 135-6; Niedermair prepares paper on subject for Adm Rock, p. 143; p. 148; Niedermair notes that Japanese were not really interested in Safety of Life at Sea, p. 144; Cochrane also member of U. S. delegation, p. 148-9;

USS SAGAMORE: seagoing tug - to tow pontoons for salvage of S-4, p. 98-9;

SARGEANT, Thomas: given charge of damage control problems in BuShips, p. 272-3;

SAUNDERS, Captain Harold E.: salvage officer for the S-4, p. 109; p. 120; p. 293;

SECRETARY OF THE NAVY: sets up special board to study designs for BBs, p. 161-2; Niedermair asked to appear solo before board - prepares at home for appearance - gives testimony without notes - his reasons (1936), p. 163-4;

SECURITY: Niedermair comments on security and the press, p. 163-6;

SENATE REPORT #184 (1934-5): on the MORRO CASTLE disaster, p. 172-3;

SHIP'S CHARACTERISTICS BOARD: p. 329;

SONENSHEIN, RADM Nathan: becomes head of Naval Ships System Command (1965-72), p. 335-6; Niedermair consults with him about Surface Effects ship designs, p. 336;

SPRUANCE, Admiral Raymond: his post WWII interest in a new type of aircraft carrier, p. 280; p. 286;

STABILITY: see entries under:
SS MANHATTAN; ADM. ROCK; SAFETY OF LIFE AT SEA; STEAMBOAT INSPECTION SERVICE; MORRO CASTLE;

STABILITY COMMITTEE: Set up for Department of Commerce (1925) with Wm. F. Gibbs as Chairman - Niedermair as member - to undertake research on the stability of merchant ships, p. 66-67; p. 125;

STAINLESS STEEL: Niedermair designs FARRAGUT Class cruiser with idea that stainless steel will be used, p. 153-4; tests proved corrosive nature of stainless steel - not used as result in FARRAGUTS, p. 154;

STARK, Admiral Harold R.: His advocacy of the CL with 6 in. guns, p. 150;

STEAMBOAT INSPECTION SERVICE: as result of MORRO CASTLE sinking Niedermair sent to reorganize Technical Division, p. 168-172;

SUBMARINES: various men who contributed to SS design and construction, p. 281-3; first postwar diesel subs carried pancake engines, p. 286-7; experiments with hydrogen peroxide and with liquid oxygen, p. 294-5; p. 310; Rickover gets started on idea of nuclear power for subs, p. 295-6; p. 307-8;

USS SUMNER: p. 297-8;

SURFACE EFFECT SHIPS: p. 336;

SWASEY, Captain Loring, USNR, p. 209; FDR interests him in the Delano idea for a merchant ship bridge across the N. Atlantic, p. 210; p. 213;

TAYLOR, RADM David W.: Chief of Bureau of C and R in WWI, p. 132; p. 316-7;

USS TENNESSEE: building at New York Navy Yard, p. 16; p. 29; her launching (1919), p. 29 ff;

SS TITANIC: p. 122-3;

USS UNITED STATES: plans called for angled deck for the fighters to go off independently of bombers, p. 184; p. 299-301;

Van KEUREN, RADM Alexander H.: becomes Chief of Bureau of C and R, p. 190; p. 193;

VICKERY, VADM Howard Leroy: becomes deputy to Adm. Land at Maritime Commission (1938), p. 181;

WALLIN, VADM Homer Norman: Chief of BuShips, p. 283; he and CDR Shade worte a paper on welding techniques, p. 284; p. 285;

SS WASHINGTON: Ernest Rigg designs, p. 147;

WEBB INSTITUTE OF NAVAL ARCHITECTURE: p. 4-6; summer work p. 6 ff; purpose of summer training, p. 13-14; RADM Rock leaves Bu of C and R to become head of Webb Institute, p. 144;

WELDING: developed as a technique in ship building largely because of treaty limitations on ship displacement, p. 283-4;

WRIGHT, Captain Henry T.: of New York Ship Yard, p. 15; p. 22; p. 33-4; p. 51; p. 89; urges Niedermair to take job in Washington in lighter-than-air field, p. 91; p. 115; p. 121;

www.ingramcontent.com/pod-product-compliance
Lightning Source LLC
Chambersburg PA
CBHW080622170426
43209CB00007B/1495